Renzo Piano 1987–1994

with a contribution by
Vittorio Magnago Lampugnani

Birkhäuser Verlag
Basel · Berlin · Boston

Originally published in Italy under the title
Renzo Piano, Progetti e architetture 1987–1994
by Electa, Milano
© 1994 by Elemond SpA, Milano

Translated from the Italian by David Kerr.

Library of Congress Cataloging-in-Publication Data

A CIP catalogue record for this book is available from the Library of Congress, Washington D.C., USA

Deutsche Bibliothek Cataloging-in-Publication Data

Renzo Piano:
Renzo Piano 1987–1994 / with a contribution by Vittorio Magnago Lampugnani. Transl. by David Kerr. –Basel ; Berlin ; Boston : Birkhäuser, 1995
 Einheitssacht.: Renzo Piano – progetti e architetture 1987–1994 <dt.>
 ISBN 3-7643-5159-4
 NE: Magnago Lampugnani, Vittorio [Mitarb.]

This work is subject to copyright. All rights are reserved, whether the whole or part of the material is concerned, specifically the rights of translation, reprinting, re-use of illustrations, recitation, broadcasting, reproduction on microfilms or in other ways, and storage in data banks. For any kind of use permission of the copyright owner must be obtained.

© 1995 for the English edition: Birkhäuser Verlag.
P.O. Box 133, CH-4010 Basel, Switzerland
Printed on acid-free paper produced from chlorine-free pulp
Cover design: Martin Schack, Dortmund
Printed in Italy
ISBN 3-7643-5159-4
ISBN 0-8176-5159-4

9 8 7 6 5 4 3 2 1

Contents

- 7 Introduction
  Vittorio Magnago Lampugnani
- 9 Interview with Renzo Piano
  Vittorio Magnago Lampugnani

Buildings and Projects

- 16 The Menil Collection Museum, Houston, 1981–86
- 30 Metropolitan Railway Stations, Genoa, 1983–94
- 38 Research Institute for Light Metals, Novara, 1985–87
- 42 Conversion of the Fiat Lingotto Works, Turin, 1985–93
- 58 Bank and Offices for Credito Industriale Sardo, Cagliari, 1985–93
- 62 Sports Centre, Ravenna, 1986
- 66 Redevelopment of the Bastions and City Gate, La Valletta, Malta, 1986
- 68 Rehabilitation of the Palladian Basilica and City Hall, Vicenza, 1986
- 72 Bay of Sistiana Redevelopment Scheme, 1987
- 76 European Synchrotron Radiation Facility, Grenoble 1987
- 80 Development of the Archaeological City of Pompeii, 1987–88
- 86 American Contemporary Art Museum, Newport Beach, 1987
- 94 The San Nicola Stadium, Bari, 1987–90
- 106 Bercy II Shopping Centre, Charenton le Pont, Paris, 1987–90
- 114 Crown Princess, Monfalcone, 1987–90
- 118 Design for Venezia Expo 2000, Venice, 1988
- 122 IRCAM: Institute for Research and Coordination of Acoustics and Music, Paris, 1987–90
- 126 Design for the Redevelopment of the Sassi, Matera, 1988–90
- 130 Guyancourt Thomson Works, Saint Quentin-en-Yvelines, 1988–90
- 136 Rue de Meaux Housing, Paris, 1988–91
- 142 Christopher Columbus International Exposition '92, Genoa, 1988–92
- 154 Kansai International Airport Main Passenger Terminal Building, Osaka, 1988–94
- 168 Science and Technology Museum, Amsterdam, 1989
- 174 UNESCO Workshop, Vesima, 1989–91
- 184 Bridge in the Ushibuka Archipelago, Kumamoto, 1989–95
- 190 Design for the Church of Padre Pio, San Giovanni Rotondo, 1991
- 196 Plan for Potsdamer Platz, Berlin, 1992
- 210 The Jean-Marie Tjibaou Kanak Cultural Centre, Nouméa, 1992
- 216 The Cy Twombly Pavilion, Houston, 1992
- 220 Redevelopment of the Ile Séguin, Boulogne-Billancourt, Paris, 1993
- 224 Pilot Scheme for Railway Stations in Turin, Mestre, Venice and Bari, 1993
- 228 Redevelopment of the Teatro Margherita, Bari, 1993
- 230 Brancusi Museum at the Georges Pompidou Centre, Paris, 1993–96
- 234 Exhibitions and Exhibition Designs

Appendix

- 245 Biography
- 246 Chronology
- 259 Renzo Piano Building Workshop, Genoa, Paris, Osaka
- 260 Collaborators
- 263 Bibliography
- 272 Photographic Credits

Introduction
Vittorio Magnago Lampugnani

Renzo Piano is a disturbing figure on the scene of contemporary international architecture, and perhaps even more disturbing on the Italian scene, in particular. After gaining practical experience in the family building business and a design apprenticeship under the expert guidance of very different architects, such as Franco Albini, Jean Prouvé, Frei Otto and Louis I. Kahn, Piano began producing his first designs and works in the late 1960s. Although that period was something of a golden age for Italian architecture, characterized by impassioned polemics, heated debates and exciting theories, the architect-builder from Genoa seemed to fight shy of all the public fervour. He took no part in public discussions, and neither wrote nor did much teaching, but simply chose quietly to pursue his work of designing and building.

Then in 1971, success in the competition for the Centre National d'Art et de Culture Georges Pompidou, jointly designed with Richard Rogers, brought him fame overnight. Over the next six years these two architects built a "cultural machine" on the Beaubourg plateau, almost the embodiment of the most daring visions of Antonio Sant'Elia and the Archigram group. The two very youthful designers were immediately hailed as the *enfants terribles* of international architecture. But this experience did not provide Piano with a comfortable niche. He might easily have made the technological expressionism of the great Parisian experiment his own personal style. But he did not; instead he chose to persevere with his unrelenting experimentation, even setting out along the hazardous way of public participation and the ephemeral.

The second turning point in his work came almost ten years after the Paris achievement. From 1981 to 1986 Piano built a museum for the Menil Collection in Houston, Texas. At first glance this building seems to be diametrically opposed to Beaubourg. While the French work is a gigantic device exalting free-ranging cultural activity, the later American building is a discrete place for the quiet contemplation of works of art: the creed of subverting through technicality has given way to a quest for normal life and silence.

The following decade was full of important projects for Piano: the IBM travelling pavilion, the Lingotto redevelopment in Turin, the IRCAM extension right alongside the Pompidou Centre, a new stadium in Bari, the redevelopment of the port of Genoa at the time of the Columbus Expo, the Rue de Meaux housing in Paris and the great Kansai international airport on an artificial island, off the coast of Osaka. After this period of intense activity, a third great turning point provided him with the occasion to rethink his approach and engage in self-renewal. In 1992 Piano won the competition to design a redevelopment scheme for the Potsdamer Platz in Berlin. This project involved him in a change of scale from the individual building to a whole urban quarter, and consisted of a single, completely new theme.

After numerous trial runs and considerable hesitation, Piano turned out an elegant master plan to be filled with buildings designed by a group of colleagues and friends. A finely balanced exercise poised between imposing strict rules but allowing sufficient freedom, between overall logic and individual taste, this plan is also a challenge to the notion of the historic city centre, an almost independent creation gradually built up over time. Fully aware of the difficulties, Piano set about artificially recreating an urban fragment, highly compressed in time, without the comfort of the unconscious spontaneity – or rather innocence – of the master builders of the past. Summarized in this fashion, Piano's œuvre might appear as being rather unsettled and elusive. And in a certain sense it is, insofar as his works reflect the insatiable curiosity and interests of a restless maker. Yet at the same time his œuvre has latent coherence, a subtle logic which comes through, not so much as a style, but as an attitude. Reminiscent of the historic avantgarde, his self-questioning brings him to approach each problem in a completely new way, and in his search for solutions, he starts again from scratch every time.

And in this sense Piano still is the *enfant terrible* he was in the 1970s. At that time what created such a stir was a brightly coloured technological box jammed into the heart of Paris. But now that Beaubourg has merged in with the city and has been accepted by public opinion, he has outraged many by doing exactly the opposite: trying to sew up a piece of city in an – apparently – conventional way. Subversion has become commonplace; now the commonplace is the truly subversive.

It is no easy matter writing about someone like Piano: his work as an architect does not rest on any elaborate theory, but on a manner (an extremely unhibited manner at that) of relating to projects. It is more rewarding, then, to relate to Piano as Piano relates to architecture: go and visit him in his studio, frequent the same places, ask questions, listen to the answers and the tone of voice. And that is exactly what I did. From such visits, frequentations, questions and, last but not least, friendship, I put together the following interview, a mosaic whose tessarae are innumerable fragments from our conversations.

Interview with Renzo Piano
Vittorio Magnago Lampugnani

V.M.L. I would like you to narrate your professional history, seen in retrospect from the beginning. I recall you once said that Beaubourg was not only a piece of architecture, but also a provocation. As an autobiographer, how would you interpret the story of your earliest buildings?

R.P. I find it all extremely straightforward and logical. First, my childhood and adolescence spent on work-sites with my father instilled in me the unspoken assumption that I would continue to do the same kind of thing. While studying architecture, I was already fascinated by the articulation of pieces.

At that time I was instinctively attracted to the challenge of lightness, and I took a delight in removing pieces as well as joining them up. A joint is visible, it is something expressed and becomes the mark of the person who made it.

My passions gradually came more sharply into focus: a passion for lightness, for making things in such a way that your own particular mark is left impressed on a piece; and a passion for the potential uses of a given thing, for its clear-cut and essential nature, plus a fascination with ports and historic centres, for building consolidated through the ages ... And these passions may have been nurtured not only by the time spent with a constructor father, but also by my childhood in a city like Genoa. In those days there was a magnificent port with plenty of ships. By definition they express the inconstant, the fleeting, lightness as well as industriousness. While still a student, I already had the chance to do some experimental work as a constructor. This was facilitated by the fact that my father's business continued, since it had been taken over by my brother.

Then from the professional point of view something very important happened - the Beaubourg episode, which was to last seven years. In terms of organization it gave me a very different awareness of team work. Previously I had been a one-man team: draftsman, constructor, engineer and architect. Beaubourg marked the beginning of a liberating development towards projects with a strong humanistic, participatory side. This development continued and eventually bloomed into a fuller understanding of the profession. That's how I began to put together the tesserae in the mosaic of the profession, balancing out professionalism, experimentation, history and form; incidentally, form is something I never discussed for years, perhaps out of some kind of reserve.

V.M.L. On the subject of form, I believe that every architect carries his own personal iconography. What are the images that you carry inside you, apart from those of the port of Genoa? Could you try and pick out your own private collection of "picture postcards" with recurrent images?

R.P. Somebody once told me that everything is already invented in childhood. As you say, we all have "postcards" which continually reappear. Earlier, I mentioned historic centres. Printed inside my head is the fact that, having been born and raised at Pegli, which is to the west and outside the city centre, going up to Genoa was a pilgrimage or an escape. When speaking about Genoa I mean the historic centre - at that time it was very close to the port - and the feeling of great weight and solid mass that I got from it. I have read some excellent definitions of this feeling, such as Paul Valéry's comment that Genoa was like a slate quarry, a cut rock. I was acutely aware of this powerful contrast between the solid mass feel of the historic centre and the lightness of the port, made up of ships, cranes, hanging loads and containers swinging through the air.

I think that most of my postcards come from these two worlds, and basically in my style of building I have opted for the second category of things - for lightness.

But it can't be said that I was only converted to historic centres after Beaubourg. I have always been deeply attracted to them, even as a boy. So much so that my degree thesis for Ernesto Nathan Rogers was on Le Manie, a Ligurian village, built after the manner of Saracen pirates. But at the same time, perhaps as a reaction to my father's profession involving work with reinforced concrete, I almost instinctively chose my field. I often see a building as a struggle between heaviness and lightness: one part is a solid mass joined to the ground, whereas the other soars upwards. For example, in the Bari stadium, the lower part is so firmly rooted in the ground that it feels as if it is the earth that is pushing upwards, while the upper part soars away.

By lightness I'm not only referring to the physical sense, to weight, but also in a figurative sense to vibration. In the Rue de Meaux housing in Paris I was interested in using terracotta because it was the right material to create the colour I wanted in the large courtyard. But on the other hand, I felt it was important to "demolish" the solid mass, making it vibrate - making it lighter. So I worked in fragmented sections, introducing splits and joining up small pieces to make a larger piece, and so on, for the whole building. This fragmenting is a kind of constant search for lightness.

V.M.L. I see a very significant difference between Beaubourg and the Rue de Meaux complex: through an emphasis on form and the polemical, Beaubourg looks like an even more industrial object than it actually is, whereas the Rue de Meaux and the IRCAM seem to explore something else. I have the impression that you are giving a craft feel to what is really an industrial product. For example, you could have broken up the brickwork with metal elements.

R.P. Yes that's true, just as in the earlier Menil Collection in Houston the iron-and-concrete element seems crafted because it appears to have been carved like a sculpture. But in fact it was produced industrially with automatic moulds, presses and counter-presses.

The Beaubourg was a youthful – perhaps rather ingenuous – work. The reference to the world of industry was almost literary: it was Jules Verne's sea-going vessel, an ironical look at technology. A taste for the polemical prevailed, and form was used symbolically to destroy the typical image of a monument and replace it with that of a factory. The factory as a place for making and, therefore, also for making culture – that was the aim.

Partly due to the previous experience of the Menil Collection, in Rue de Meaux I set my sights differently, and sharpened up the technique of the piece. Prior to Beaubourg I had designed buildings that weren't architecture but the sum of several pieces. But then the final organism gains priority over the piece, and at that point the technician has begun to make way for the architect. This change occurred gradually, and the Menil Collection is still the exact repetition of a piece.

V.M.L. But even the Rue de Meaux housing is the result of assembling detailed elements, almost "industrial bricks".

R.P. I learned to focus attention on the underlying element generating the organism and then explore it thoroughly. The pieces for Beaubourg are designed in a rough way, those for Rue de Meaux are much subtler. And without being precious, I hope that the Church of Padre Pio at San Giovanni Rotondo will be even subtler. In this case the choice of stone was prompted by the collective imagination, because everyone thinks of a church as being a stone building. But nowadays you can cut stone with computer-controlled machines and, more importantly, you can cut the stone as you like, making each piece different from the others. The planes come out in such a way that you can line the pieces up perfectly and make the system much more coherent. I would like to use stone from a quarry not far from Foggia. By resorting to this local material the Church of Padre Pio will have a far from industrial look, but will actually have been built using the most advanced industrial system imaginable: an intelligent tool will ensure that the individual piece disappears and the repetition will be effected by the automatic gesture of the machine.

The evolution of my work runs parallel to the new developments in construction processes. I have interpreted them as coherently as possible, mastering them through the Workshop – through continuous cooperation with highly-skilled and well-informed experts. Today's architect must have such instruments.

I have matured by remaining faithful to a permanent underlying thread in my work: the art of making. With the passing years I have greatly benefited from the experience, sensitivity and close support of a number of people. What is architecture, if not a set of closely interwoven disciplines? Yet at the same time I have become increasingly aware that architecture is made up of contexts, humanity, relations with people, spaces and forms.

V.M.L. On one hand, you use the latest technologies ....

R.P. Yes of course. If I didn't use modern systems, I couldn't possibly build a Japanese airport with a throughput of a hundred thousand people a day. But that's not always the way it is. Sometimes the focus is more on contexts and transparencies and on lightness in the literal sense of the word.

Your question contains an observation you already made four years ago: that there is a desire to do something complicated, as a challenge, a puzzle which is then solved.

V.M.L. Or embracing the latest technologies to feel nearer the pulse of our age, as if that were a guarantee of modernity.

R.P. That might be the case. But the fact remains that doing something complicated just to have fun solving it is a real trap. And since I have become increasingly conscious of this, I am more careful. I adopt a rather wary attitude and continually question what I'm doing.

It is probably true that following the latest technological and scientific developments gives you more confidence. I am not ashamed to own up to that; to my mind it reflects an intelligent choice. And anyhow it is not the only way of connecting oneself with

the evolution of our time. Other factors are the observation of people's behaviour and the greater awareness that the city is a fragile body which must be conserved. These are other important elements the shipwrecked creator can cling to.
Given the bewildering number of choices open to us today, we look to knowledge acquired from the fields of science and technology, from memory, history and anthropology. We are always in search of certainties.

V.M.L. Recently you have been showing a new propensity for the traditional materials of architecture, but you employ them in a wholly unusual way. Do they now interest you because you believe they affect people's behaviour, that is, you are engaging in a kind of populism? Or is it because you consider architecture only has dignity with materials like stone?
R.P. I could show some sketches from fifteen years ago when I was musing with the idea of building with clay. It is true, however, that this interest has only come through in my projects over the last ten years: there is the same intuitive attraction to the buildings of the past that I have always had for historic towns and traditional materials. For example, I have always been greatly attracted to wood.
Such materials have always been used in building and they give architecture a sense of permanence without necessarily being something monumental. I am more attracted to *cotto* – brick, terracotta and ceramic – than stone. With *cotto* you can demystify solid mass. In the sun it becomes exuberant, and the resultant colour I find very beautiful. Stone lacks this quality.
Using these materials is tantamount to admitting that architecture is never invented from scratch, but has a number of constant elements. If there is something opportunist about my choices, I think it lies in the awareness that these materials are intuitively adopted by everyone. But perhaps you can't really say that wanting to please people is being opportunist.
And then, at a time when the idea of the modern is shrouded in self-deception, there is the challenge of demonstrating that the architecture of the future will not necessarily only be made of completely new materials: plastics, special glass fibres or stainless steels. The future will not only belong to these materials but also to materials that have always been around. In the past skis were made from wood, and today you can still make fantastic skis from wood.
In our age the true and the false are confused. For twenty years there was talk of the year 2,000 and space travel, and then we discover that we will continue using things that have nothing new about them: the latest domestic iron with its aerodynamic form is no more modern than the kind used in the past. The tram is more modern than the bus which replaced it. This confusing modernity and progress with what are basically changes in form and consumer fashions is all a great illusion.
I rather relish the absurd and contradictory, so I like to show how seemingly old materials can actually be more modern than many other so-called modern materials. Terracotta, for example, is an extraordinary material: it is really very modern – it lasts for ever and breathes. You can extrude it, as we did in the IRCAM in Paris or mould it in various ways. The same may be said of wood, which can be laminated. These materials have incredible potential.

V.M.L. How are materials connected with typology? For example, the choice of wood for the scenography of *Prometheus*? Or to what extent did the fact that Rue de Meaux was a housing project influence your choice of material there?
R.P. With *Prometheus* there was never a moment's doubt. We all immediately thought of wood and its associations with the lute, music and the soundbox. It was not only a question of a return to wood, but the fact that wood is the most congruous or compatible material and this justified the use we wished to make of it. Similarly, we immediately and intuitively thought that the area of the Rue de Meaux courtyard should have a warm colour, because warmth is the intrinsic quality of that sunny space where birch leaves play with the light. Terracotta was the only material possible because it emanates a feeling of warmth and peace typical of a sheltered place and so important for life in it. And then, of course, the Church of Padre Pio could only be of stone, because it is to be built in Apulia, where all the monuments are made of stone.

V.M.L. Was it this image of the courtyard, the warmth, the play between birch trees and the terracotta cladding that dominated Rue de Meaux, or was it also an opportunity to pursue in a logical and appropriate way the experiments with brick and terracotta begun in the IRCAM project?
R.P. The urban development plan for the area doesn't include a courtyard. But fortunately the head of services at the Regie Immobilière de la Ville de Paris understood my idea. To get the right scale

in that context I only needed to work on a single fragment – just one courtyard – and this came intuitively, just as it was intuitive to choose only one material. Of course, other materials were used, such as the GRC (Glass Reinforced Concrete) panels supporting the moulded terracotta tiles. When I ponder the colour of light, I immediately begin thinking about how I will mould the pieces and assemble them. Jean Prouvé was fond of telling me that you don't begin with the general to get to the particular. You don't think first of the city and then the inner courtyard, then the appartments, then lastly the bricks or components to be assembled. You think of the city and the bricks at the same time. You blend all these things together in a kind of circular process. In practice I have never begun a project only from an overall view. Right from the start, I begin thinking about the materials, modalities, the techne and the kind of process I will use, because along with the climate, history and context, one of the first elements you relate to is the material. At least that's what happens to me.

V.M.L. Even in Berlin? After all Berlin was a very clear theme – a pure piece of urban planning.
R.P. Yes, this even happened with the Berlin project. I started off by thinking about the material, how to join up the roofing or how copper behaves in the roofing, and the structure of the terracotta components. For the small square in front of the theatre I tried to create mobile roofing elements so that in summer they would protect from the sun and channel the breeze from the north, while in winter they would be closed to obtain the opposite effect. There was nothing fanciful about this idea, because it was based on a semi-built structure. At the same time, I began to focus on how to make the fronts interplay with those of Scharoun's Staatsbibliothek. All of these are purely building considerations about materials, but they merge in with the broader themes of the heterogeneous nature of the urban profile or of the whole city.

V.M.L. While working on the competition design did you have in mind a plan of the city able to absorb any kind of architecture, or was the plan of the city in some way linked to given volumes or even a specific piece of architecture?
R.P. While preparing the project I always imagined a big colourful quarter. My ideas were still confused, however, and I didn't realize at the time that the colour I was looking for was very similar to the colour quality of the Berlin air. It was variable, changeable – different. The idea of *cotto* as a partially unifying element came later. But the thought that the architecture should be coloured was there right from the start, along with the idea that it should be raised up from the ground, that at least part of it should soar upwards. At ground level there are streets and arcades – there is transparent communication with the activities contained inside.
Without seeming contrived, the external spaces have to express peaceful urbanity, and trees play a crucial role in this. The play between trees and water gives a very important sense of vibration, of sparkling – the same thing that can be felt in the old port of Genoa – and that would appear to be of fundamental importance. In the initial design the square and streets were not yet clearly defined. But the premises were there: lines that later were to guide us. In complex projects you need a compass and the compass readings become premises you include in the project and which you must always bear in mind.
In addition to colour and the themes of upward movement, of transparency, and the nature of the existing structures and streets, the profile of the city was of fundamental importance. In a confused kind of way I felt the need to give the city a powerful and articulated presence. The Weinhaus Huth was the starting point for the project. Now I realize that along with the Staatsbibliothek in other ways, the Weinhaus Huth was our life-raft, and we clung to it like survivors of a shipwreck. The theme of articulating the profile grew stronger, partly because we wished to establish a relationship with these buildings, and partly to obtain a more acceptable relationship with the streets. If you then ask me if this implies already having the architectural form in mind, then the answer is no. Even at the risk of seeming irresponsible, I must confess that I rarely know with any certainty where the project will end up. If you already know at the outset, it is because you have applied a model, your own if you are a clever architect, or someone else's, if you are not so clever.

V.M.L. How did you set about the competition? What did you already know about it? Did you go and explore the site and its history?
R.P. As always, when you work on a design there is a combination of various influences. A mixture – as the venerable Borges said – of memory and oblivion, of things you have already got inside you and others that you have never known, or have forgotten and

re-discovered. When you work on very complex projects you must spend a long time "digesting": you accumulate knowledge and learn to wait in silence.

And in fact everything begins to happen during this period of silence: you absorb the historical and climatic aspects – the things which have influenced the surrounding area for centuries – and they gradually begin to piece themselves together.

The part I already had in mind was the conviction that in designing a neighbourhood for 30,000–40,000 people, there was a need for collective spaces with convivial activities as well as urban spaces, such as the square and the streets. I was also aware that colour and water were important, and later I discovered that Berlin is also made of water. When I went there for the competition I spent a lot of time wandering about with my hands in my pockets, and I rediscovered water. This is what I meant by a mixture of memory and oblivion.

Then I had to face what I could never have imagined without visiting the city: the incredible challenge of measuring up to Scharoun. This was not a question of engaging in "heroic disobedience", but a sense of adventure that intuitively drew me to Scharoun's great cultural complex. And although his building was not in the competition area, I wanted to link it up with my project. In the 1920s the competition area was a mythical place, where all sorts of things were invented. Everything that happened in it was remarkable: from theatre to cinema and music hall. The most important cultural events took place in that part of the city. And although designing a building for a historical site may often be a rather daunting prospect, at least you can take advantage of the existing axes, rules, rhythms and scales, since you only really need to complete them. But here these elements are missing. So there is an even more powerful need to gather life round a centre, only to find you have nothing to graft on to, not even those famous rules – which contrary to what some short-sighted people claim – help by giving you discipline.

Then there is German culture and what you know or learn about it. How can you forget that Germany is the home of expressionism, of great cultural movements? And even if extraneous to my basic way of looking at things, something of this is sedimented in the design process.

I went to see Mendelsohn's work, and did all the architectural pilgrimages. Not in search of any formal inspiration, but to try and grasp the nature of the city. I felt the need for a sense of a built mass, which isn't necessarily heavy. Yet it would be a mistake to build a "paper-thin" Berlin.

V.M.L. How do you think you will achieve this sense of body and so realize the ambition not to create cladding but massive volumes? Will you use the materials and technologies you have already tried out, at the IRCAM, for example?

R.P. No, not at all. I definitely won't work with the technique used in the IRCAM, because it is a "paper-thin" technique. Nor will I use the technique of Rue de Meaux, because it, too, basically involved creating a surface – a vibrant surface but a surface nonetheless. I already know that Kollhoff and Lauber und Wöhr are going to use traditional brick. I am more interested in knowing what the state of the art is in reinforced ceramics and reinforced or moulded terracotta. But any approach becomes incoherent if you fail to consider the different relationships between outside and inside in the office or at home. The question of the theatre is much easier, since it is an inverse volume expressed blindly. But when you come to the functions for living in a house or working in an office, there is a more important relationship with the outside. All this concentrating on the façade is very risky, if it doesn't take the inside as a starting point.

What is the meaning of the view outside for a seven-metres deep office, or how important is the lighting or the relations between the positions of the door and the window? We have been reflecting on these points, because ideally we would like to devise something that didn't simply follow the rather banal solution of ribbon windows. I'd rather work on the interplay between transparent and opaque sections in the façade. In this way, since the components have their own width, you continually switch perception from the inside to the outside.

I don't think we'll use brick in the traditional sense of the word. We definitely won't repeat anything we have already done. The technique of reinforced moulded pieces might turn out to be much more interesting. One of the great recent inventions is composite materials, made either by conglomerating or laminating. GRC is one example of what you can do with concrete when you reinforce it with glass fibre as opposed to steel, which entails working with large pieces. We used GRC for the panels in Rue de Meaux. They are thin, bear loads and can even be made into profiles. Reinforced terracotta is another material we might use. It would help us overcome the usual limits of size imposed by fragility and high firing temperatures.

This constant blending of purely building, scientific or productive themes with aesthetic aspects involves a kind of very stimulating mental gymnastics. For example, you can now cut stone to only three millimetres thick and support it with a base to give it body. The material is full of potential and the technique can also be applied to ceramic. I would like to open up the way for this kind of research which might even lead to some wild variation since we have to design very different buildings: a theatre, a casino, housing, a shopping centre and offices. I believe that once you set out in this direction something new will be invented, otherwise you just end up with the conventional curtain wall.

V.M.L. But if you don't come up with anything new, don't you just resort to the solid sandstone wall?
R.P. No, and this is something very important. It has nothing to do with being frightened of indulging in nostalgia, it is simply because there is no-one who can do it for you any more.

V.M.L. All the buildings in Potsdamer Platz are very different from each other because they reflect different functions and situations. And of course there are other architects involved in your project.
R.P. As coordinator, I find it difficult to impose a very strict master plan. I don't want to interfere too much with the other architects' freedom to design. That would mean impoverishing the project.

V.M.L. But isn't that a typical feature of Berlin – this setting limits to the creativity of architects working on the city?
R.P. Ideally it would be nice to exercise discipline without curbing creativity. There is only a very thin line between being naturally tuned into the city and being boring. Naturalness can easily degenerate into boredom, just as invention might become idiosyncratic excess. Being natural, tidy, straightforward and disciplined is fine. Being boring is not. Similarly we want inventiveness and creativity, but not excess. In this sense all of us – Isozaki, Kollhoff, Lauber und Wöhr, Moneo, Rogers and myself – take risks, each in his or her own way. The overall result may be a little untidy, but that doesn't bother me. The reality is much more beautiful than the drawings, because you can't draw the living atmosphere. There are six of us building this corner of the city, and after each project had been presented, I asked what material they had chosen. It was at that point the fairly spontaneous idea of terracotta came to me. I am not at all convinced by the rather literary idea that the unity of a city derives from using the same materials throughout; the colour we give the air is more important. If we all really work at these things, the atmosphere will have a single colour, which is rather like the fragrance of a city's mulberry trees or the sound of a river. Some elements unify not by making uniform but by holding things together.

V.M.L. This Berlin experiment is basically an attempt to concentrate into a few years the centuries-long development of the European city. But no matter how good the designers involved are, I wonder if this is not an impossible task?
R.P. This is very much a problem. Perhaps it is a rather venturesome undertaking, but I have no choice than to carry on regardless. The city's beauty is due to the unity of its materials, the collective culture, but above all to the passing years – to time. The architects involved in my project are very different and that is why I have to impose a certain discipline. But in addition to architectural considerations, another fundamental theme must be respected: life. Only half of the city is stones and bricks, the other half is people. We are living through a dramatic contradiction: if building a city in five years is very difficult in architectural terms it is even more difficult in human terms. The only solution is to attract people to the area. The usual way to do so is by creating a great shopping centre: a supermarket which acts as a magnet, but which also closes people into the belly of a system, leaving the streets outside bare. When you talk to shopping-centre experts, they tell you that their target public is the middle class. But this is a mistake. The human value is not only introduced by combining functions – shopping, housing, hotels, culture … – but also by sharing them out among people from all walks of life.

The fabric of a city takes hundreds of years to be woven; life will slowly come back, just as it slowly left. Unfortunately, to speed up this process you need an urban machinery capable of immediately attracting the multiplicity of life. But will we be able to control this process so it doesn't gradually suffocate all the rest of life? Can we justify advocating a rapid but effective machinery, or should we resort to a slower and less effective method? This contradiction is perhaps even more dramatic than the architectural problem. And together, the two make the challenge we face doubly difficult.

Buildings and Projects

The Menil Collection Museum, Houston, 1981–86

Site plan.

In 1981 Dominique de Menil commissioned Renzo Piano to built a new museum in Houston for one of the finest collections of Modern, Surrealist and Primitive art in the world. John de Menil and his wife Dominique had begun collecting in Paris in the early 1930s, and as the collection grew they had felt an increasingly strong desire to make a home for it.

The main design idea was to create a space that encouraged a direct and relaxed relationship between the visitor and the works of art: a familiar setting stripped of all monumental rhetoric and surrounded by nature. The chosen site was a green area in a nineteenth-century residential quarter. A number of existing buildings on the site were converted to be used for complementary museum activities, and together with the Menil Collection they form a kind of "museum village".

The whole project hinged round the need to use natural light. The problem was how to handle the natural light from the roof in the climatic conditions of Houston, characterized by very hot sun and high humidity. The solution was ferro-cement. The special properties of ferro-cement, such as its thin structure, lightness, and malleability, met the design requirements for the structural and environmental aspects.

The museum roof is transparent, the basic element being a ferro-cement "leaf" supported by a pliable steel structure, repeated three hundred times to form the covering for the whole building. Above this structure is a glass element able to filter out ultraviolet rays. The profile of the ferro-cement elements prevents direct sunlight from shining on the exhibited works, but at the same time provides natural lighting, which changes with the atmospheric conditions. The air conditioning functions by introducing slow flows of air through conduits in the flooring. Air comes from the outside at ambient temperatures before rising slowly to be gathered at roof level in the interspace between the glass and the ferro-cement leaves. In this way the temperature and humidity are kept constant. The tree-system adopted is based on the continuous refrac-

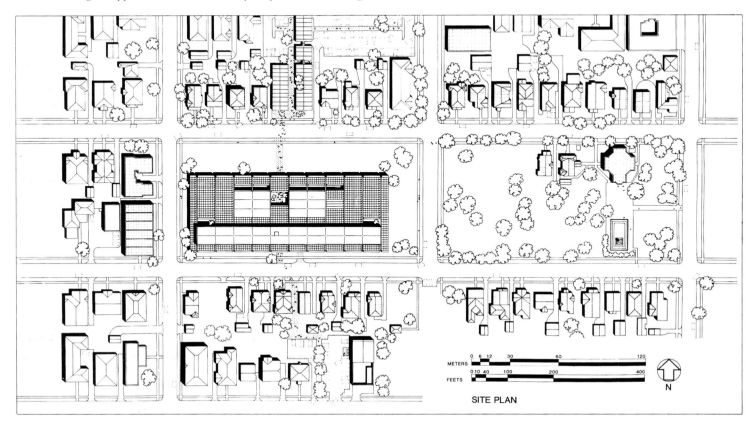

SITE PLAN

Aerial view of the museum.

tion of light from one leaf to another; thus areas of shade are created without blocking the ventilation. The roof screens are basically leaves arranged in such a way that air passes through but the harmful ultraviolet rays are filtered out. The roof structure is extended outside to form porticoes stretching into the tropical garden. They are thus a vital link in the intimate relationship between architecture and nature. Inside, the main circulation corridor or "promenade", runs the length of the building (150 metres) and feeds into more articulated areas used as additional exhibition spaces or places where visitors may meet or rest.

The museum was integrated with the surrounding buildings by keeping the profile low and using the same kind of treatment for the outside walls: the steel structure is painted white, while the external surface is clad with traditional clapboarding.

The collection is set out in two distinct areas: on the ground floor are the public exhibition rooms, whereas in the upper-floor Treasure House the rest of the collection, permanently stored in special containers, may be consulted by visiting scholars.

Design sketches.

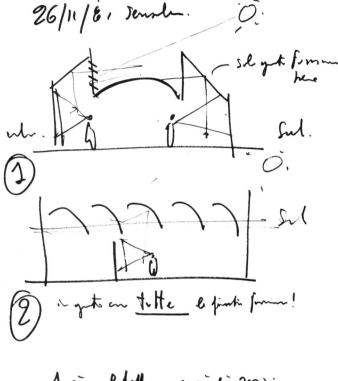
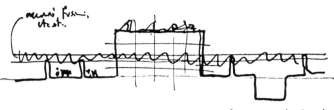
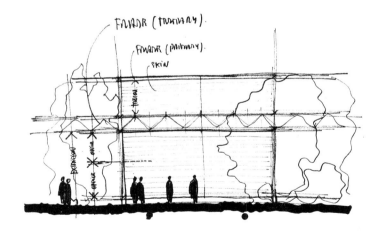

View of east façade.

Front view.
Detail of the roofing system.

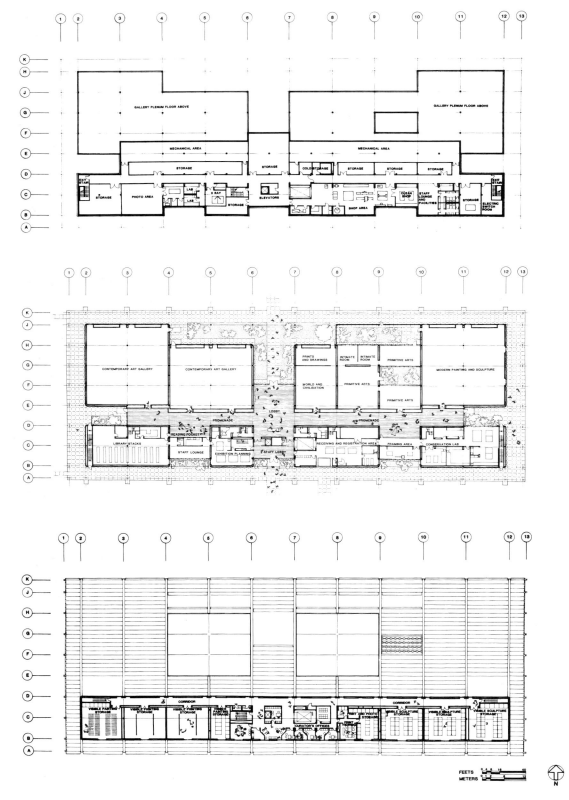

Plans of lower floor, ground floor and first floor.

The entrance portico.
Detail of the roofing system.

A workshop at night.
South elevation.
Two first floor windows.

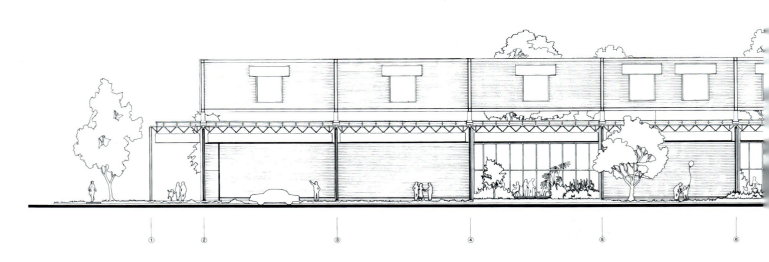

24

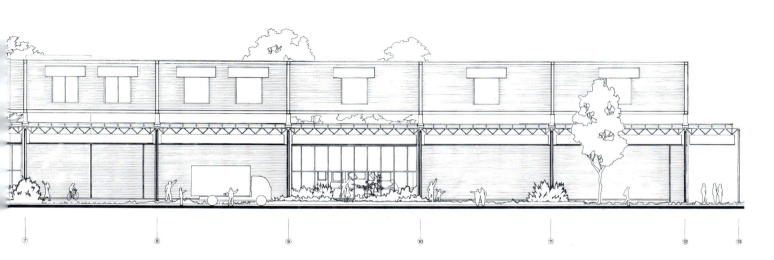

Cross section.
Drawing of daylighting system.
An exhibition room.

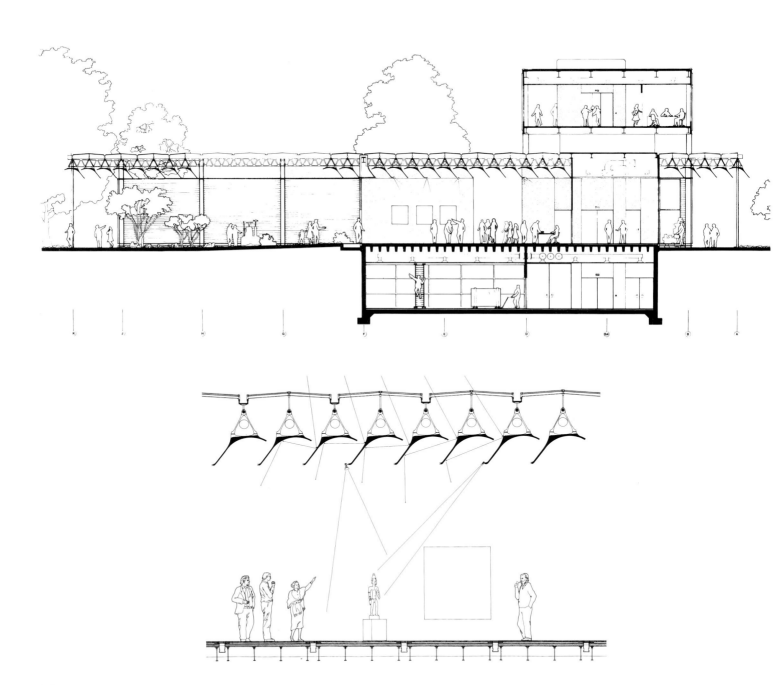

Exhibition spaces.

The circulation spine.

Metropolitan Railway Stations, Genoa, 1983–94

Brin station in its urban context.

The very dense urban fabric of Genoa (population 800,000) is concentrated on a narrow strip of land between mountains and the sea. The city's need for a more efficient urban transport system was met by this project for a new metropolitan railway with eight kilometres of tracks, eleven stations and a capacity to transport 25,000 people per hour in both directions.

The line is partly underground – on converted existing structures (old railway lines and tunnels) – and partly overhead on completely new raised sections (overpasses and bridges). The project divides the metropolitan system into modular sections. In this way an economy of scale is introduced with consequent time saving in construction schedules.

The stations were analyzed and arranged into individual structural elements. These were then grouped into families according to their various functions (cladding, lighting, graphics, etc.), and a catalogue of all the components was produced. Each station's design is a combination of these components, which are instantly recognizable for users and thus ensure easy orientation and safety.

The stations are divided in two parts: the first consists of rails, platforms and entry points; and the second of the access areas from the street level forming a link between the station and the city. The design of the access areas has been influenced by the surrounding urban context and consequently their form varies from one station to another.

Brin station: view of the platforms and cross section.

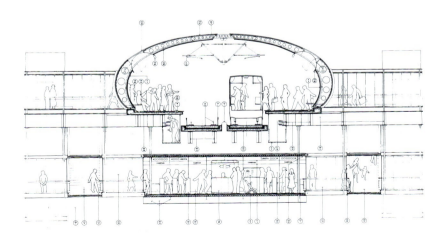

Plan of Genoa with the new metropolitan line.
Brin station: elevation and roof-level plan.

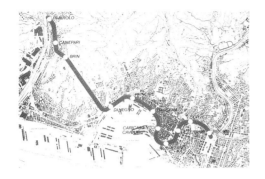
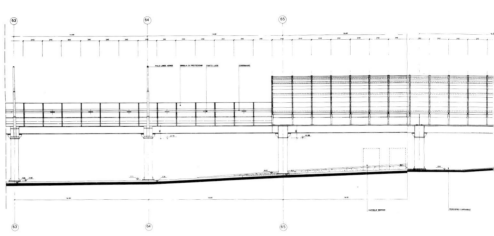
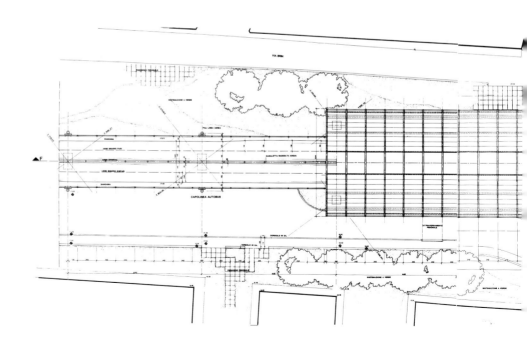

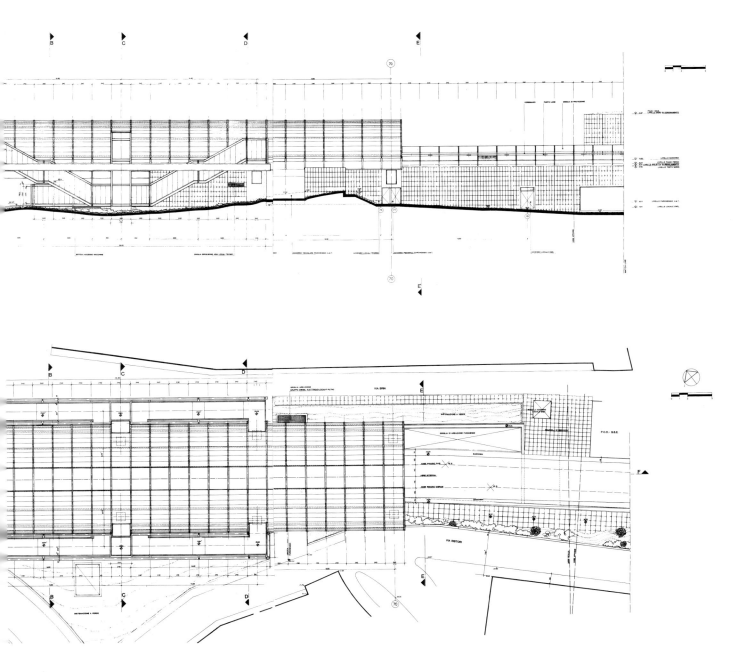

Detail of Brin station.

Section of a typical station.
Section of the Porta Principe station.
Model of a station.

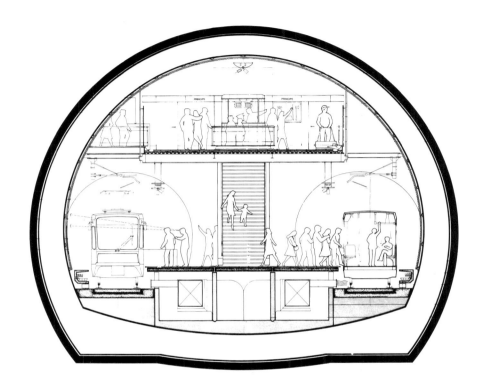

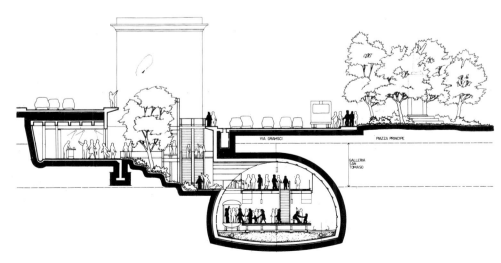

*View of the station access system.
Longitudinal section of a stretch
of metropolitan line.
Detail of footbridge.*

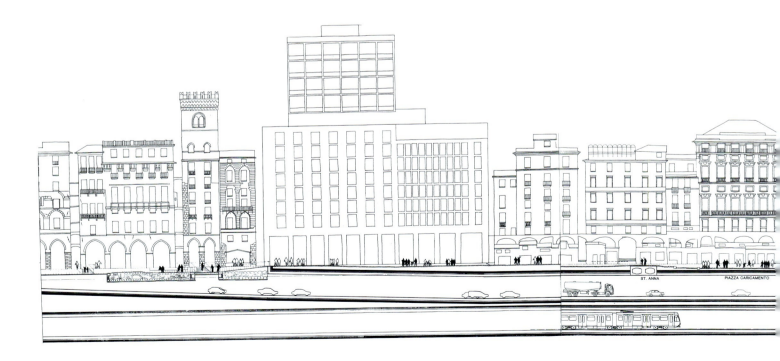

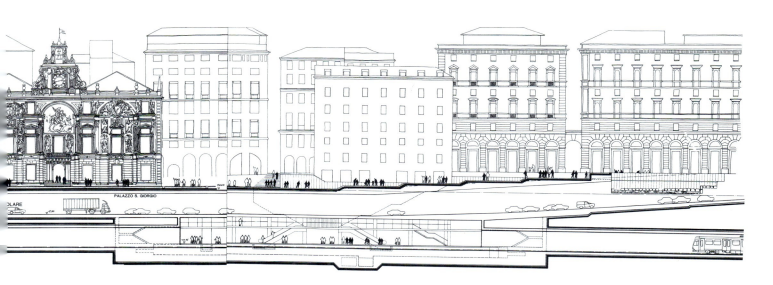

Research Institute for Light Metals, Novara, 1985–87

Model and façade showing the extendible prefabricated system.

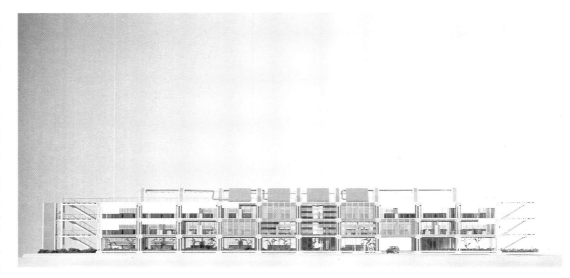

The design for the institute was based on two well-defined objectives: to create a highly flexible building and to design, develop and apply a new aluminum frame façade, which could later be marketed by the client.

The first objective was met by dry assembling an entirely prefabricated raw reinforced concrete structure. Consisting of hollow beams, columns and flooring, the structure is highly flexible within the main grid (8.40 metres). The hollow pillars (section 1.20 × 1.20 metres) were all assembled in a single piece. Thanks to this system, the skeleton was completed in only three months.

To meet stability, flexibility and vibration resistance requirements, the prefabricated concrete structure had to be relatively heavy.

The building is heated and cooled throughout by a pulsed air system. Air is driven through convector vents situated in the central corridor ceiling. Each bay is equipped with four adjustable-flow convector vents.

Lighting is fitted into the flooring ribs. Since the building stands on an industrial-estate road, the ground-floor offices are all positioned on the courtyard side. A covered garden, the length of the ground-floor façade, creates a filter between road and offices.

The second objective – the development of a new aluminum frame façade – provided the opportunity to try out new structural glazing techniques based on the fundamental principles of the curtain wall.

The façade, whose key structural element is the aluminum frame, not only has to meet the needs and constraints imposed by users, envi-

Plans of roof, second and first floors, ground floor and basement.

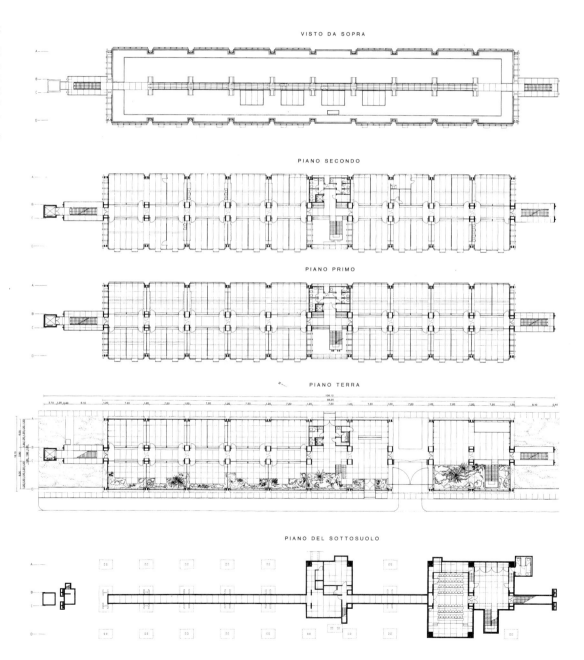

ronment, climate and exposure, but also has to be lively and attractive. The cladding was thus uniform and transparent, a kind of backbone supporting numerous functional but also decorative features: screens, blinds, doors, heating services, sunshades, cleaning robots etc.

Using layers with various degrees of transparency, the building completely loses its static aspect and becomes a lively expressive element in the urban context.

The façade is composed of factory-assembled 7.2 × 3.6 metre frame and silicon bonded glass units which hook onto an aluminum bar set into the nosing of a concrete slab.

Both inside and out, the prefabricated system will accept any type of rigid screen or sun-blinds. At Novara moulded aluminum stiffeners were chosen, and their sleek elegant finish reveals the full potential of this technique. Lastly, some other moulded or extruded aluminum elements were developed for stairs, rails etc.

Partial view of the main façade.
Cross section.

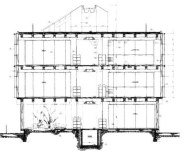

Views of the internal stairs.

Conversion of the Fiat Lingotto Works, Turin, 1985–93

Aerial view of the factory before redevelopment.

The former Fiat factory of Lingotto, an historic landmark symbolizing the industrialization of Turin. In future, it will continue to play an important role in city life.
The new Lingotto project has two objectives: to make a multi-use complex and to preserve the building's architectural identity.
After seventy years of car manufacturing, the great Turin factory is thus to be given a new lease of life as a multi-use centre whose facilities bring together and encourage interactions between education and industry, technological services and cultural events, and research activities and conferences.
Lingotto is a monument in its own right, a proud symbol to its history of pragmatism, engineering and hard work. No matter what its future function will be, its roots in the past must be conserved. The common denominator of all its new facilities is thus the connection with industry: no longer in the traditional manufacturing sense, but as a place offering services closely related to industrial activities.
The underlying aim of the structural modifications is to establish close links between the building and the city, nature and work, and technology and the environment.
Matté Trucco's original design with its repeated geometric pattern is completely conserved, whereas the incongruous later additions are demolished. The south ramp is stripped of all superfluous elements and becomes the essential link with the old press shop.
The city enters the factory again through the unifying element of nature: trees are planted in areas once dominated by industrial plants and railway lines, thus healing wounds opened up when the factory was originally built. This triumph of na-

The worksite.
Internal courtyard.

ture is emphasized by a tree-lined avenue leading from a park to gardens inside Lingotto.

The main entrance of the complex passes through the former office block in Via Nizza and continues by means of a ramp from the street level to the first floor, which now contains the public passageways connecting the renovated enclosed area to the rest of the city. The pedestrian walkway leads to two columned passages which, in turn, provide access to the services sector and the goods lifts, which are set into the building's grid.

The general public will mainly visit the exhibition spaces, conference centres and air-conditioned areas on the ground floor; the vehicular entrances are also situated on this level.

The redevelopment of the Lingotto complex is to be carried out in several independent stages. This means that after each area is completed, it can become fully operational without waiting for the rest of the project to be finished as well.

This decision was made on various grounds: technical – the most rational approach to the operations involved; economic – to obtain the quickest returns on investments; and philosophical – Lingotto as work in progress, symbolizing the continuing modernization and evolution of Turin.

The various stages are unified, however, by using a homogeneous set of components (window and door frames, lighting systems, flooring and partitions). These components are integral parts of the project and thus ensure that the building has an overall formal unity.

The new Lingotto centre has been designed in such a way as to optimize communications, synergies and capital investment. It is an open

Longitudinal section.
Elevation.
Design sketch.
Diagram of functions.

space able to meet the needs of a wide range of functions, such as fairs, exhibitions and other services. To optimize communications with the outside world, applications from the latest developments in technology, information technology and telecommunications have been introduced.

The public also has access to some parts of the advanced computer network at the heart of the building's control system, which also regulates heating, ventilation, lighting, entrances, car parks and security.

A telecom network enables users to consult major Italian and international data banks. Videophones and close-circuit television equipment are available for international video-conferences.

On completion, Lingotto will be a complex "machine" able to interact with the urban environment and link up with some of the most advanced communications systems.

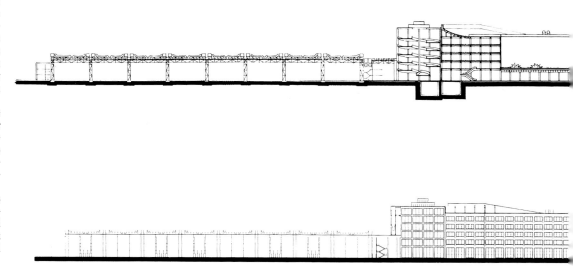

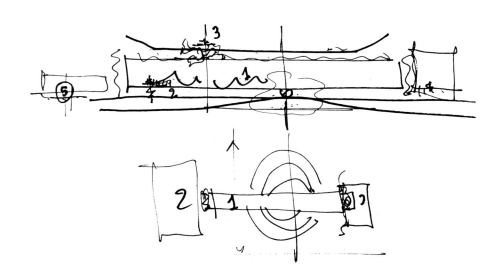

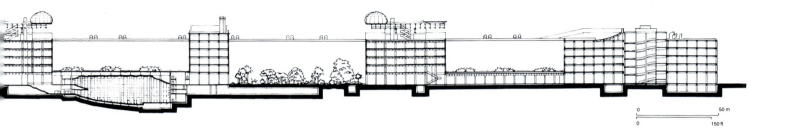

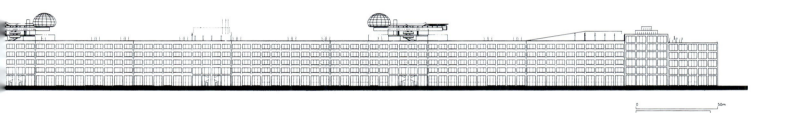

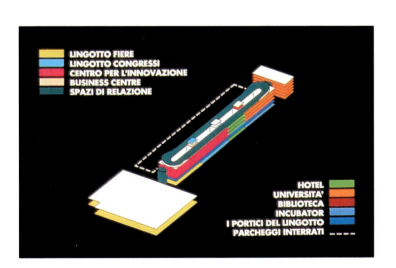

The auditorium: model and detail of section.

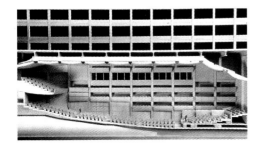
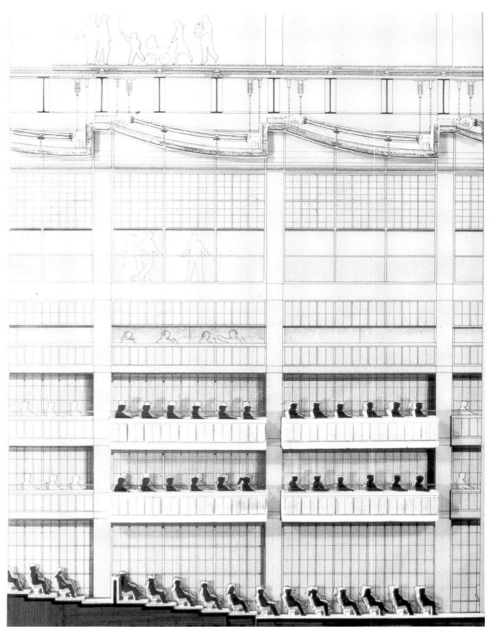

Work in progress on the auditorium.

Auditorium: longitudinal section and floor plan.

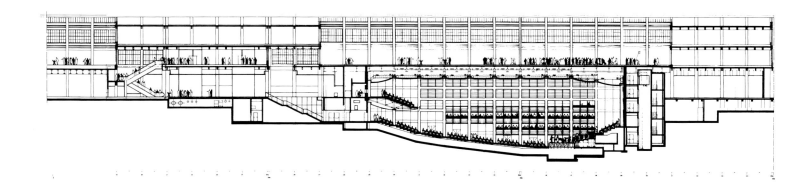

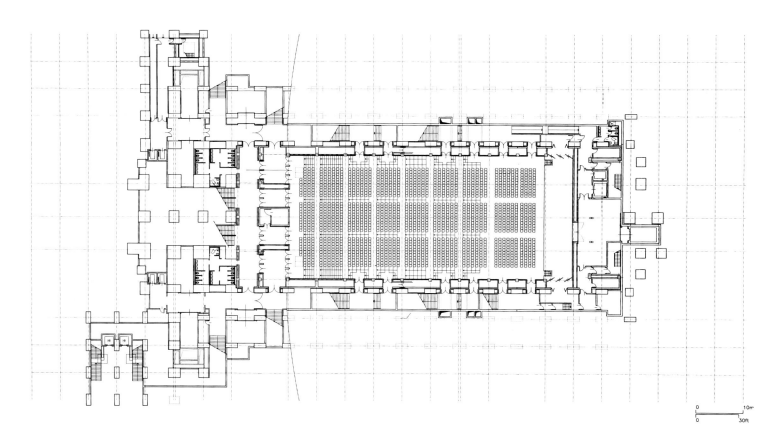

Section through the galleries.

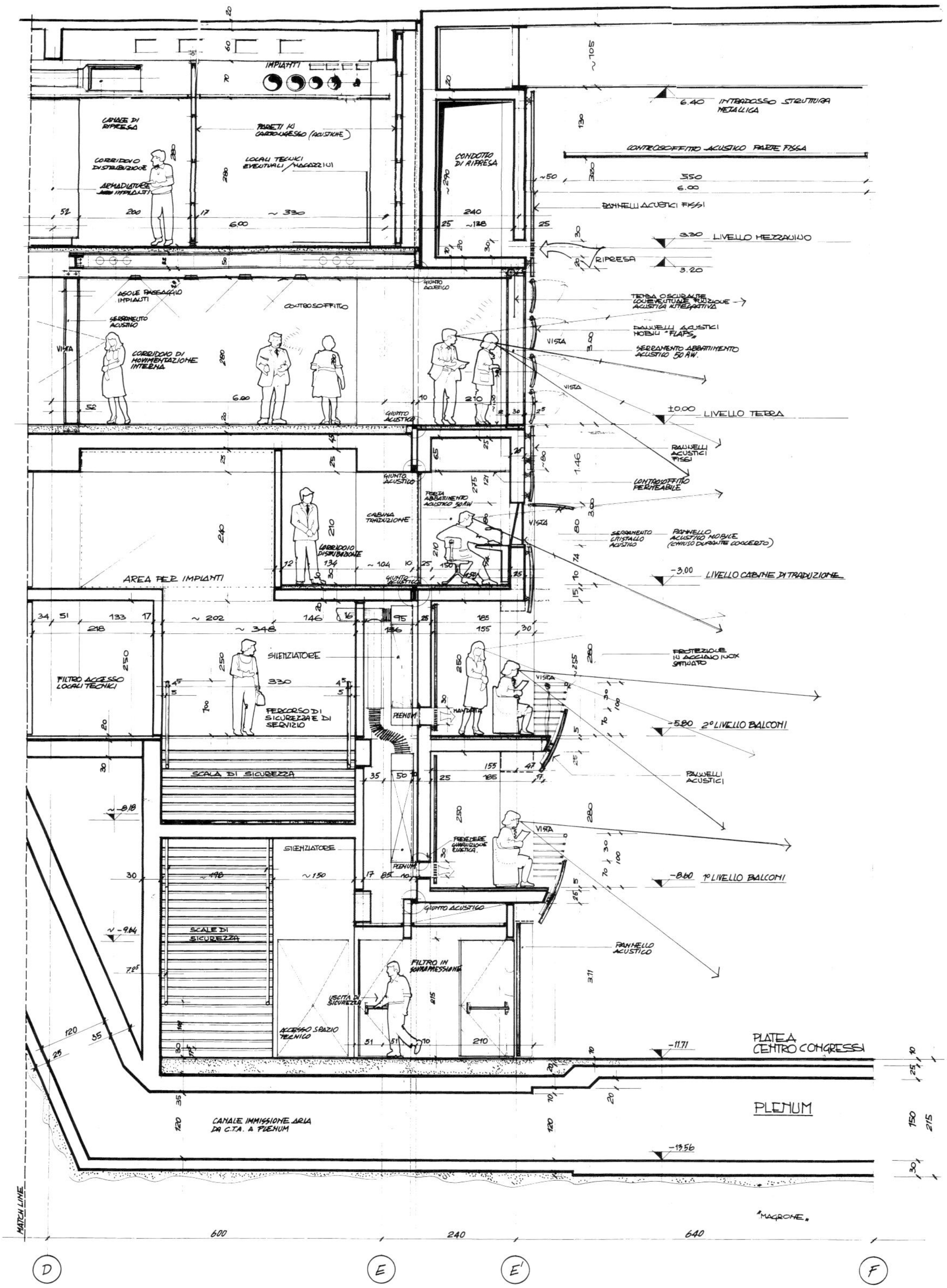

Views of the auditorium interior.

Section through the movable stage.

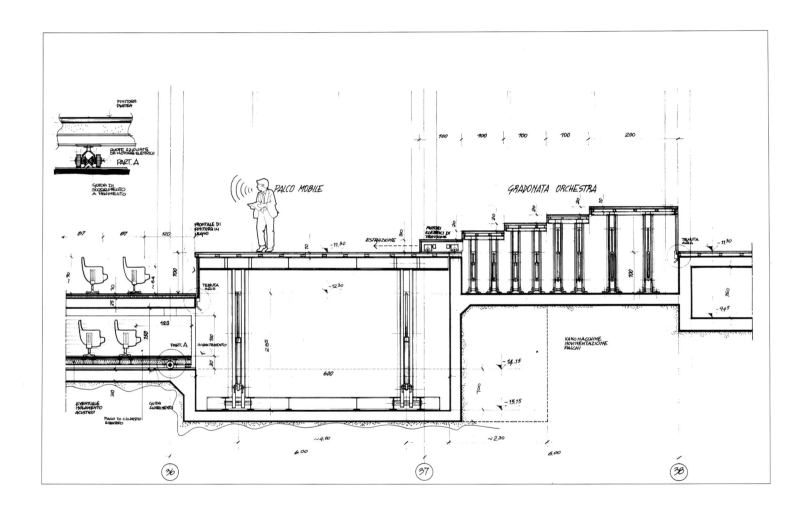

The Fairs Centre at night.

Section through façade segment. Section and plan of the bubble structure on the roof.

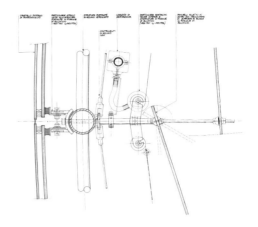

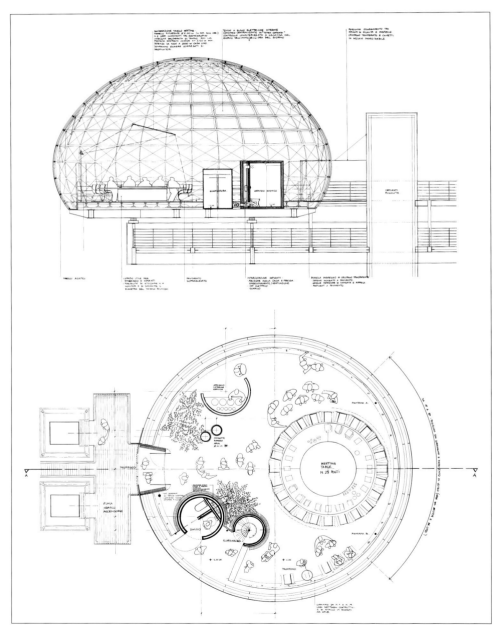

*Section through circulation system.
Diagram of the bubble structure.*

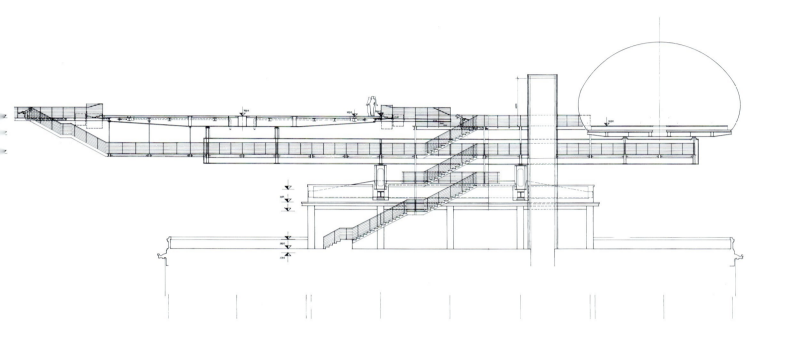

Work in progress on the historic roof test-track.

Detail of an internal ramp.

Bank and Offices for Credito Industriale Sardo, Cagliari, 1985–93

Front façade and entrance.
Façade of a lateral building.

The winning design for the 1985 "Piazza for Cagliari" competition, organized by a Sardinian Bank, consists of two parts: a public area and a private area. The public area is composed of a large pedestrian square over a two-storey underground car park. The square is bounded on two sides by buildings and on the other sides by large green areas that provide a connection with the part of the city oriented towards the sea-front.

Although on the edge of the project area, the green areas are an important link with the context, since they are the natural continuation of a hill with a sanctuary (Bonaria), which overlooks the complex, and of the city's palm-lined central promenade.

The private area contains the three volumes of the bank building. The first two are low blocks along the sides of the area, while the third part stands transversely and rises above the other two. The ground floor is mainly occupied by activities involving exchanges with the outside world and thus constitutes a large public concourse.

The top floor of the highest block contains the management offices of the bank, whereas the other floors accommodate offices and services also used by the public. There is no rigid division between public and private areas. People can move freely between the two by crossing the open-air and semi-covered squares used for recreational and entertainment facilities, including a 250-seat auditorium for conferences, shows, meetings and congresses.

The large porticoed space under the highest block is a kind of stage structure containing the production box, lighting and sound equipment both for open-air shows held in the

Front and lateral elevations and a cross section of the complex.

square and for activities inside the auditorium. This structure is available for both private and public organizations.
The bank building has three parts: the two three-storey lateral blocks and the central six-storey block. The appearance of lightness of the collective areas is contrasted by a more solid appearance for the private offices: here the exposed reinforced concrete structure results in a modular grid pattern on the façades, infilled by glass surfaces or screens and sunshades made of local stone.

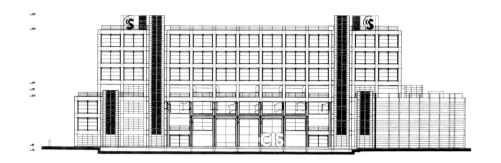

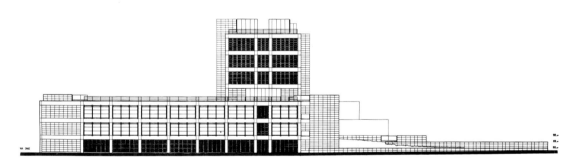

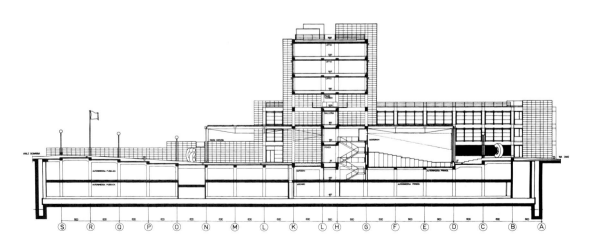

Plans of ground and first floor of the complex.
Plan of the central block.

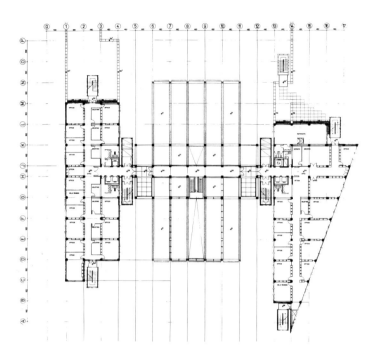
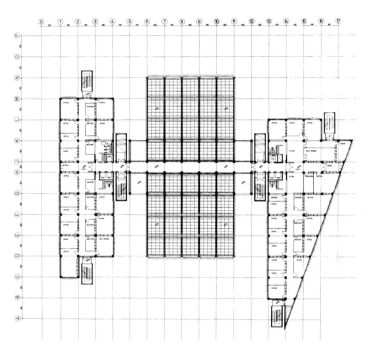
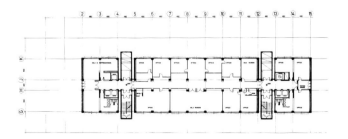

Variations of the auditorium interior.

Sports Centre, Ravenna, 1986

Design sketches.
Site plan.

This new sports centre in the southern suburbs of Ravenna is situated next to a football stadium. The centre consists of two buildings: the first, which gently traces the curve in an adjacent avenue, houses all the services facilities for the users; the second is a gymnasium (with 4,000-seat spectator capacity) whose roof is made of a broad shell-shaped structure.

The main entrance is situated at the junction between the two buildings and is an important pivot in the design, not only from a symbolic point of view, but also in structural and functional terms.

The building's formal system is based on part of a trochoid. Studies were conducted to ascertain how a variable number from ten to twenty prefabricated V-shaped beams could be combined in a single cast. Each beam was around eight metres long; their width began with sixty centimetres in the middle, became gradually wider towards the outside, reaching two and a half metres at the edge. The order of the beams was calculated so that the weight of each would be balanced by the gradual change of width.

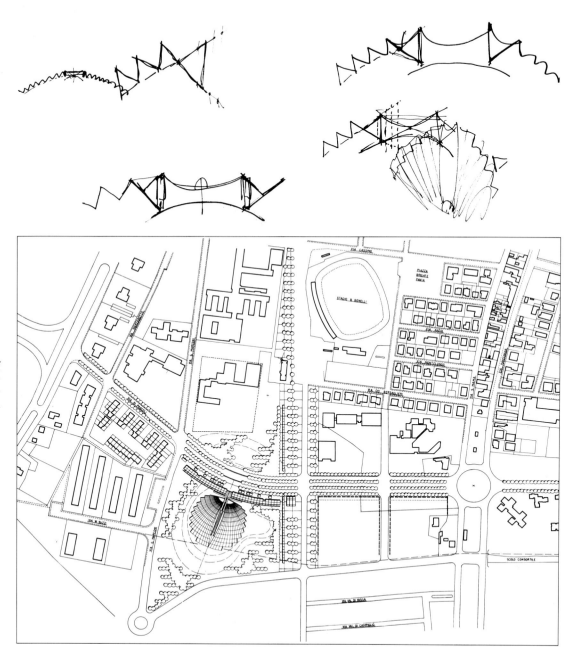

Model of the sports centre.

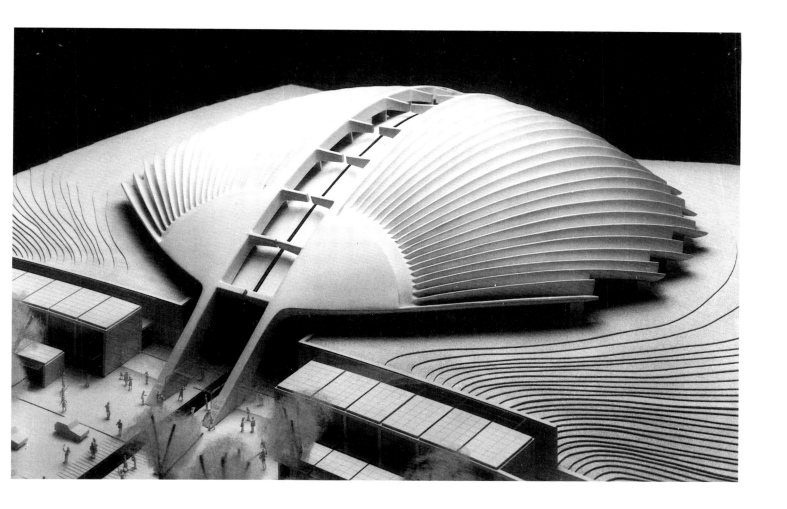

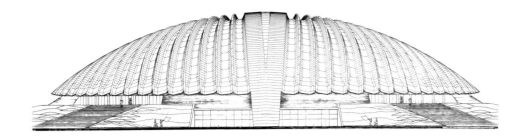

Elevations and sections.

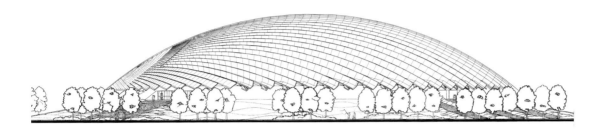

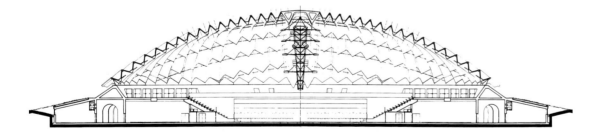

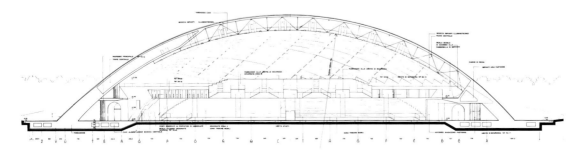

Design sketch and floor plans.

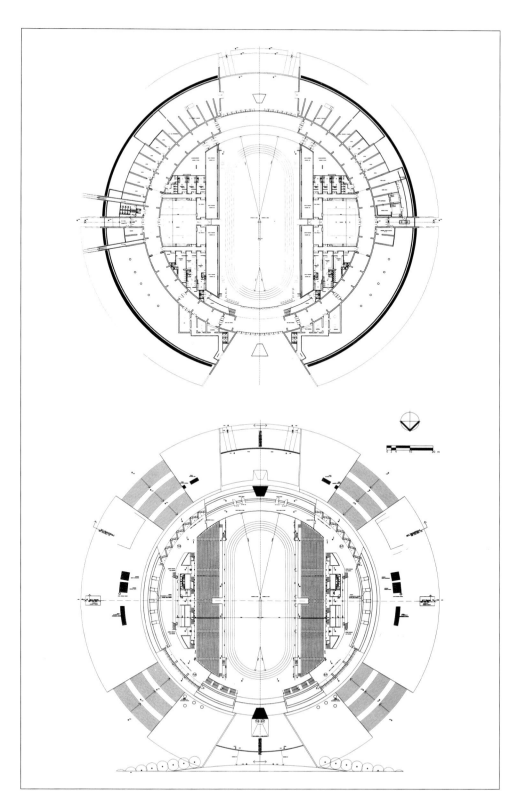

Redevelopment of the Bastions and City Gate,
La Valletta, Malta, 1986

The project area.
Section through bridge and moat.

The island of Malta lies halfway between Gibraltar and Alexandria in the stretch of the Mediterranean separating Sicily from the African coast. In the early nineteenth century the island became a British colony and despite gaining independence in 1964, it still conserves many British customs with English being widely spoken.
The reopening of the old port of La Valletta would join up the expanding modern city with the historical nucleus. The works envisaged should be part of a larger project to redevelop the whole historic centre, from the fortress of St Elme along the sea-front as far as the Floriana botanical gardens. The gate would thus be a pivot on the communications axis between these two points. The approach adopted was to reestablish the original plan of the historic walls erected to defend the city from Turkish invasions but badly damaged by the reconstruction of the gate. Now that Malta no longer needs to defend against marauding enemies, it wishes to conserve its heritage.
Designed to contrast with the solid mass of the fortress and the walls, a new light narrow bridge takes visitors up over the moat and bastions – giving them the impression of having vaulted over the mighty city defences – into the historic centre. Narrower than the existing structure, this new bridge provides splendid views of gardens in the moat area at the foot of the walls.
From underground parking beneath the gardens stairs leads up to Freedom Square, an empty area to be transformed into a cultural complex and destined to become the liveliest quarter in the city.

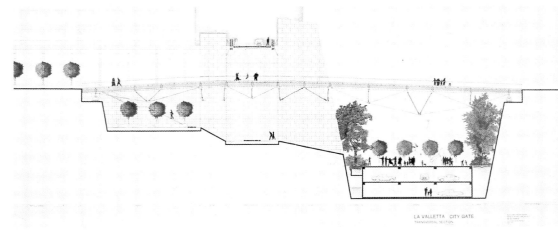

Section showing underground car park.
Plan of project area.

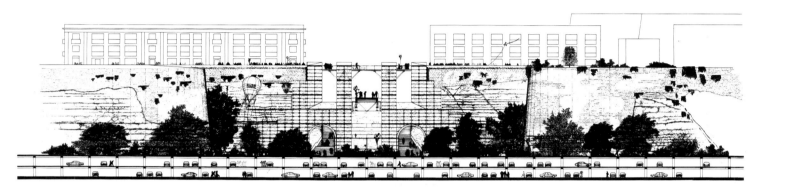

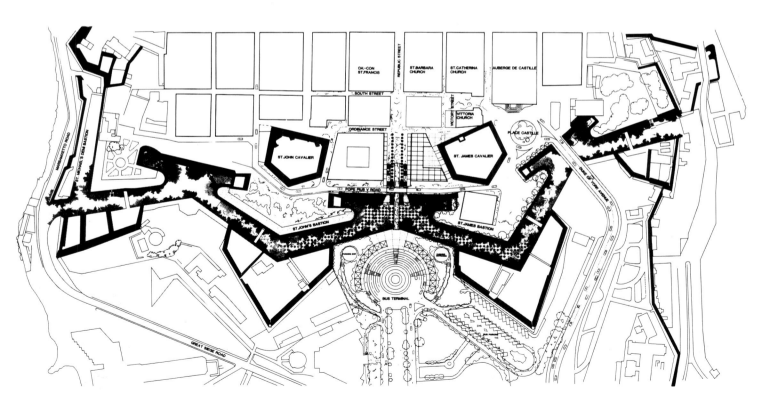

67

Rehabilitation of the Palladian Basilica and City Hall, Vicenza, 1986

Longitudinal and cross sections.

The Basilica of Vicenza has never been a religious monument. The ancient Roman term signifies a place for public business and administration, and in fact in Mediaeval times the Vicenza Basilica was the seat of the Council of Five Hundred and the law courts. In 1546 the thirty-eight-year-old Palladio won his first commission and fame by designing a two-storey loggia round the existing Gothic building.

The rehabilitation project (with Ove Arup & Partners, London) focused on analyzing non-tangible elements of the space such as the light, sound, and air movements inside the Basilica at various times of the year. Acoustic and reverberation studies in the fifteenth-century hall revealed that it was an ideal space for performing Renaissance music. Lighting experiments conducted inside measured the intensity and colour of light and the temperature caused by it to ensure there would be no damage to the existing structure and to obtain the desired effects by taking full advantage of this superb space.

The project thus reintroduces activities to the Basilica without endangering its integrity. The proposed cultural and civic centre covers 5,500 square metres: 2,200 for cultural activities, the rest for civic and administrative functions. The complex includes a large auditorium, a theatre, spaces for dance shows and exhibitions, a study centre, a library, shops, restaurants, city-council offices and small meeting rooms.

Other buildings connected to the Basilica, such as the Domus Comestabilis, the tower in the Piazza delle Erbe and the city-council offices are given new functions, thus creating a small but lively civic and cultural centre in an area destined always to be the heart of the city.

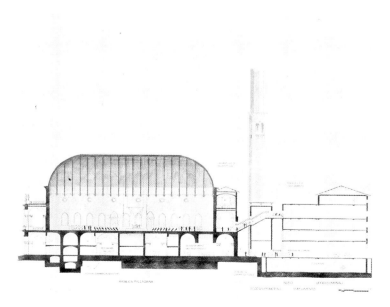
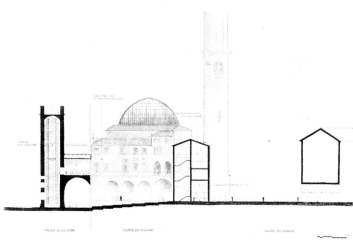

Roof-level plan.
Axonometric section.
Ground-floor plan.

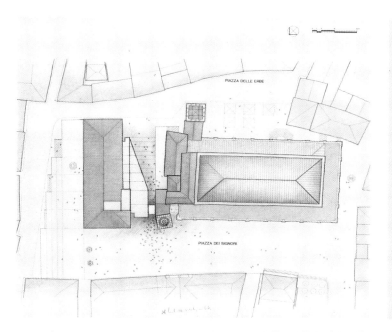
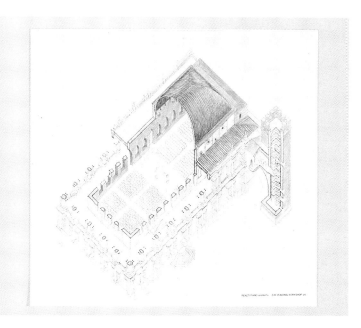
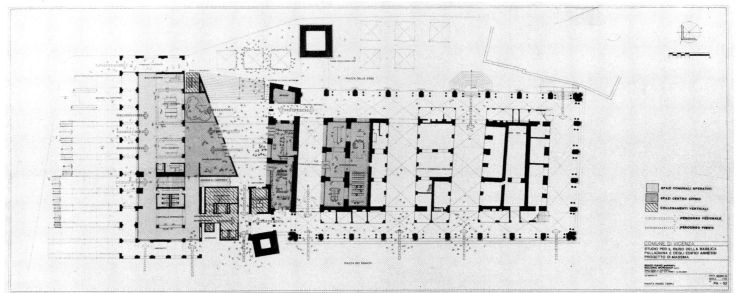

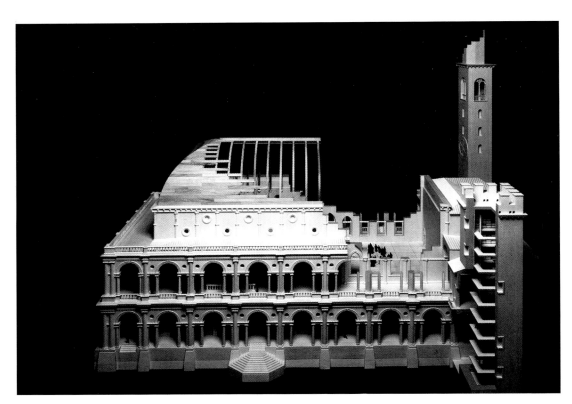

Views of sectioned model.

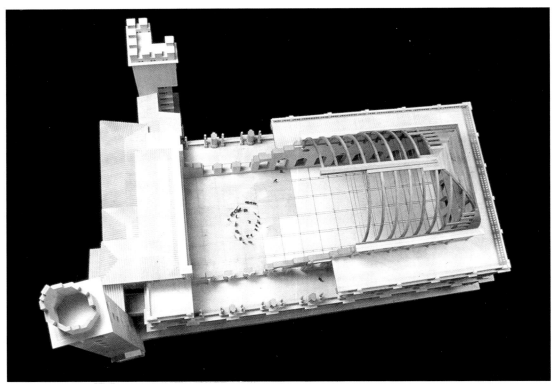

Longitudinal section.

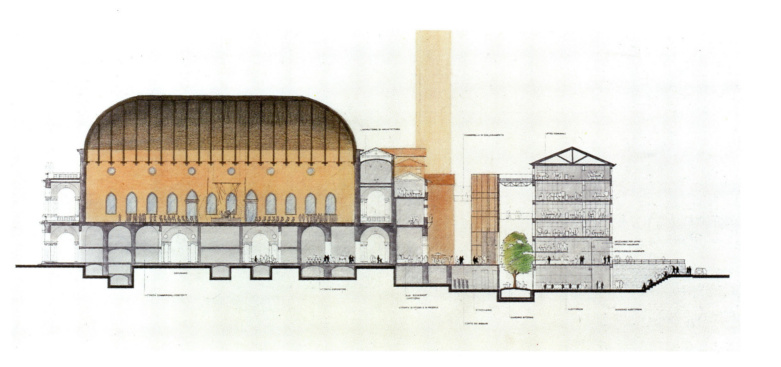

Bay of Sistiana Redevelopment Scheme, 1987

View of the bay with insert of the development area.
Diagram of site plan.

This redevelopment project concerns a large and very attractive area in the Bay of Sistiana, where the natural beauty of the sea, cliffs and green areas is marred by the presence of an enormous abandoned stone quarry; one objective of the scheme is therefore to enhance tourism in this area near Trieste.

Located between the pine woods of Duino and the Costa dei Barbari, two adjacent coves – one natural (the marina of Sistiana) and the other man-made (the stone quarry) – are the main features in this area of around sixty hectares whose overall characteristics are to be conserved.

The aim of the project is to rehabilitate the pre-existing landscape and make nature once more the prevalent element.

While fully respecting the natural environment, the scheme creates an integrated tourist complex for 2,500–3,000 people. The planned structures are hotels, residences, and various shops intended for upmarket Italian and international visitors.

The basic idea is to set an example of how high quality results may be achieved through relatively low-cost projects: once completed, the high-standard facilities on offer will be reflected in appropriate but nonetheless competitive prices.

The development in the former quarry centres around the creation of a great teflon sail stretching over part of the artificial sea with approximately 3,000 square metres, in which islets, ponds, fresh-water fountains and various kinds of plants and flowers will create a "garden of wonders". A greenhouse effect is generated by the combination of three factors: the teflon curtain, the natural ventilation system

Compositional diagrams and site plan.

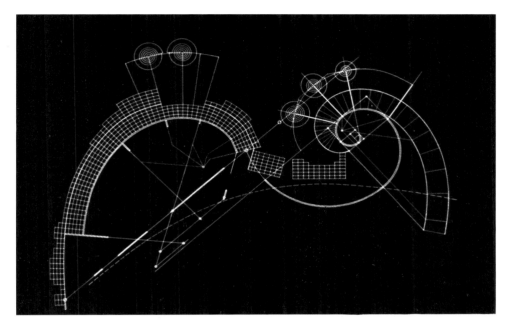
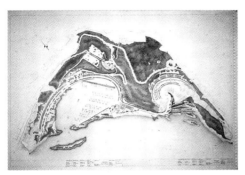
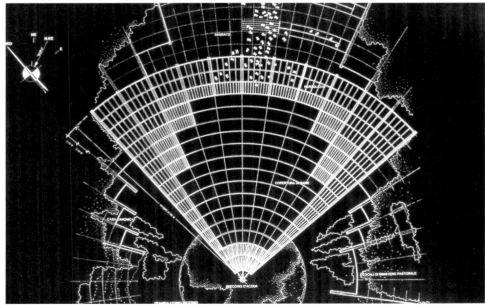

Design drawings of the tourist complex.

and the existing microclimate suitably exploited by the project. The sea water may thus be heated, providing warm sheltered bathing even in winter.

In the holiday low season the complex will continue to be utilized through the creation of a conference centre and auditorium, each with a capacity of 1,000 seats.

The beaches used for summer bathing will be consolidated and reshaped, taking into account the sea currents. Environmental conservation will be guaranteed by the fact that the areas have the status of a public domain traditionally accessible for everyone from both the land- and the seaside.

The number of boats allowed to moor in the port will be limited to avoid overcrowding. The Rilke promenade, a historic walk from the Carso hills to the sea, is extended so that the whole bay may be crossed on foot. The nature conservation scheme will ensure that building can only take place in the abandoned quarry in the form of low-profile, well camouflaged constructions, thus safeguarding the spectacular steep green descent from the hills down to the sea.

Section through a terraced building.

European Synchrotron Radiation Facility, Grenoble 1987

Design sketches.

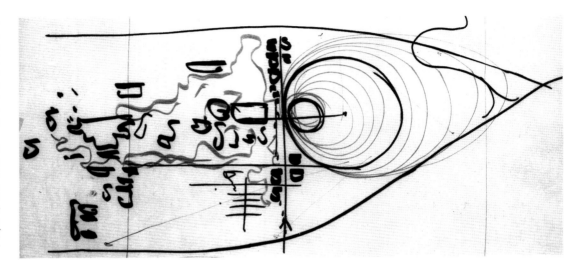

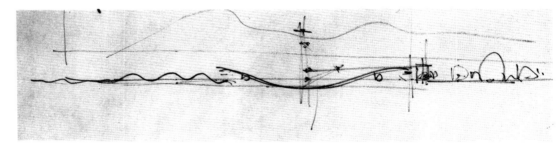

If a highly-charged electron or positron is diverted from its natural path to a precise degree by a carefully calibrated magnetic field, it will emit coherent X-rays called synchrotron radiation. These high-energy invisible X-rays are a very effective tool in biological and medical research and in studying the properties of matter.

The decision to build a large new synchrotron radiation research centre outside Grenoble received backing from France, Germany, Italy and Spain. Since the aim was to make the facility available for external research organizations, the building had to meet a number of requirements to offer suitable services to users.

The basic scheme of the competition-winning design by the Renzo Piano Workshop (Paris) was further elaborated in collaboration with the research institute.

The principal scientific installations are a storage ring, in which the energy of an accelerated electron is stored for around eight hours, and the synchrotron, which accelerates the electron or positron up to 6 GeV. The synchrotron circumference is 299 metres and the storage ring 855 metres. At sixty points the synchrotron-emitted X-rays are "straightened" out of the storage ring, and therefore sixty research areas can be set up to make use of the available X-rays at those points. The installations are situated inside this citadel of scientific research, where two rivers meet outside the city of Grenoble to the backdrop of mountains. Although the site layout is as simple as possible with very direct access roads, attempts were made to make the most of the splendid natural environs.

Given the predetermined form of the scientific installations and the

Model and site plan of the storage ring.

features of the site, the basic design idea led to the creation of two "horizons": one seen from inside the complex and the other from outside.

The main entrance leads from a courtyard to the centre of the storage ring, a large, gently dished, outdoor space. Set apart from the roads and offices, this outdoor garden area has splendid all-round mountain views. A similar kind of separation effect is obtained in the intermediate space between the installations and the motorway, in this case by planting trees and landscaping the space.

A raised walkway from the administrative block crosses the research ring and extends as far as the dished garden area, where a group of dome-like buildings – a library, conference hall, restaurant, café and other services – are arranged to create a special environment in which scientists can meet and exchange ideas; at the centre of the group are the installations control room and the main computer centre.

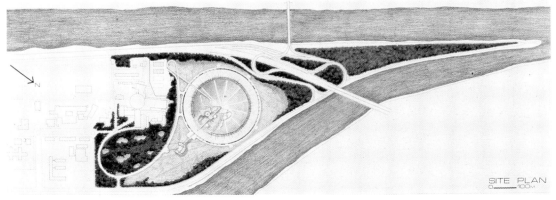

SITE PLAN
0 — 100M

Perspective views and section through the storage ring.

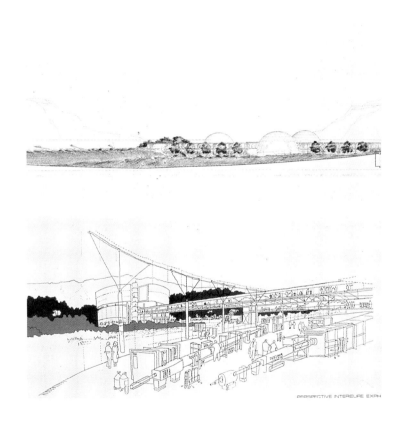
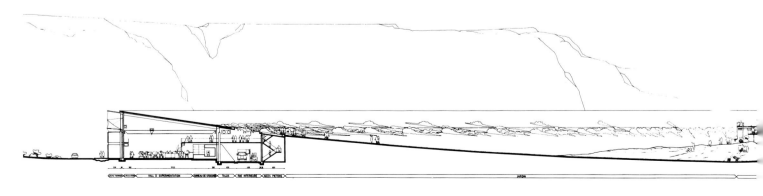

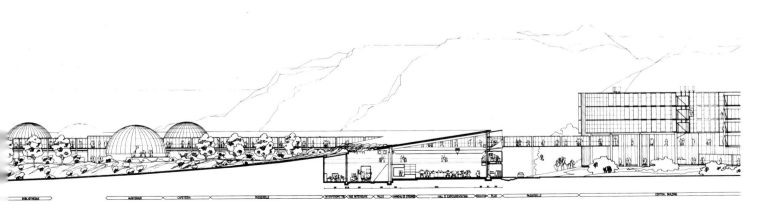

Development of the Archaeological City of Pompeii, 1987–88

Aerial view of the archaeological site of Pompeii.

Pompeii is the most famous archaeological city in the world. The aim of this scheme was to improve the management of the vast excavation site both in regard to visitor participation as well as to overall efficiency and economic viability.

The brief was divided into four chapters: create access roads to the excavated area; make the archaeological visit more enjoyable; allow visitors to observe work in progress; and lastly, devise a more efficient system for preserving finds.

The proposed access route is a circular road round a section of the city. It contains the various surface services such as ticket offices, guides and parking. In addition to these services are four underground blocks for various functions: a three-hundred seat auditorium for films or plays recounting the story of the eruption in AD 79; a small museum illustrating daily life in Pompeii; a data bank with an audio-visual library of all the treasures of Pompeii continually updated with new finds; and lastly, the nerve centre of the whole system – the control room for excavation operations.

The main problem to be tackled in making the visit more pleasant and effective is improving the urban furniture. This involves designing unobtrusive new signs, seating and protective elements for the ancient city. Given the need for discretion, transparent glass is the principal material used.

The problem of allowing as many people as possible to enjoy the thrill of watching a dig has been solved by extending the excavation schedule. A third of the city is still to be unearthed and small groups of visitors will be admitted to watch work in progress.

Lastly, new finds will be conserved in a Treasure House consisting of mobile air-conditioned containers with private access for specialists.

Overall plan of the project area.

Site plan of the archaeological centre.
Design sketch.
Compositional diagram.

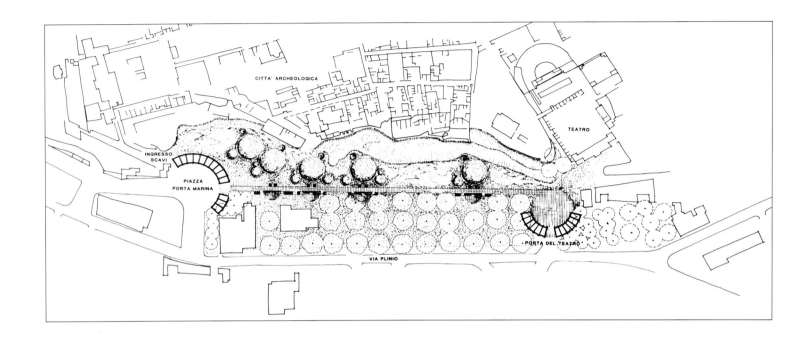

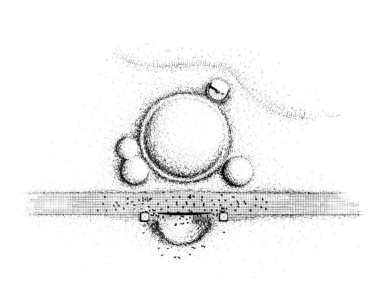

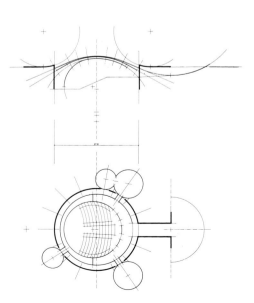

Axonometric section and details of the protective system for the excavations.

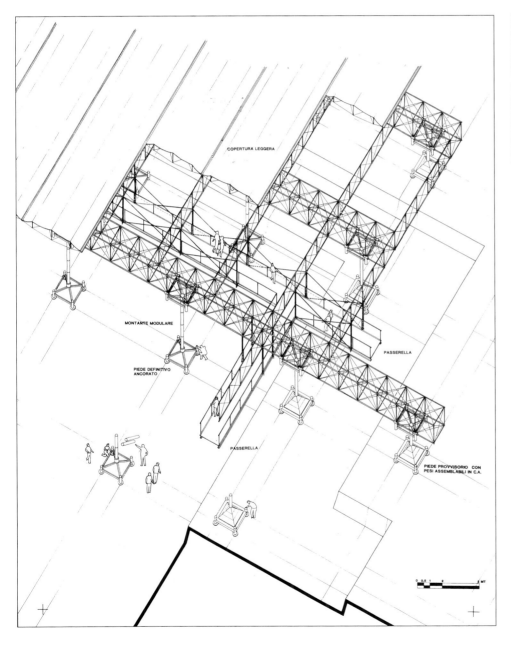

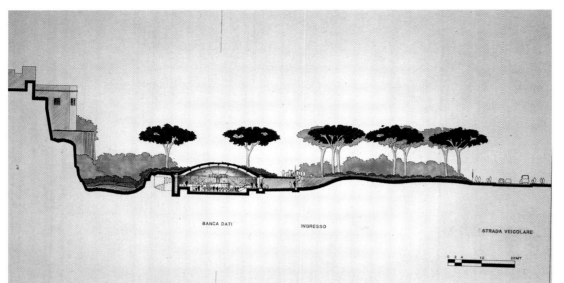

Sections through the data-bank room, auditorium and museum.

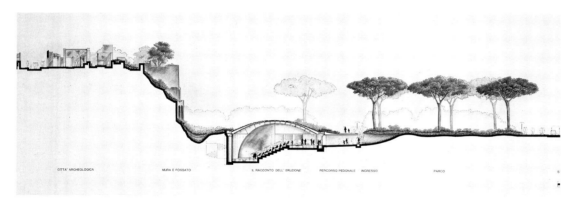

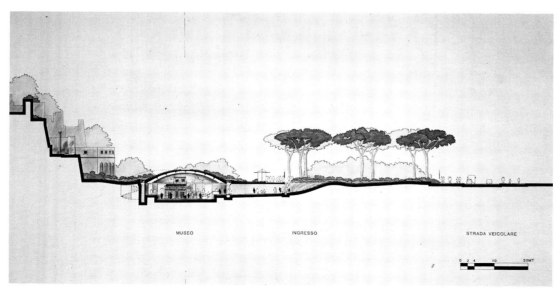

Typical street section.
Chart of signs and street furniture.

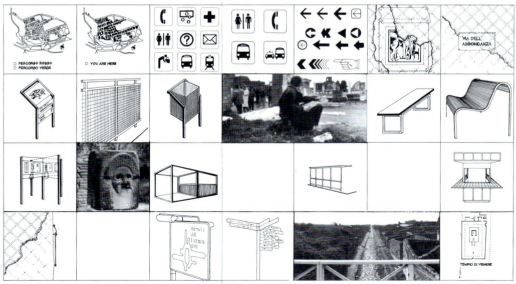

American Contemporary Art Museum, Newport Beach, 1987

Aerial view of the district with the project area highlighted.
East elevation.

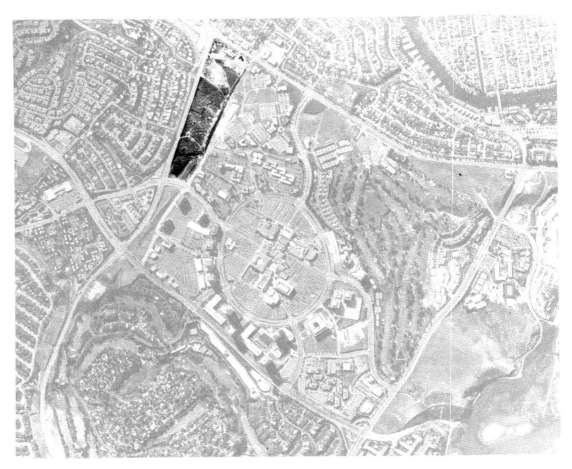

The site of 40,000 square metres for a Museum of American Contemporary Art, located at Newport Beach, south of Los Angeles, is bounded by three large motorways: the Pacific Coast Highway to the south; MacArthur Boulevard to the east and Avocado Avenue to the west.
The new museum is meant to be a place of discovery, a sheltered microcosm inviting visitors to wander and explore. The design takes into account the fact that the car is the main means of transport in southern California, but also includes a secluded pedestrian entrance far from noisy traffic.
Taking advantage of a number of site features, such as the mild climate, the large area available and an existing panoramic terrace, a low-slung one-storey building was planned, plus a mezzanine, which fits in with the landscape and natural environment. The spaces are delimited by load-bearing walls running from east to west at intervals of approx. twelve metres.
The main entrance opens to the north-south passage through the building, which alternates views of art with gardens, restaurants, auditorium, shops, educational facilities and laboratories. In this way visitors are offered a highly varied slice of museum life.
The key architectural theme is the two-sided platform-roof slotted into the hillside: a "flying carpet" meant to protect the exhibition spaces from direct sunlight and atmospheric agents and at the same time support the service installations. In the upper half of the platform a second space has been created: here visitors can walk round enjoying views of the Pacific Ocean and experiencing the relationship between art and nature.

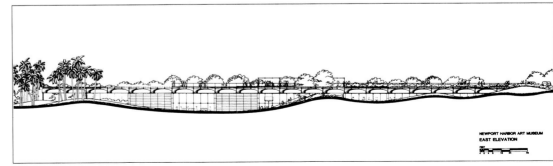

Site plan.
Ground-floor plan.

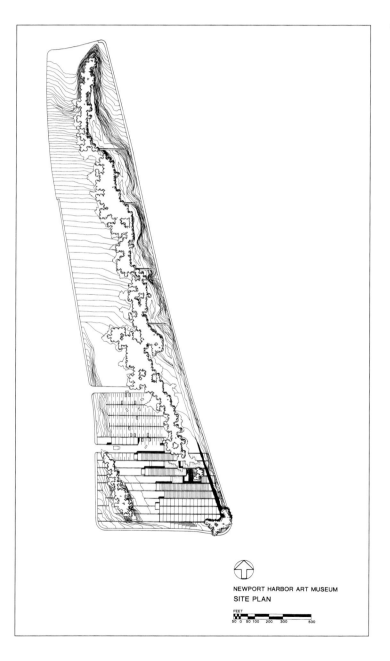
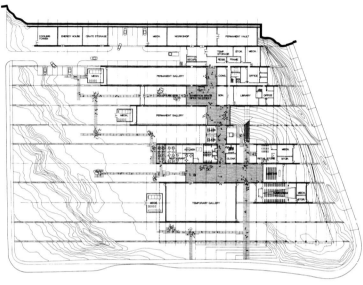

87

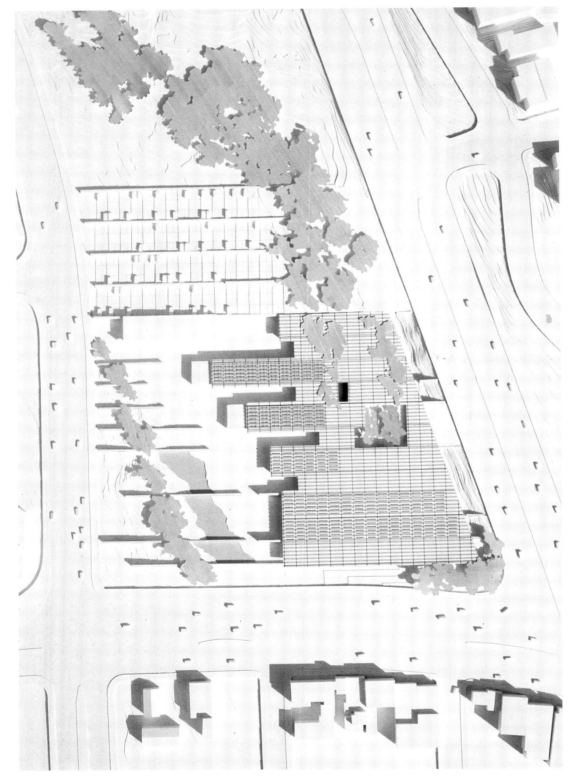

Views of the models.

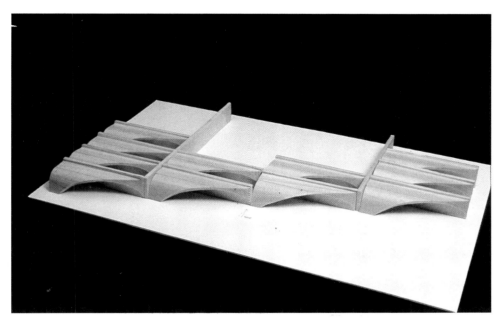

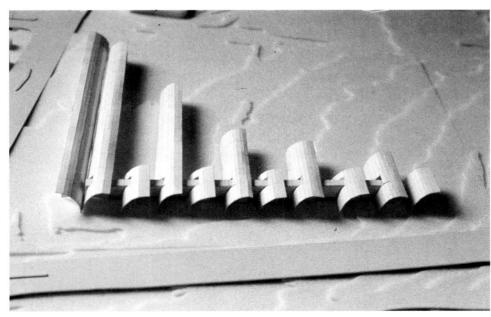

Cross and longitudinal sections of the museum.

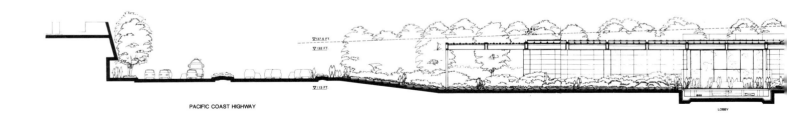

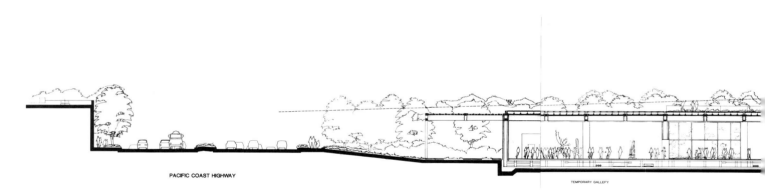

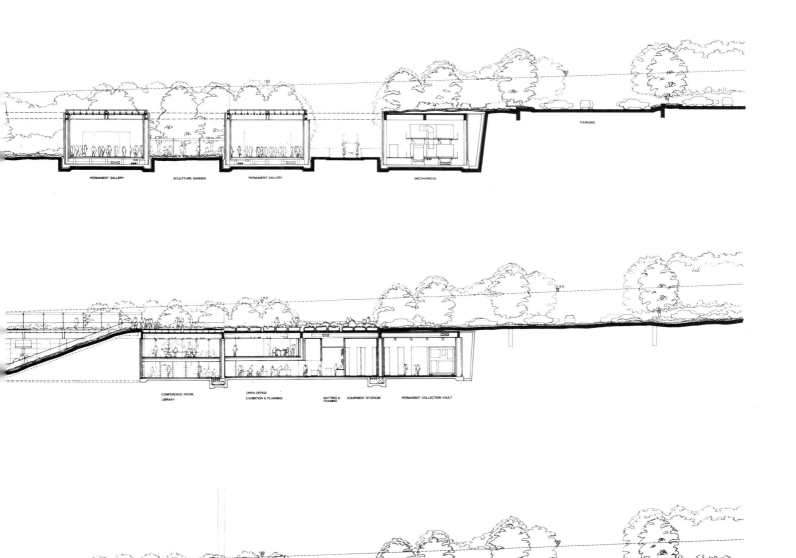

Section through the exhibition rooms.

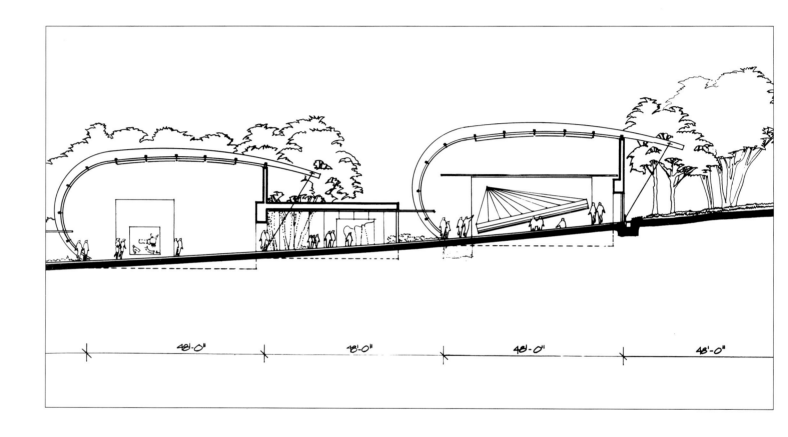

Section through exhibition room showing ductwork. Design sketch.

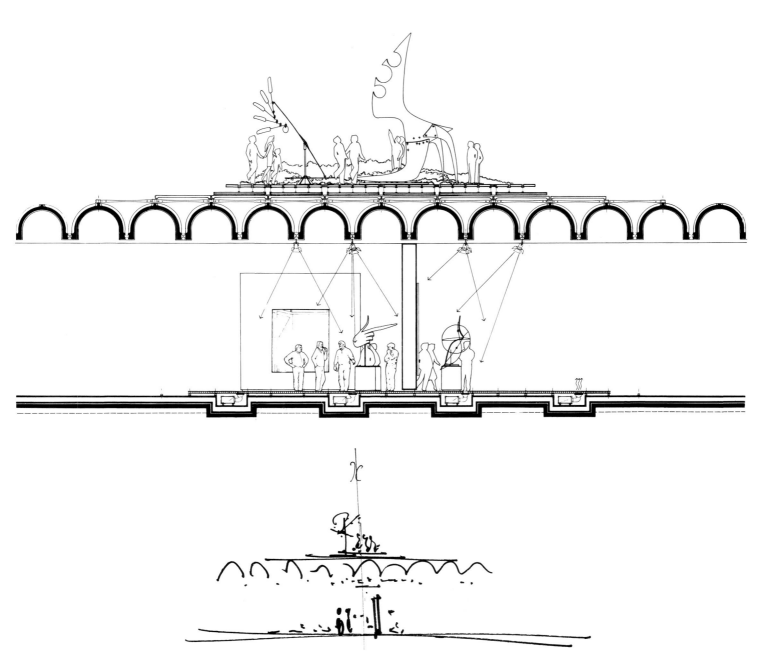

93

The San Nicola Stadium, Bari, 1987–90

Petal segment.

For the 1990 World Cup in Italy eight existing football grounds were renovated and three new stadiums built, including the San Nicola Stadium in Bari.

Situated just outside the city, the Bari stadium is immersed in a typical landscape of olive and fruit groves in the broad Apulian plain. The 60,000-seat ground is embedded in a natural depression, rather like a crater. The upper tier is only 3.6 metres above ground level and therefore the environmental impact is minimal. From afar, the structure looks like a great flying saucer borne aloft by the trees crowning the embankment. The unobtrusive concrete shell is reminiscent of the traditional stone façades in the region. The green elements are particularly effective in attenuating reflected heat in this fiery part of the Adriatic.

The structural eclipse holding the stands is composed of 310 elegant precast crescents made on the site; the upper level is divided into 26 "petal" segments, thus creating the overall impression of an open flower.

The gaps between the petals contain the dramatically highlighted entry stairs. The steel and teflon canopy has been carefully studied to protect spectators from the rain and the intense Mediterranean sun, and the football pitch from swirling wind. The various services – ticket booths, information offices, toilets, etc. – are arranged along the radial accesses between the stands. The large area under the stands organizes circulation to the dressing rooms, service installations and emergency exits.

*Models of the stadium and of a stand.
Design sketches.*

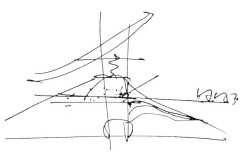
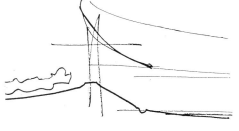

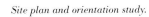
Site plan and orientation study.

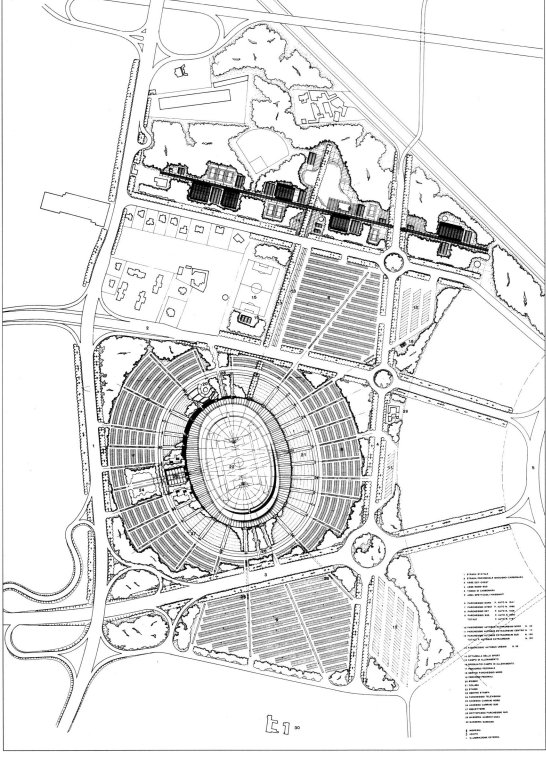

*Overall view of the stadium.
Design sketch.*

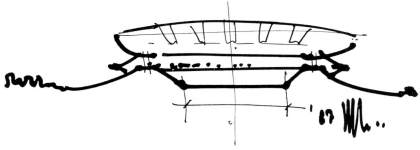

View of the access stairways.
Design sketch.

One of the stand entrances.

Views of the stepped seating and teflon-covered canopy.

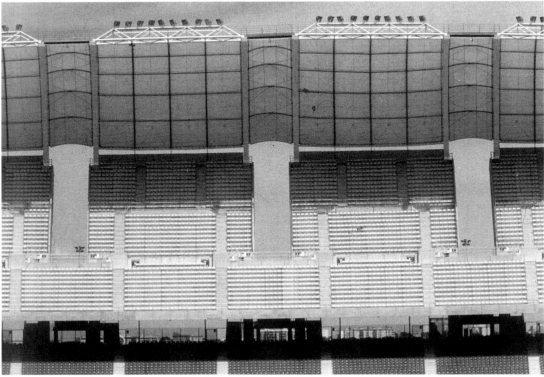

Interior of the stadium.

Section showing the underground service areas

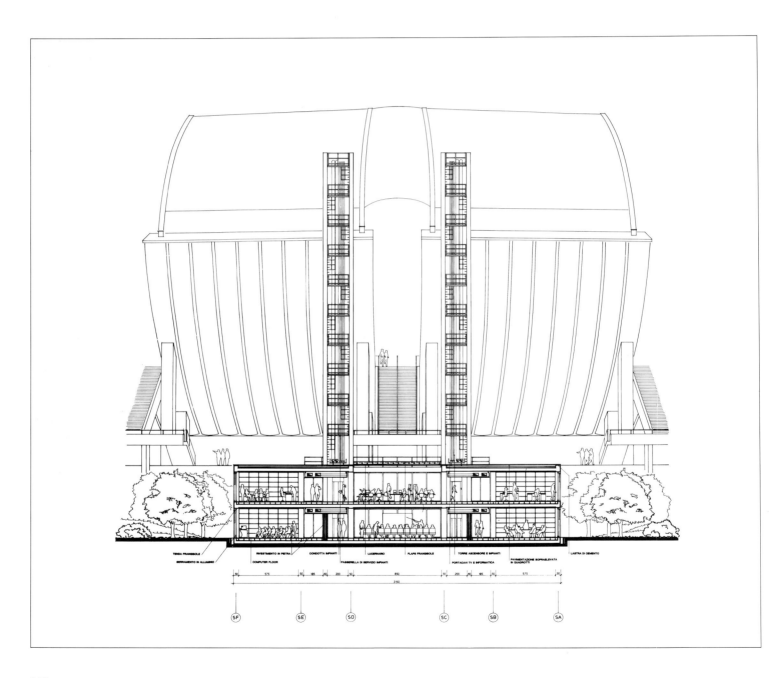

View and perspective drawing of the stands.

Design sketches and section of a stand. *View of a stand.*

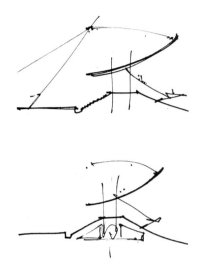

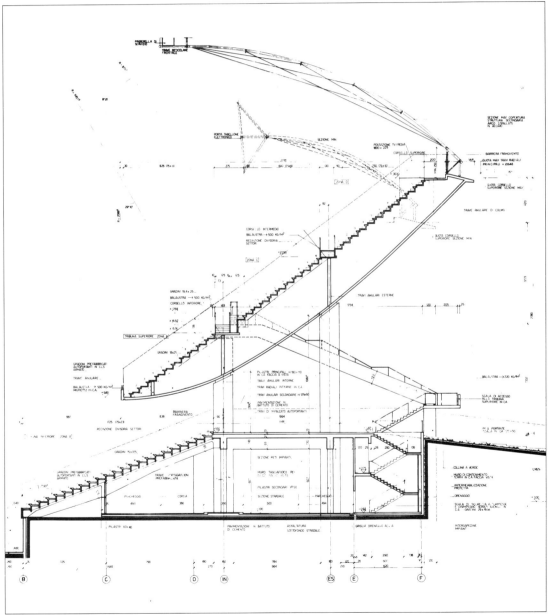

Bercy II Shopping Centre, Charenton le Pont, Paris, 1987–90

Aerial view of the project area. The completed building.

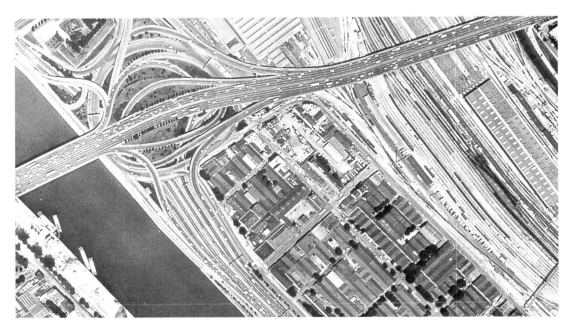

The Bercy shopping centre is situated where the Charenton suburbs begin on the eastern edge of Paris. The complex stands on a corner site bounded on both sides by the chaotic interchange between the Boulevard Périphérique ring road and the A4 motorway.

The form has been dictated by two factors: the need to link up with the important artery of the Boulevard Périphérique and the desire to make the complex visible from the great ring road itself.

Initially, a building was constructed so that the volume and form, shaped round the curve of the road, brought to mind the image of an airship just landed on the site. Subsequently, in search of an idea to make the overall form easily recognizable for people travelling by car and to give the building the appearance of a well-defined object, a skin with a grid of standardized metal panels was designed.

The greatest problem created by the project was defining the curvilinear form. This was solved by the logical extension of the building system and the precise subdivision of the grid of panels. As the project developed, a constant close link thus was forged between form, structure and geometry. In some ways the main problem was giving the building an overall visual form – almost like a sculpture – from the observer's point of view.

The geometrically generated skeleton for the outer skin consists of three circular sections with different lengths and radiuses. Consequently, the roof had to be made up of three independent elements: a timber structure of laminated beams with a solid natural wood core (the purlins following the curved line of the building), an impermeable inner membrane and,

West elevation.
Site plan.

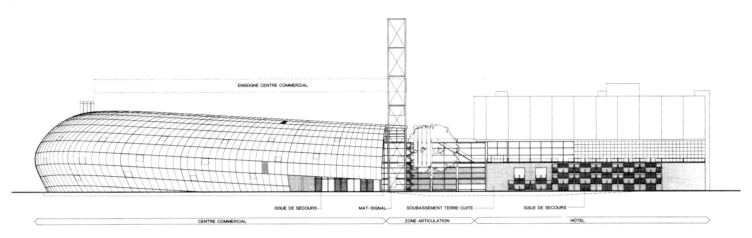

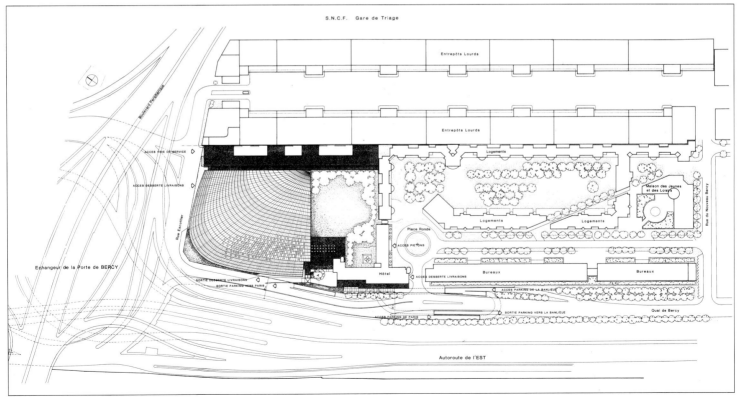

*Longitudinal section.
Second-floor plan.*

lastly, a laminated stainless-steel skin.
The internal plan of the shopping centre was devised to enable customers to find their way around with ease. It is arranged in bands running parallel to the Seine: service installations, shops, a central avenue and small boutiques. The avenue is broken up by three atriums containing central gardens with trees. Most of the visitors arriving by car in the underground parking are guided towards the shops by the lights in the avenue. In each atrium escalators gently ascend to the upper floors. From the escalators and the two sightseeing lifts, there are views of the imposing curved roof, rising up like the upturned wooden hull of a ship.
Lastly, thanks to a series of openings in the roof, the atriums and trees in the garden are bathed in natural light.

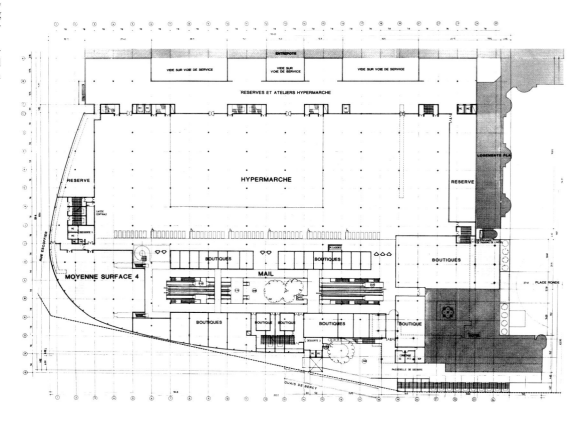

Bercy II seen from across the Seine.

The structural skeleton.
Model.

*The worksite.
Detail of a joint.*

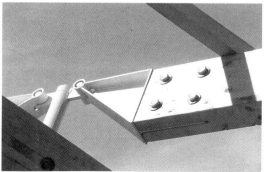

The curved corner of the complex.

View of the galleries.
Detail of the roofing system.

Crown Princess, Monfalcone, 1987–90

The cruise ship at sea.

The cruise ship *Crown Princess* was launched at Trieste in June 1990. The most striking aspect of the liner is its overall size: 70,000 gross tons, 246 metres long, 32 metres wide, 37 metres of draught, 22 knots top speed, and 50,000 square metres of usable surface arranged on thirteen levels with 798 cabins for 1,750 passengers and 656 crew.

The design for the ship entailed original ideas both for the instantly recognizable profile and the internal communal spaces, arranged along the length of the ship from prow to stern.

The observation lounge – both outside and inside – is one of the most important and exciting spaces on the ship. Moreover, it embodies a typical feature of the design: instead of resorting to decoration, the refined structural system is exposed and highlighted. With an interior like the belly of a great white whale, the aluminum shell of the lounge rests on top of the bridge and seems to be shaped by the wind.

From the curved observation-lounge windows there is a view of the ship's prow and the sea beyond.

Plan of the upper bridge and side elevation.
Cross section through the stairs.

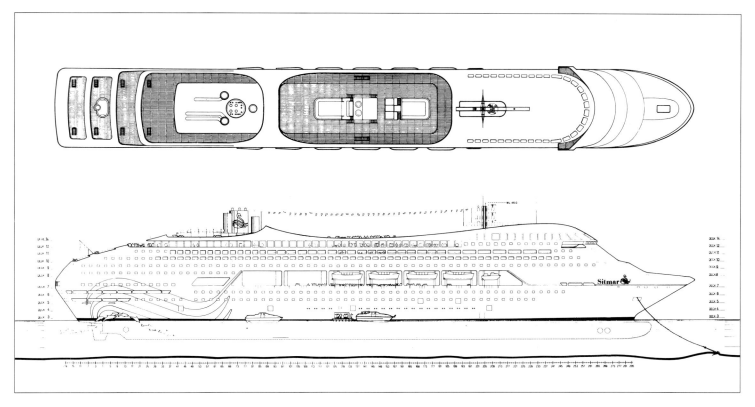

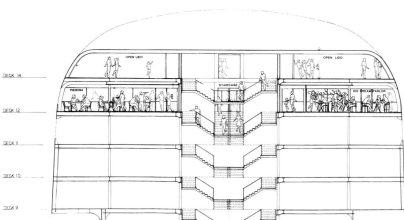

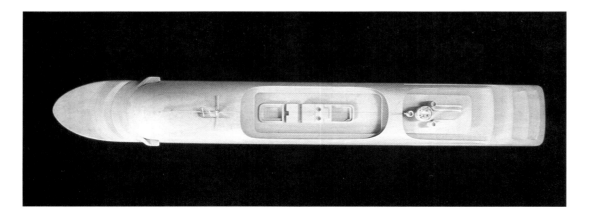

Model views.
Studies of form: from fish to ship.
View of the observation lounge under construction.
The bridge and observation lounge.

Design for Venezia Expo 2000, Venice 1988

Localization of the project in the Venetian lagoon area.
Site plan.

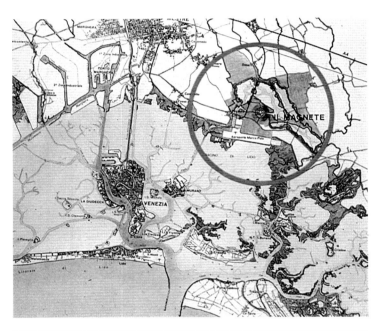

"The idea of a 'Magnet' on the lagoon coastal belt was based on three separate but convergent factors: a new approach to organizing Venice's proposal to host the Expo 2000; the creation of an effective filter for entry to the city of the future; and the need to provide the surrounding Veneto region with a fully equipped logistic centre for its fast growing economy." (Renzo Piano)

The term "Magnet" is intended to denominate the space actually hosting the exposition reception area. At the centre of a telecom network linking up decentralised exhibition or activity areas, the Magnet provides visitors with an overall picture of what can be seen at the Expo. They then choose the events of particular personal interest and plan their visit accordingly. The Magnet is situated in the countryside near Tessera, mainly consisting of large tracts of farmland with an important access feature: its proximity to the Venetian lagoon.

As the reception area and organizational centre for the Expo, the Magnet will attract 20–30 million visitors. It thus requires a very large-scale new structure and spaces, compatible with such a "fragile" context as the Venetian lagoon environment.

The discreet presence in the lagoon landscape of several small nineteenth-century Austrian forts consisting of simple – now tree-covered – embankments suggested working along similar lines for the Magnet spaces.

Accordingly, the proposed development is completely horizontal and kept at ground level by constructing a green mound approx. thirty metres high, which opens up into a large central crater of approx. fifty metres diameter. All of the covered spaces of the Magnet are situated under the artificial mound and overlook the large central crater containing the open spaces.

A navigable channel from a new artificial lagoon passes through two openings in the sides of the mound to the centre of the crater, thus creating a lagoon habitat inside the Magnet.

The large ring building will host samples of all the experimental activities, exhibitions and shows that the Expo has organized throughout the Veneto region.

The ring building has two levels modulated by a precise grid and organized to offer very high-standard and flexible technical services in varied spaces with different geometrical and functional features. The adjacent building has a single space and large mobile lighting. Thanks to a controlled microclimate, it can host exhibitions and activities in complete continuity with the outside space.

The main circulation system for the whole complex is in the central area of the ring building. This zenith-lit gallery between the upper and lower levels of the Magnet links up with the vertical communications systems and accommodates seating, restaurants and bars.

Plans of the lower, upper and roof levels of the Magnet.

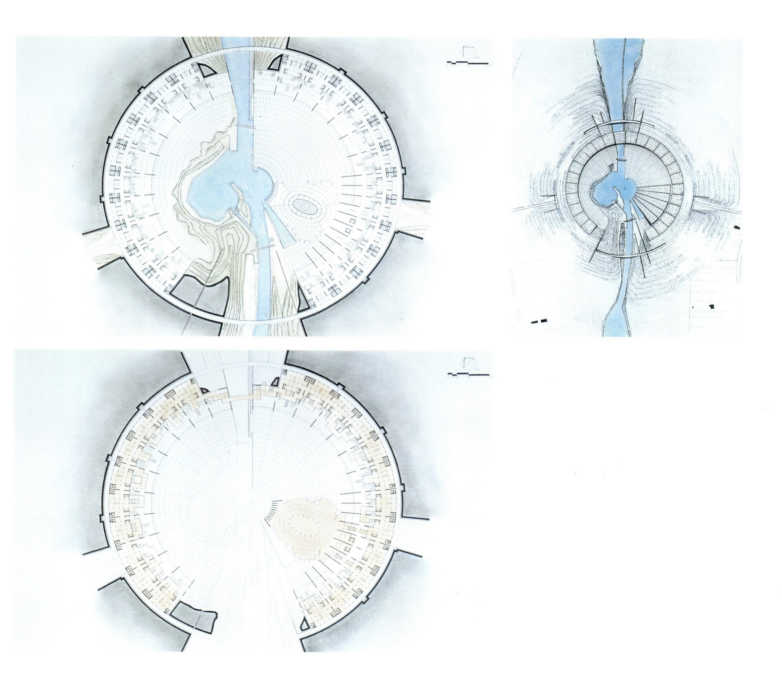

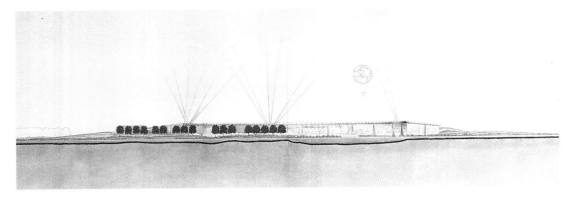

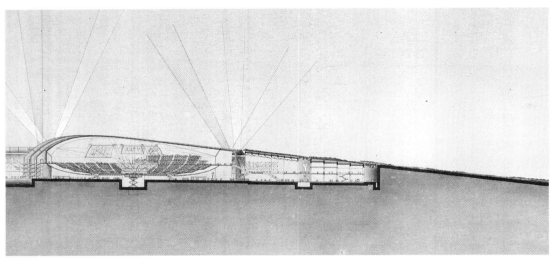

*Elevation.
Sections through the Magnet.*

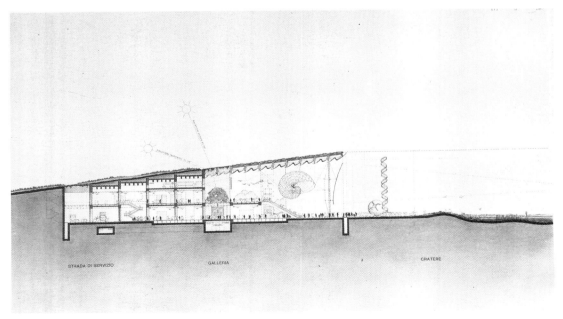

Model views with different degrees of insolation.

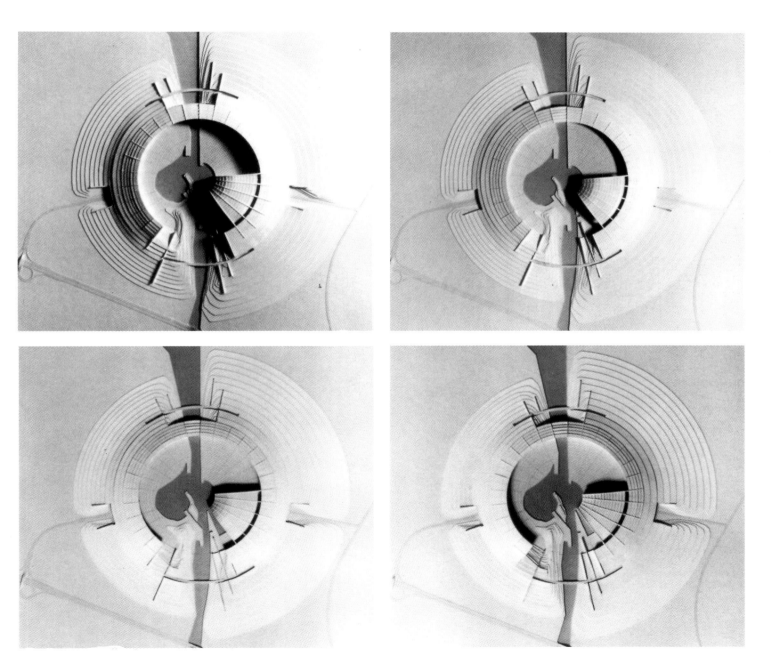

121

IRCAM: Institute for Research and Coordination of Acoustics and Music, Paris, 1987–90

Longitudinal section.
Site plan.

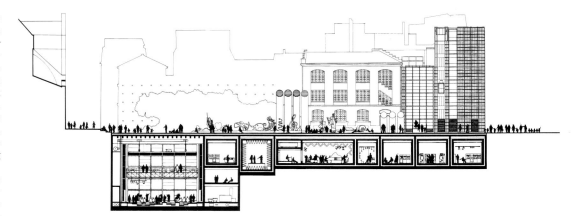

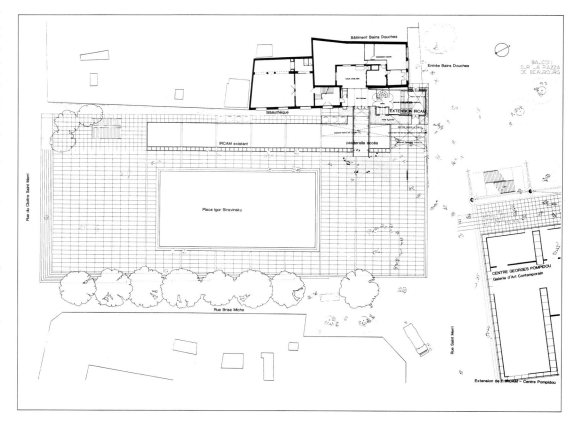

During construction work on the Pompidou Centre, a project was also begun to design a building for musical research and experimentation sited in the adjacent Place Saint Merri (now Place Stravinsky): the building is part of this great cultural centre in Paris. The square, hemmed in by an old school, was made into a pedestrian precinct, thus restoring urban dignity to the church and the surrounding cityscape.

On the scientific grounds that the best insulation against the transmission of sound is the earth, the IRCAM was designed as a subterranean structure. Vibrations generated by underground trains and overground traffic, however, created a major problem for absolute acoustic isolation in a structure on an urban scale, and the decision to build underground was only a partial solution. A further structural solution had to be found: the research studios were mounted on elastic joints, rather like car suspensions, able to "absorb" vibrations. To protect against noise inside the building, the rooms were arranged on three levels: the two upper levels (i.e. closest to the surface) contain offices and circulation structures, but also function as sound absorption chambers, while the research and experimentation studios are on the lowest level.

The research space is the heart of the whole complex. It is equipped with state of the art soundproofing technology, developed by interdisciplinary cooperation involving several experts, including acoustics-specialist Victor Peutz and composers Luciano Berio and Pierre Boulez.

Each studio is an acoustic tool whose main feature is flexibility, enabling it to produce an extensive

View of the office tower.
Perspective sketch.

range of sound types to meet various acoustic requirements. The volume and acoustics can be varied by modifying the floors, walls and ceiling. Each wall is equipped with rhomboid panels faced with different materials so that reverberation times may be modulated from 0.6 to 6 seconds.

Although subterranean life is ideal for acoustic research activities, the same cannot be said for offices. Consequently, several years after the underground complex was completed, the offices where "taken up for air", by transferring them into a kind of "conning-tower" for the underground institute. The new tower was built within the limits imposed by the site, which was basically the missing corner of two pre-existing buildings.

The tower block is a smallish nine-storey building with the three lowest levels underground. The street entrance is reached by a bridge across the glass roof of the original subterranean building.

The two pre-existing corner buildings have been renovated to house a library and meeting rooms. The tower thus completes the corner and is a pivot for the adjacent converted buildings, which have the same permeable terracotta brick cladding protecting the masonry underneath.

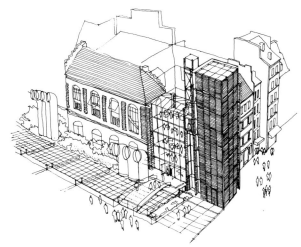

Views of the tower extension from the Pompidou Centre and from Place Stravinsky.

View of the fountain in Place Stravinsky.

Design for the Redevelopment of the Sassi, Matera 1988–90

Localization of the project in a plan of Matera.
Section of the quarter.

The Sassi is a celebrated troglodyte quarter dug out of rocks in the southern Italian city of Matera. The original cave settlement dates back to 2000 BC, but in the sixteenth-century a town was built out of the earlier rock structures. With good exposure to the sun and well ventilated, this area once had a flourishing agricultural economy, and the underground structures were used as stables and food stores.

In the nineteenth century, however, the agricultural crisis upset the social and sanitary balance as the underground structures began to be used as dwellings again. In the overcrowded town people had to put up with inadequate, unhygienic living conditions with no light or air. After the Second World War the situation deteriorated further and became totally unsustainable. The local authorities evacuated the area and transferred the inhabitants to a new residential estate built outside the city. At present only fifteen percent of the Sassi area is inhabited and the rest has virtually been abandoned.

The rehabilitation of the complex to acceptable living standards would be extremely difficult, given the present conditions: there is only a very poor communications network and services are non-existent. The aim of the project, therefore, was to find a compromise solution for the problems of architectural restoration, given the total lack of services. The first unit to be redeveloped covers a very narrow but important area, since it includes all the principal architectural features to be found in the Sassi: a *palazzo*, ordinary dwellings, cave structures, vegetable plots, micro-gardens and squares.

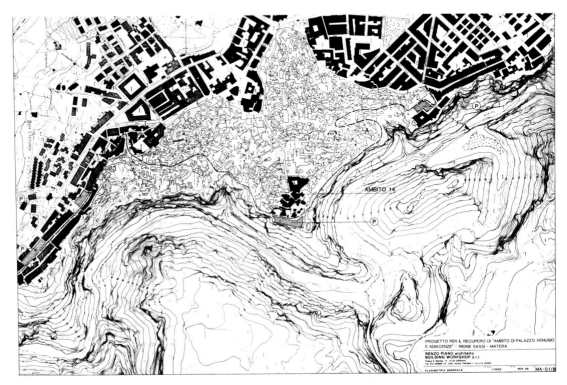

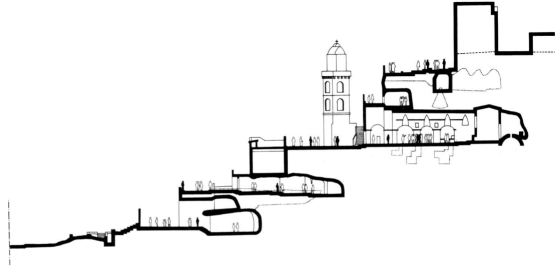

The Sassi quarter of Matera.

Drawing and plan of a typical redevelopment area.
Semi-underground plan of the Palazzo Venusio.

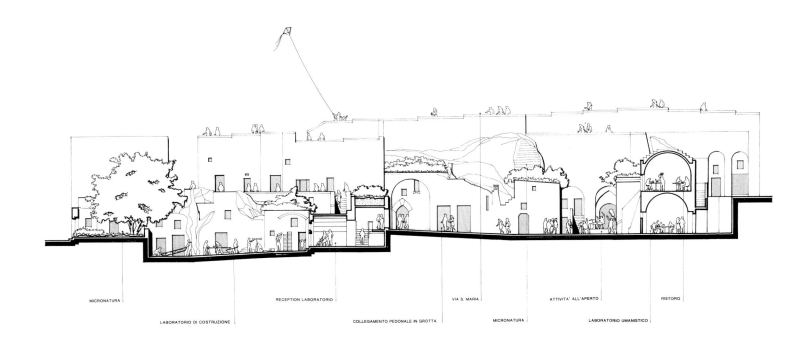

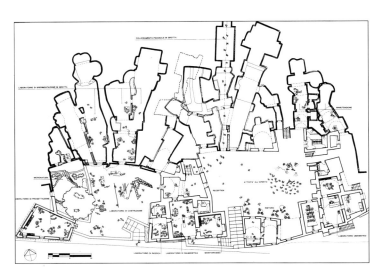

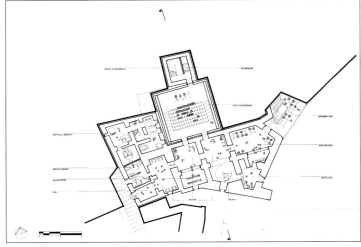

Section through a redevelopment area.
Section through the Palazzo Venusio.

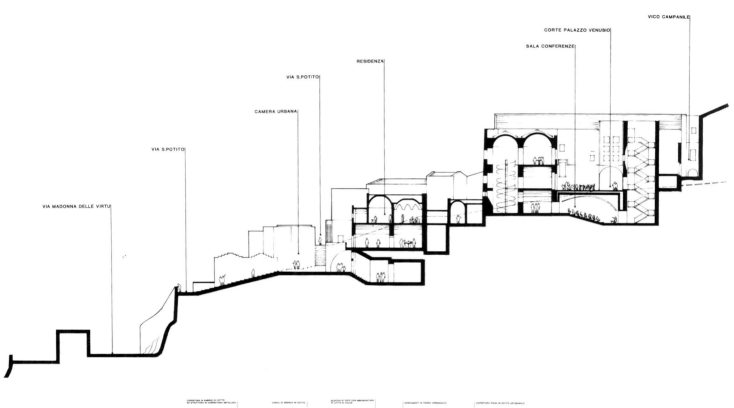

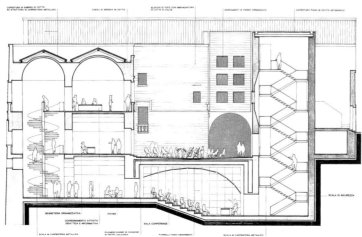

Guyancourt Thomson Works, Saint Quentin-en-Yvelines, 1988–90

Site plan.
Aerial view of the factory.

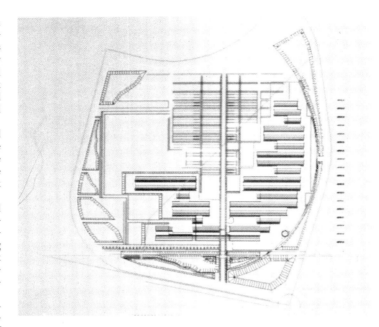

Thomson's optoelectronics division at Guyancourt near Saint Quentin-en-Yvelines, a suburb of Paris, is situated on a plateau punctuated by rows of poplars and a few scattered woods. The factory is designed to fit into this natural context, an island of greenery reflecting the rural landscape of the plateau.

Saplings have been planted round the building in rows, following the design grid for the project. The trees have been arranged so that the vegetation will be much denser at the edges of the site.

Broken up by open areas to be used as car parks, lawns and factory patios, the overall vegetation generates well-balanced alternating spaces within the grid. At the foot of the southern façade an ornamental lake collects rain water channelled from the roofs.

The well-being of the people employed in the factory is of primary importance. Accordingly, the aim of the design was to provide a high-quality work environment. The project is developed over an extensive park interrupted on the eastern side by a large stone wall forming a kind of sleeve for the buildings. This curved structure becomes the generating element for the whole scheme: the long building blocks stretch westwards away from the wall towards the park, hinting at possible future extensions. Each rectangular block has an "umbrella", open on the north side. This simple structural solution is the outcome of studies on natural phenomena. The structure is a frame (30.6 metres) anchored to the ground plus the umbrella skeletons (14.4 metres), which may be combined to form large sheds with extensive glazed walls.

The great flexibility for the internal spaces and the mechanical structural system made it possible to develop and integrate the network of internal and external services during assembly.

Articulated under these steel structures, the building can accommodate a variety of functions: from two floors of offices to highly sophisticated laboratories with mobile levers and clean rooms.

View of the model.
Section showing umbrella structure.

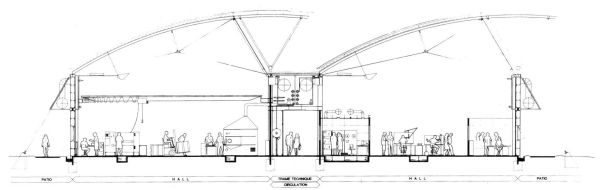

Views of the factory embedded in countryside.

View and detail of the office building.

View of a glazed façade.
Wind-braces.

Corner of a factory block.

Rue de Meaux Housing, Paris 1988–91

Site plan with garden.
Typical floor plan.

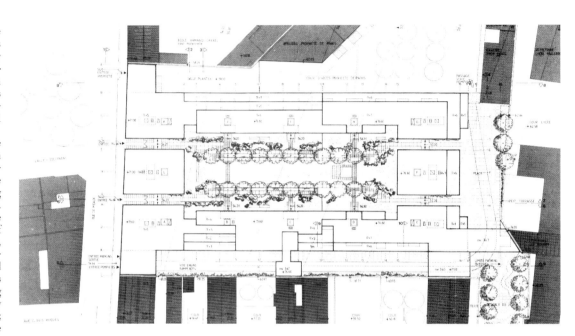

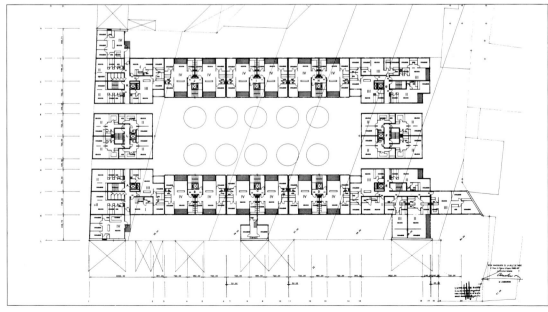

The main design aim was to create an inner garden for the inhabitants of a new building in the densely populated nineteenth *arrondisement* in Paris. The perimeter of a rectangular shaped block is thus made to fit into the surrounding urban fabric, whereas a large enclosed garden is created at its centre.

The bustle of the street and the peaceful inner space provide a pleasant contrast for the inhabitants, who enter and leave the building across the garden, passing by bushes and white birch trees. The volumetric organization of the building generates a great variety of apartments. In the longer blocks, from east to west, dwelling typologies were designed with simple and flexible plans. Most apartments have a large living space running north to south with a small balcony at one end and a porch at the other; adjacent to the living space is the night zone. All of the 220 apartments look in to the garden and out to the city.

The building is characterized by various fronts. From the second to the seventh floor, the garden façades are made of slightly projecting modular panels of precast GRC (Glass Reinforced Concrete) whose grid is 90 by 90 cm, 30 cm deep and 5 cm thick. The grid is covered with opaque isolating elements clad in terracotta tiles with natural colours (each tile is 20 × 40 cm) or by painted white GRC panels. The architectural effect of this façade is based on rigorous geometry, the uniform materials and the intricate patterns created.

On the ground and first floors of all the façades, glazing (with treated surfaces to ensure privacy) has been set in a frame similar to the structure bearing the terracotta tiles. Behind these glass fronts are

Elevation of main façade.
Design sketches.

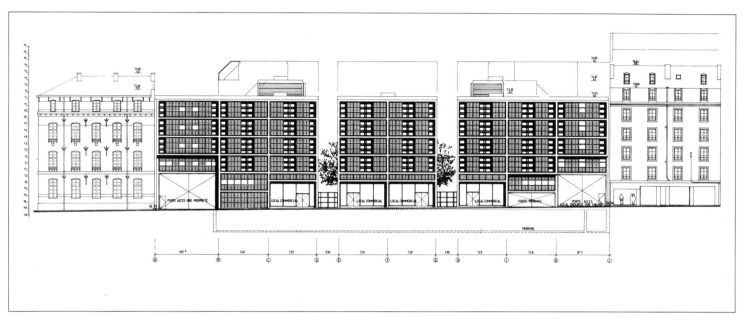

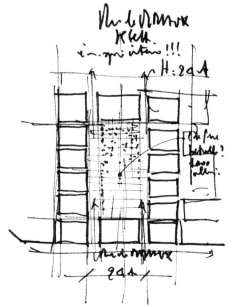

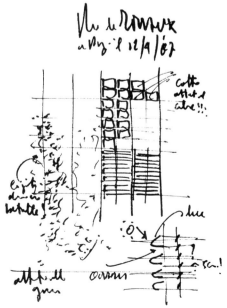

Overall view of the enclosed garden.

offices and homes. On the street façade the same materials and grids from the garden side have been used, but the frame no longer projects forward. The overall effect is more sober, despite the use of the same rich materials.

View of garden façade.

Detail of garden façade.
Louvres in garden façade.

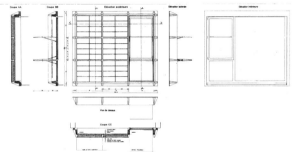

Views of garden façades.
Detail of infill system.

Christopher Columbus International Exposition '92, Genoa
1988–92

The port of Genoa before and after the exposition.

Expos and their relationship to cities are a recurrent theme in modern architecture. Not surprisingly, in the project for the 1992 Genoa international exposition – "Christopher Columbus: the Ship and the Sea", held under the patronage of the Bureau International des Expositions, Paris – the real subject turned out to be the relationship between the expo and the city. In this case the theme was elaborated in such an innovative way that it may provide a model for a new generation of expos: the logic of building provisional structures only meant to last for the duration of the event has been totally abandoned, and the new structures as well as rehabilitated and converted buildings have remained after the expo to be used by the city.

"When invited to work on the Columbus celebrations", writes Renzo Piano, "I thought how these international expositions are usually banality fairs and an excuse for trying to break records, so I considered revising the underlying logic for this kind of event. I suggested organizing the exposition in the old heart of the city so that it could become an opportunity to restore the historic centre, starting from the inside. Genoa is a city of the sea. It has always had a mediated relation with the sea: people worked on the sea and in the port. Then after a day's work, they returned to take shelter in the narrow reassuring streets of the old city centre.

Genoa – a city with no large public squares – had the port for a great meeting place. Now at the end of this century, thanks to the Columbus celebrations we have an opportunity to reconnect the city with the old port. The scheme for the Genoa expo is very complex and sophisticated. It affects the urban plan and

Site plan.
Design sketches.

landscape, and its modernity lies in the fact there is an attempt to continue the history of the city without inflicting traumas or deforming its very suggestive historical context. After the exposition ninety percent of the structures built for the occasion will be re-used for various functions (cultural, commercial, services, crafts and leisure), making this part of the city perfectly integrated with the rest of the Genoese urban fabric."

Among the works for the exposition are the aquarium, the most important of the new buildings and the largest of its kind in Europe, and the Grande Bigo (a kind of giant crane), the symbol for the whole event, which also supports the adjacent tensile tent-like structure in Piazza delle Feste.

The rehabilitated buildings include the cotton warehouses, which have been converted into a conference centre, and the seventeenth-century pavilions making up the customs depository in the old district beyond the Millo area. A number of old wharves have also been brought to light, revealing the potential for the creation of the first port archaeology park in the world.

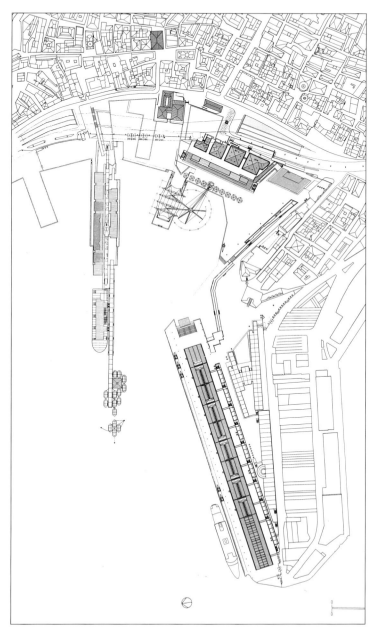

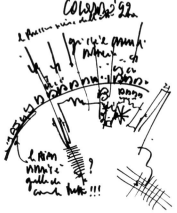

*Plan of the western section.
Cross section, elevation and view of
the cotton warehouses.*

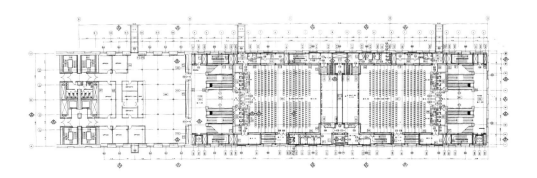

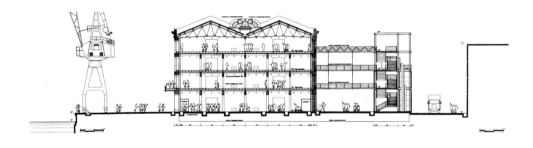

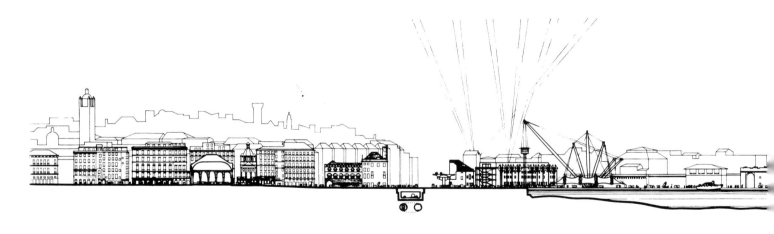

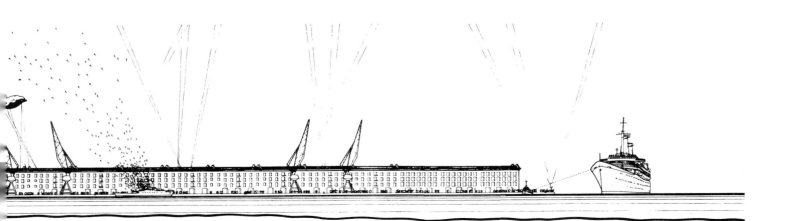

Conference centre auditorium.
Cross section of the conference centre.

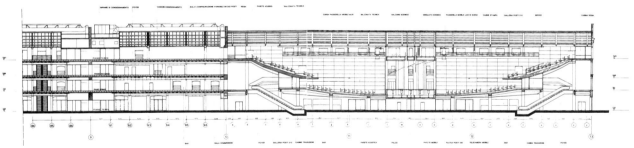

The cotton warehouses: an exhibition room and detail of cross section.

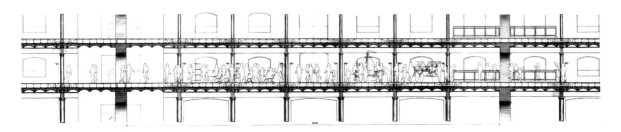

Elevation of pavilions in the customs depository.
Ground-floor plan of pavilions.
Section of the Quartiere San Desiderio.
View of the restored seventeenth-century pavilions.

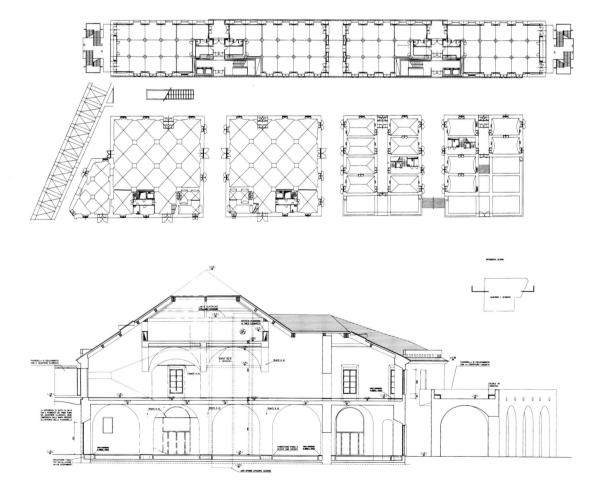

Plans of ground, first and second floor of the aquarium.

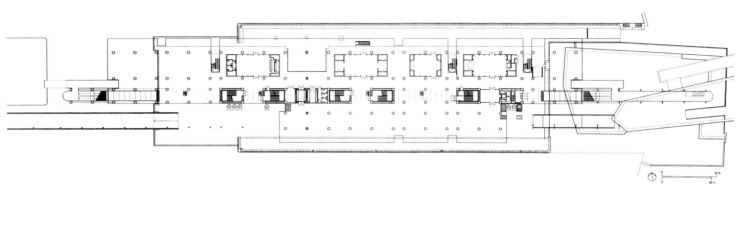

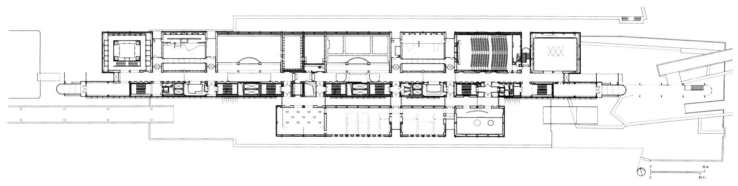

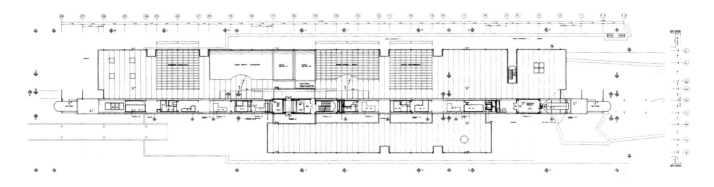

The aquarium.
Cross section through the aquarium.

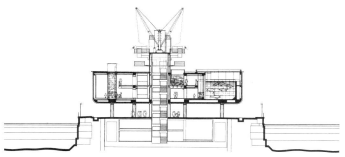

151

The Grande Bigo
Elevation of the Bigo with panoramic lift.

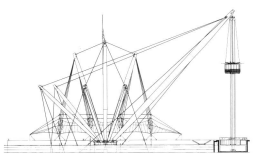

The port at sunset.

Kansai International Airport Main Passenger Terminal Building, Osaka, 1988–94

The island during construction and the airport worksite.

The design image for the main terminal building of the Kansai International Airport is the aerodynamic profile of a landing jet. At the dawn of the air-travel age in the early twentieth century, Futurists as well as Russian avantgarde artists gave visual shape to the general excitement over flight. The great Romanian sculptor Constantin Brancusi (1876–1957) also addressed this long-cherished twentieth-century dream, producing the stupendous form of the abstract aerodynamic *Bird in Space*. The poetic perfection of that work is a constant source of inspiration for all those in search of fluid forms.

When the international competition for Kansai airport was held in 1988, the project site had still to be created in the water and the only ongoing work was excavations involving thousands of tons of sand on the seabed, eighteen metres down. Situated in this unusual geographical context, the 511-hectare island-airport (1.5 × 4.37 kilometres) consists of an immense and elaborate integrated circuit. In terms of speed and technology, its features are far removed from the spatial-temporal dynamics shaping cities and landscapes.

Designed as part of a high-density functional nucleus, the main terminal building is like a precision tool. Given the absence of restrictions connected to urban surroundings or site features, the volume was simply determined by the dimensions and spaces required by planes manoeuvring on the island. The terminal consists of a main block with a long wing-shaped linear extension (the total span is 1.7 kilometres) containing the circulation spine for the forty-one boarding or disembarking gates. The interior of the main block is divided into four levels to accommodate the circulation and functions such as check-in for domestic and international flights, immigrations control, customs, luggage transfers, etc. The large internal space under the continuous roof structure of 90,000 square metres is completely open-plan; the roof design was developed from the dynamics of air flows along the ceiling. The volume of the curved section of the main hall increases towards the runway side, providing a sense of direction for the passengers as well as new exciting spatial experience. The asymmetric reticulate roof trusses (82.8 metres long) trace the invisible volume described by the airflow in the building.

To ensure that the control tower has complete all-round visibility, the tips of the "wing" containing the boarding gates dip slightly; the shape of the wing roof was derived from the geometrical form of a toroid generated by a series of arched sections rotating round a single pivot. In this way the entire roof structure could be covered with around 82,000 stainless steel panels, all of the same size.

The completed airport.
Site plan.

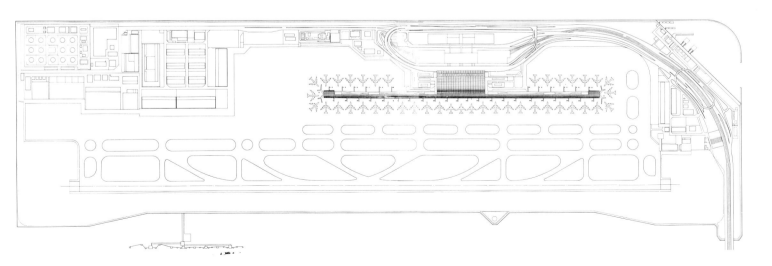

Model views.

View of the sectioned terminal model.
Design sketch.

Section through the main terminal building.
Section showing the wing extension.

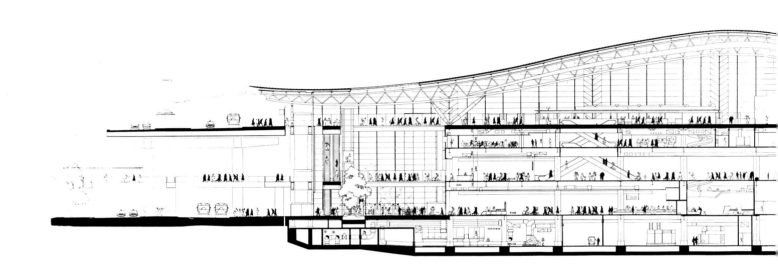

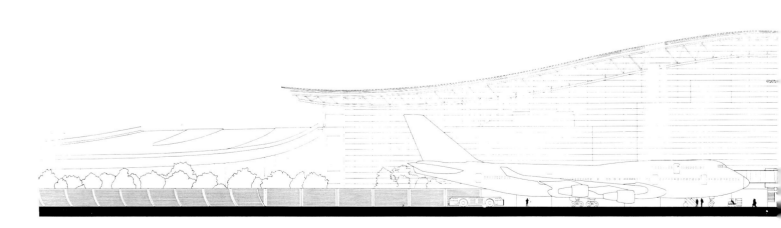

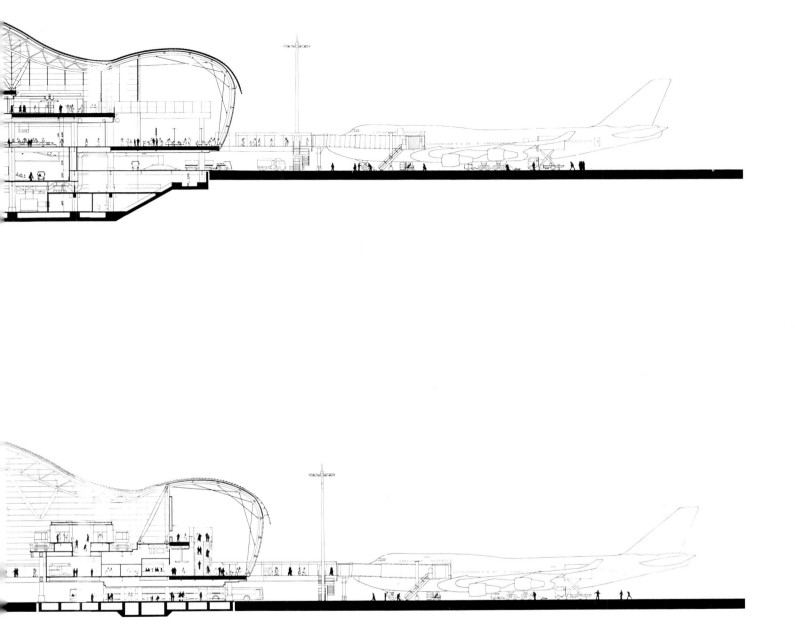

Computer graphic studies.
Cross section.

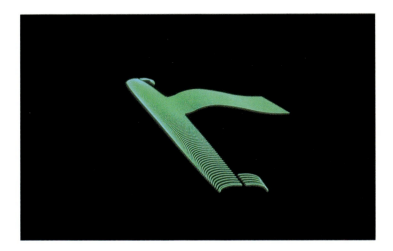

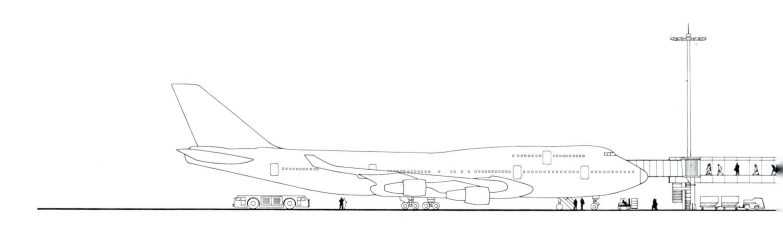

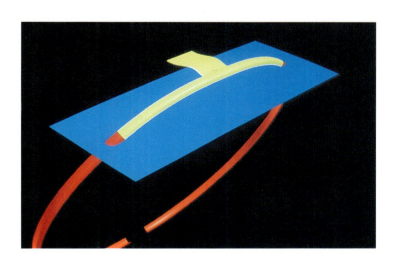
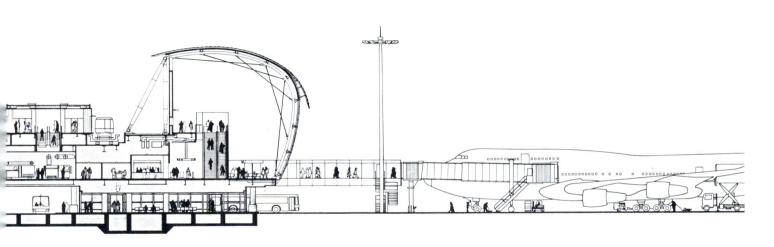

View of the airport complex
View along the "wing" of the terminal.

Detail of the structural system.

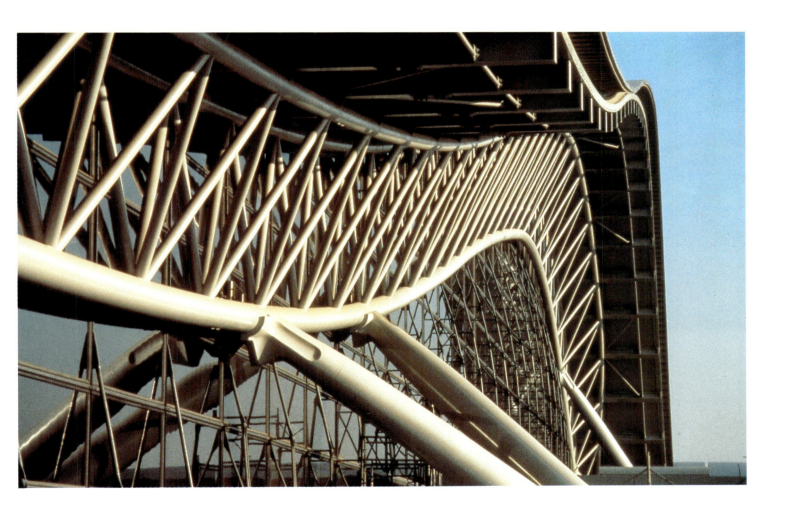

Detail of structural elements.
Interior views of main passenger block.

View of the roof trusses.

Details of the roof structure.

The airport at sunset.

Science and Technology Museum, Amsterdam, 1989

View of the project area.
Site plan.

This new building for the Amsterdam Science and Technology Museum is projected above an underwater tunnel, an important engineering work from the 1970s in the heart of the port.

The chosen site is where the road tunnel emerges into the port and a pedestrian ramp leads up from the opposite direction providing a panoramic view of the whole port. The museum spaces have been created in the wedge-shaped area between the pedestrian ramp and the tunnel. This area can be reached from the city centre by walking across the museum roof whose sloping plane will host interactive displays making use of the wind, sun and rain. Other structures on the roof are a restaurant and the entrance to lifts leading down to the main hall on the ground floor.

Following the example of other European and American science museums, the Amsterdam museum will accommodate on its 10,000 square metres permanent exhibitions on communications, energy, electricity and biotechnology using interactive presentation techniques.

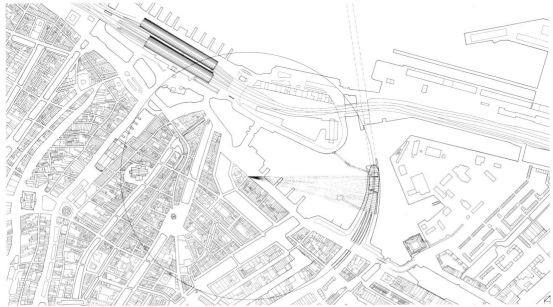

Longitudinal section through the tunnel.
Cross section through the tunnel looking towards the city.
Design sketch.

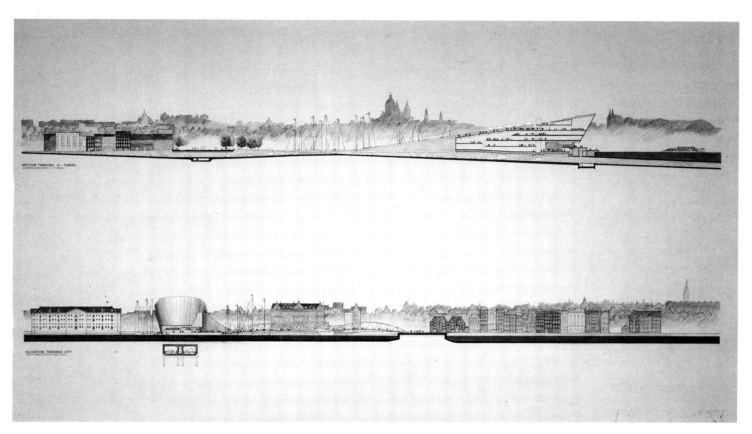

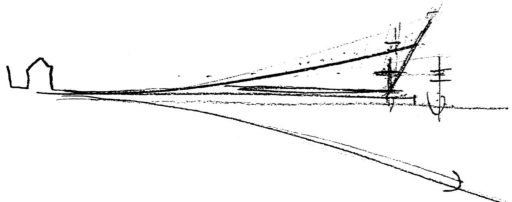

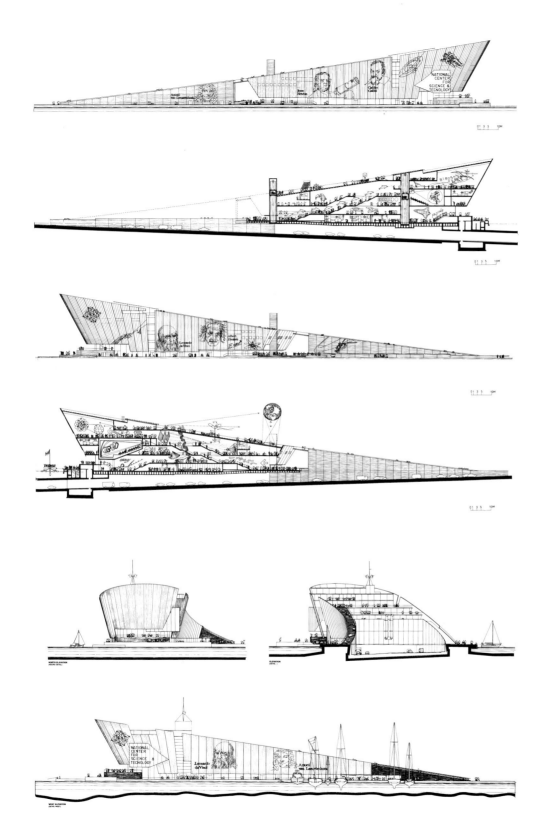

Elevations and sections.

Cross sections.

Model of the port and museum.
Perspective drawing.

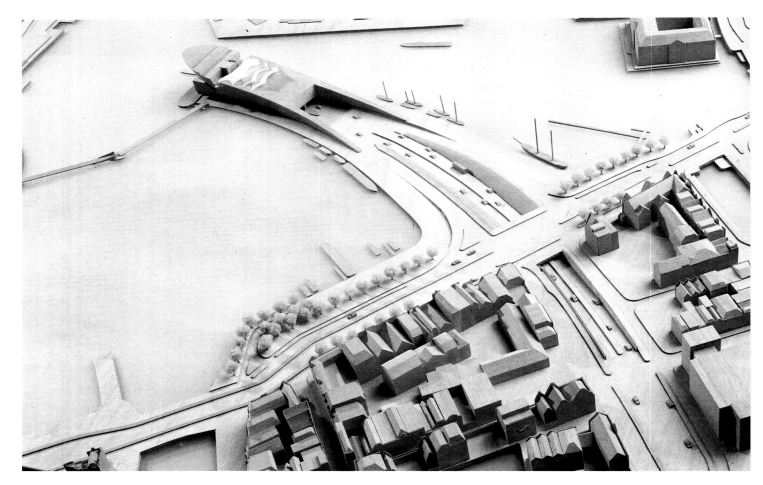

Model views.

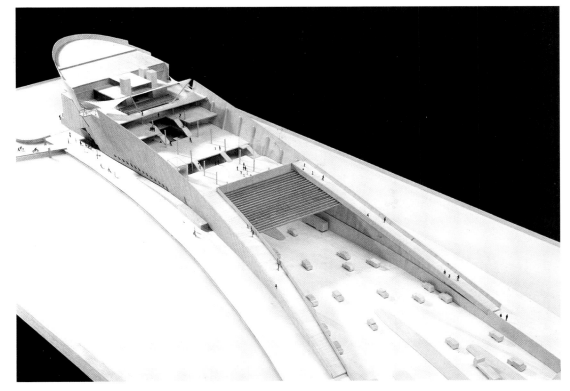

UNESCO Workshop, Vesima, 1989–91

Aerial view of the project area.

This UNESCO workshop is specialised in the field of building materials: a research centre for studying old materials to reach new and modern solutions able to combine light earthquake-resistant structures, wood laminates, concrete, stone and new applications for traditional materials in modern constructions.

Situated on a beautiful point on the Ligurian coast, the workshop can be reached from the coast road by a cable-car. The smallish site is around 1,000 square metres, consisting of terraced land originally dug out of the steep descent to the shore by Ligurian farmers. The sloping transparent roof follows down the shape of several terraces, bringing to mind the image of giant butterfly wings.

The roof is composed of a wooden structure filled with plastic-frame panels covered by thin membranes, chosen for their properties in filtering light and insulating against heat. A system of louvred blinds is controlled by photoelectric cells to protect the roof in adverse weather. The design evokes the agricultural history of the area through the terraces, traditional materials and structures on various layers.

Axonometric section.
Design sketch.
Site plan.

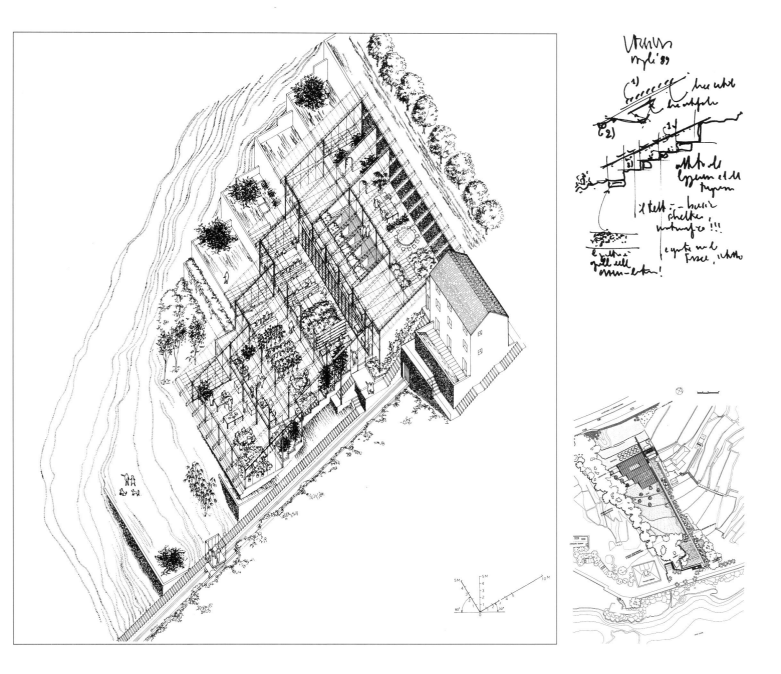

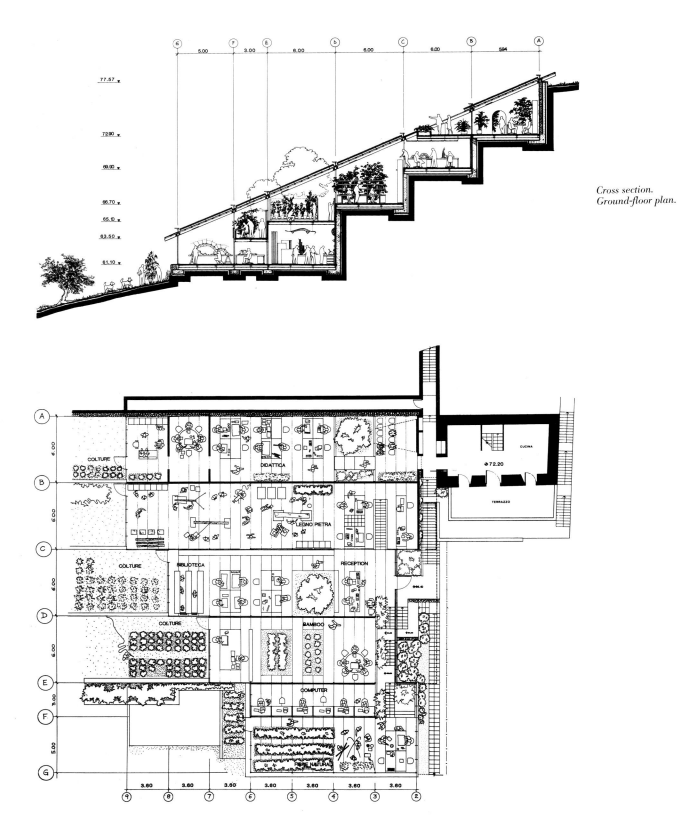

*Cross section.
Ground-floor plan.*

Views of outside areas.

*Views of the cable-way.
Section through the slope.*

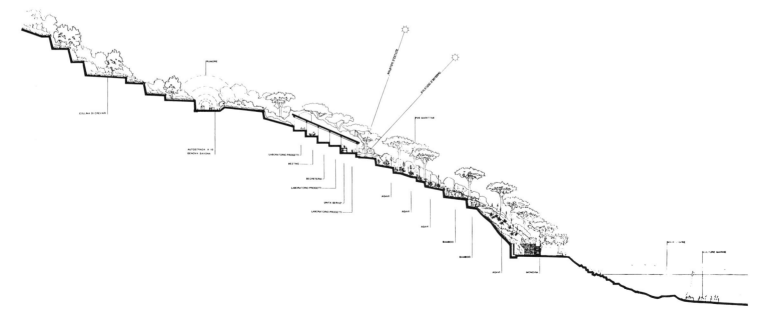

The research centre at night.

Views of the interior.

*Detail of the wooden roof structure.
Views of the interior.*

Bridge in the Ushibuka Archipelago, Kumamoto, 1989–95

*Aerial view of the project area.
Site plan.*

Situated on the southern point of the Amakusa headland, Ushibuka-shi is a medium-sized fishing port set in magnificent scenery. The new link bridge is designed to take the main state highway across the bay to the southern part of the town on the opposite shore. A further link with this area is provided by prolonging the road to the southeast. Given the risks of upsetting the delicate formal equilibrium of the bay, the design seeks to follow the landscape very carefully: the bridge thus traces a distinctive bend suspended over the sea.

To make the bridge's structure as unobtrusive as possible, a system of continuous trusses (150 metres each) supported by pillars was adopted. The lower sides of the trusses (19 metres above sea level) are curved – making them almost float above their supports – thus giving the structure lightness.

At each end of the bridge, windbreaks protect the pedestrians, whereas the curved lower part of the structure eliminates air friction. Light reflected by the windbreaks and the interplay of shade on the trusses establish a subtle rhythm all the way along the 900 metres of the bridge. Trees planted in three areas around the bridge heads help to blend the construction in with the scenery of the bay.

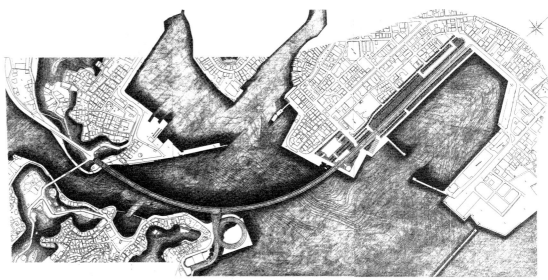

*Model.
Photomontage with the bridge included.*

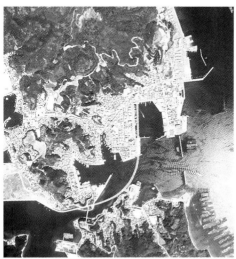

Section through land and sea.
Model views.

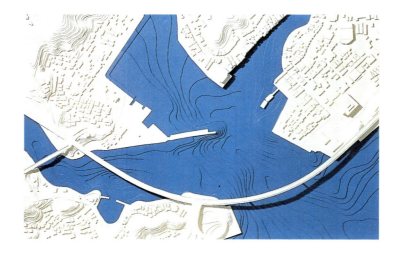

*Model view of pillar and trusses.
Cross and longitudinal sections.*

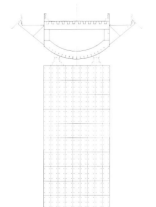

Construction details.

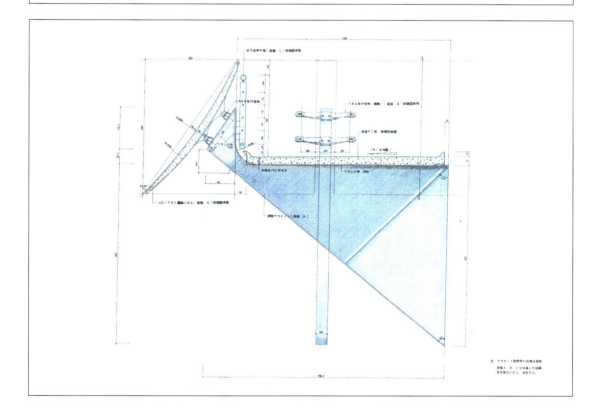

Church of Padre Pio, San Giovanni Rotondo, 1991

Design sketch.

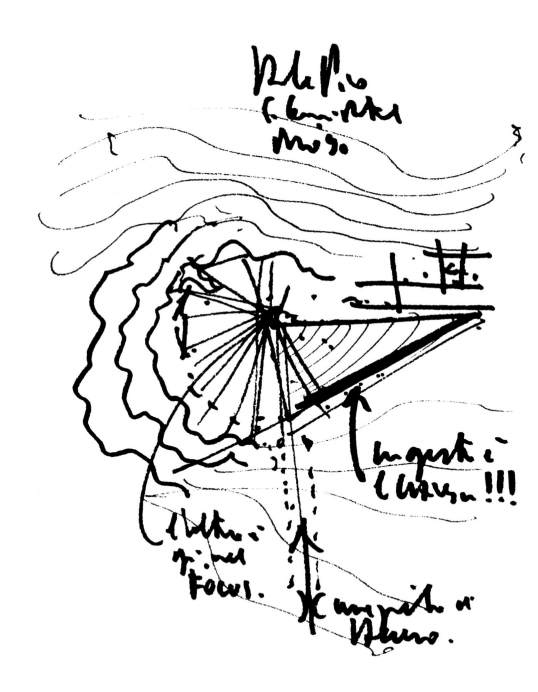

This Church dedicated to Padre Pio is to be built at San Giovanni Rotondo, an important pilgrimage centre and home town of the "miracle priest" (1887–1967). The site is up among the foothills rising out of the Tavoliere delle Puglie, the Apulian plain. Here massive low arches constructed from enormous stone blocks erected on concave flooring will bear a great church at the end of a large triangular *piazza*; from this position it will overlook the plain and welcome the faithful. From afar the church will appear semi-concealed by trees. By contrast, a huge supporting wall will be very conspicuous: almost twenty-five metres high, its buttresses will provide belfries for a dozen massive bells. As in Assisi, the wall will be an important landmark for pilgrims. From the foot of the hill, following the wall will take them up to the monastery where Padre Pio once lived and, more importantly, towards the chapel where he preached for the first time. The wall does not extend as far as the monastery, but ends at the top of the square, which is intended to accommodate the crowd overspill on feast days. The square's sloping paving will guide the faithful down towards the church. The paving continues into the church, curving into the concave floor bearing radial arches arranged in concentric circles. From the entrance onwards these rings become increasingly tightly interwoven, creating a kind of spiralling space tapering into the sacristy.

The traditional materials are measured and cut using computer-controlled machinery. The stone arches bearing the cupola are the modern version of a centuries-old form. They have been studied to bear uniform loads and analyzed on the ba-

Plan of the underground level.
Plan of roof level.

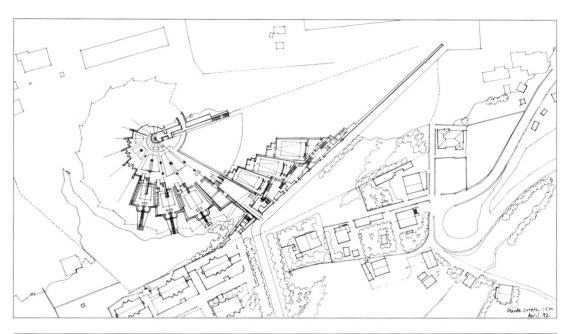

sis of new knowledge about the dynamics of the arch; their constituent stone elements measure 4.20 by 1.80 metres. All of the fixed weights will be supported by a wood and steel-cable system. The supports are tensed at the ends of each arch to bear the sections of the roof. Apertures in the roof diffuse natural light, flooding the great arches and creating a suitable atmosphere of religious awe and mystery.

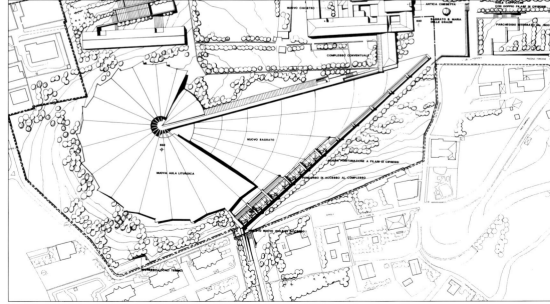

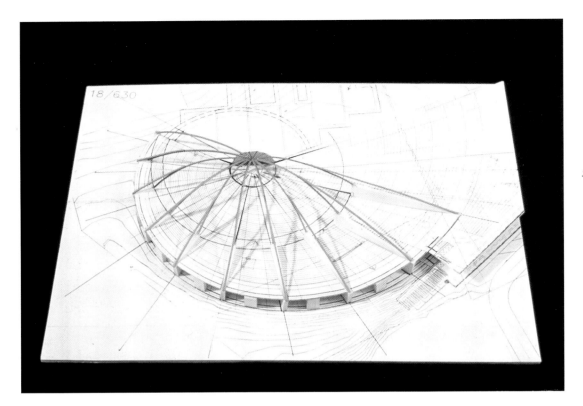

Study models of the roofing.

Models of structural elements.

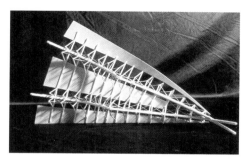

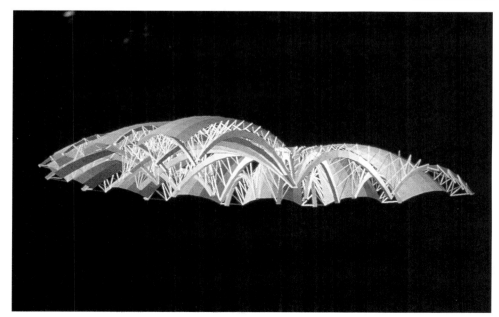
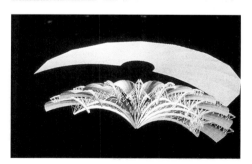
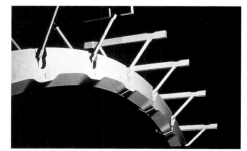

Section through the church.
Detail of the lighting system.

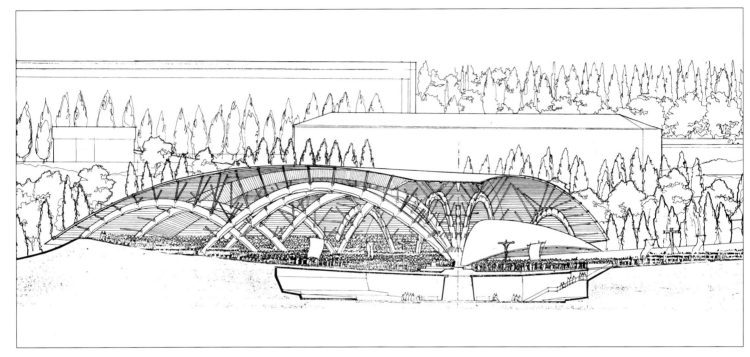

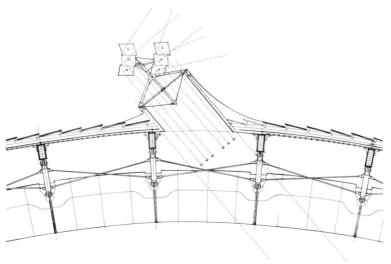

Section, detail and perspective drawing of the structural arches.

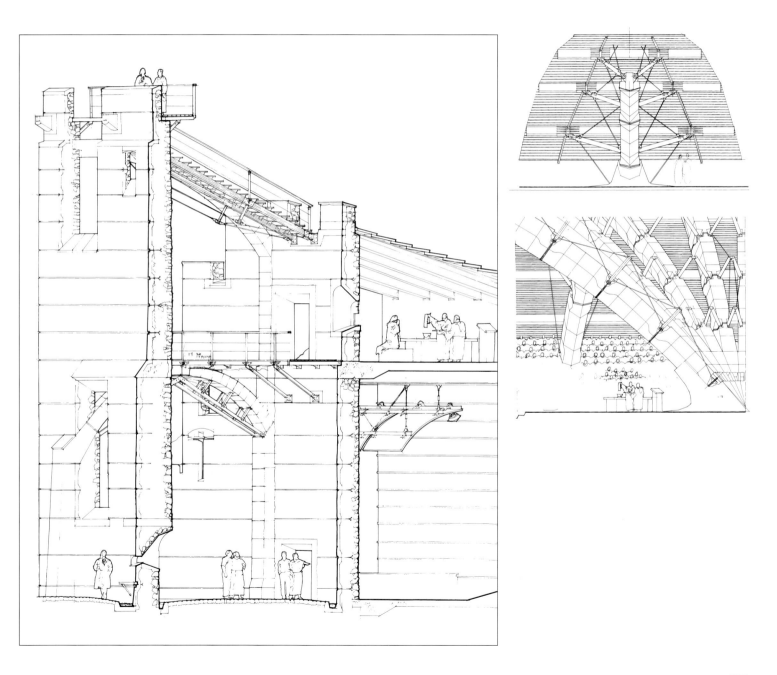

Plan for Potsdamer Platz, Berlin, 1992

Aerial views of Potsdamer Platz from the 1930s and 1920s.

A metropolis can never be created out of nothing, nor from one day to the next. Cities develop with their own history, and that takes time. Accordingly, initial design work chiefly involved identifying the main planning guidelines in the hope that the synergies present in this particular quarter would eventually serve to fill it with city life.

The best starting place is a careful examination of what already exists: Scharoun's Staatsbibliothek – a huge "mountain" on the eastern edge of an autobahn planned but never built – a "fortress" that would have been inconceivable if East Berlin had never come into being. The site is a square defined by built volumes forming a focal point for the vital urban and architectural functions of the quarter. The whole area is open to the force of the natural elements, such as sun and wind, whereas there is water to the south, towards the Landwehrkanal, and trees and greenery to the north, along the edge of the Tiergarten.

The urban scale – that is the size of the buildings, the hierarchy of streets of varying widths and heights, and the fragmentation of the street blocks – has elements used in endowing the quarter with variety and laying the basis for the development of a truly urban centre.

The combination of different but partially overlapping uses creates a balanced relationship between the buildings and will enhance the area with a variety of activities and people. Urban density is not only the expression of economic interests but also the desire for a city way of life. Private cars, taxis, buses and bikes are all part of the cityscape we are familiar with.

The masterplan is modelled on cities characterized by a finely woven texture consisting of the social fabric and a wide range of contrasting functions and uses, which paradoxically result in an overall appearance of coherence.

The modern city is not only a nostalgic jumble. It is related to the past and bound to the present by utilizing all the available technologies, by homogeneity and discipline in the use of materials, and by introducing a variety of perspectives.

Site plan.
Detail of the competition design.

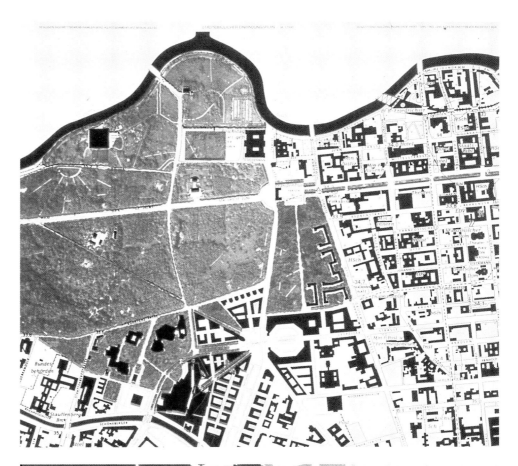
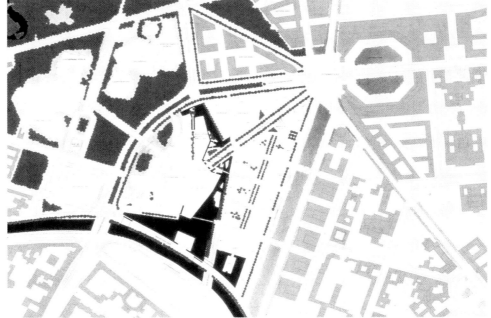

Design sketch.
Competition design model.

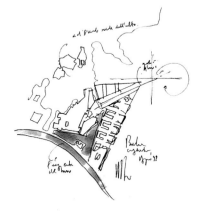
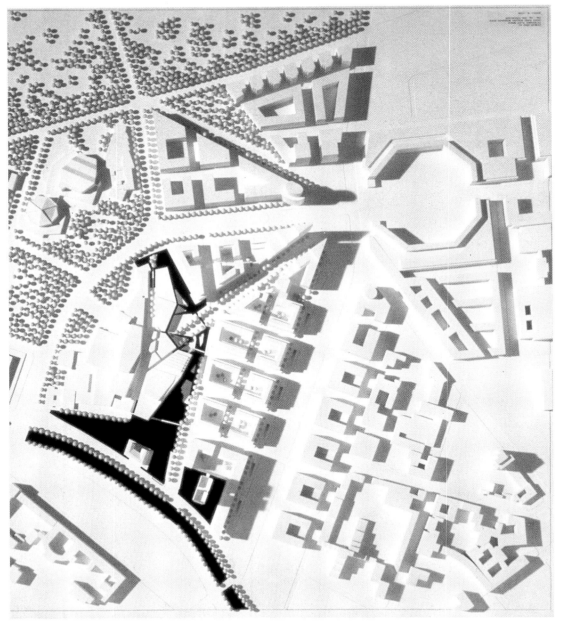

Competition design sections.

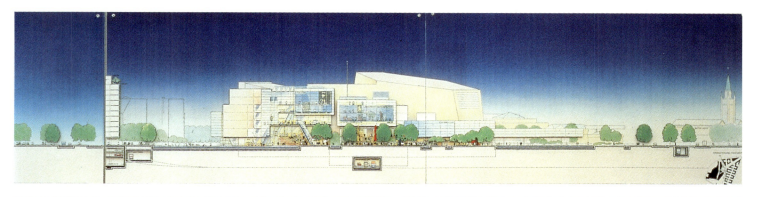

*Design sketch.
Photo with scheme inserted into area.
Site plan for Potsdamer Platz master plan.*

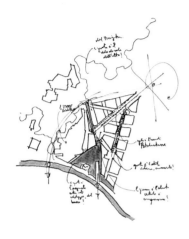

View of the model.

Master plan sections.

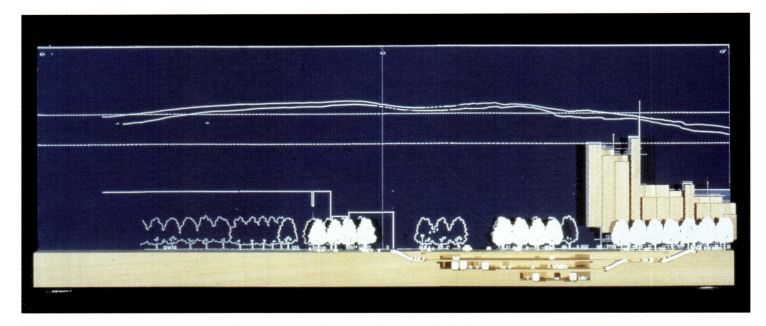
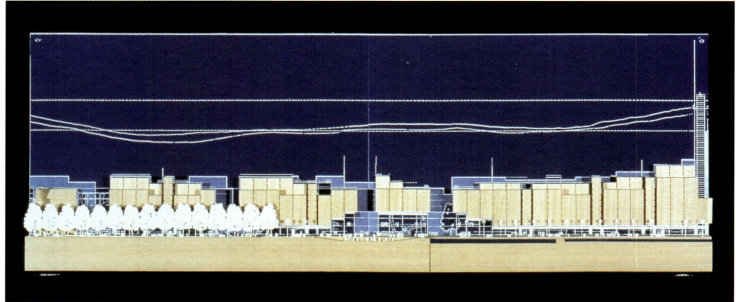

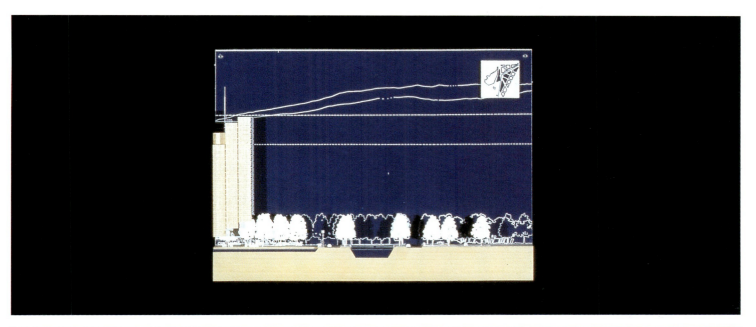
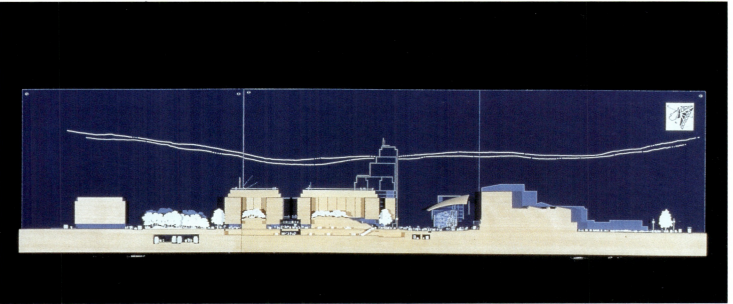

*Plan-site with typical street sections.
Model of the theatre and library.*

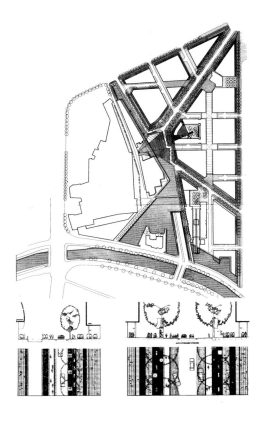

Overall view of the model.

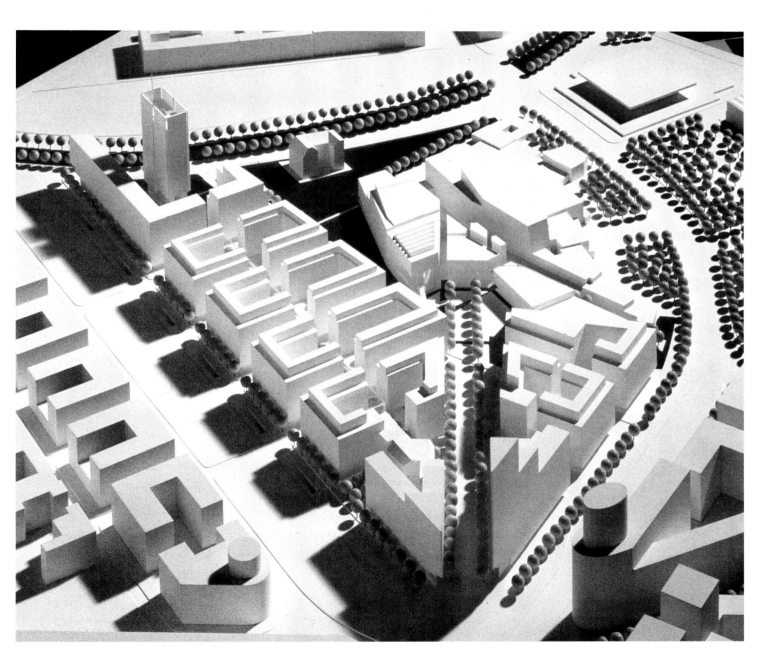

Master plan models (1992/1993).

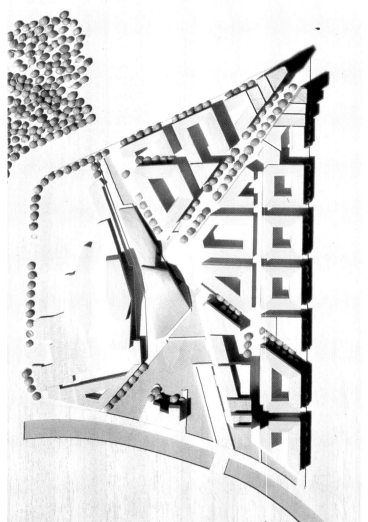

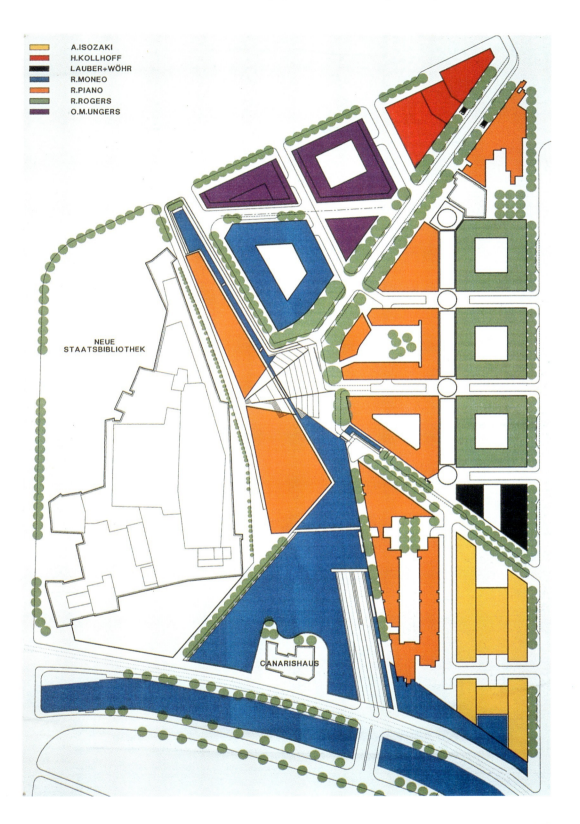

Site plan indicating the architects and their buildings (1993).

*Sketches of the roof.
Cross and longitudinal sections through the theatre.*

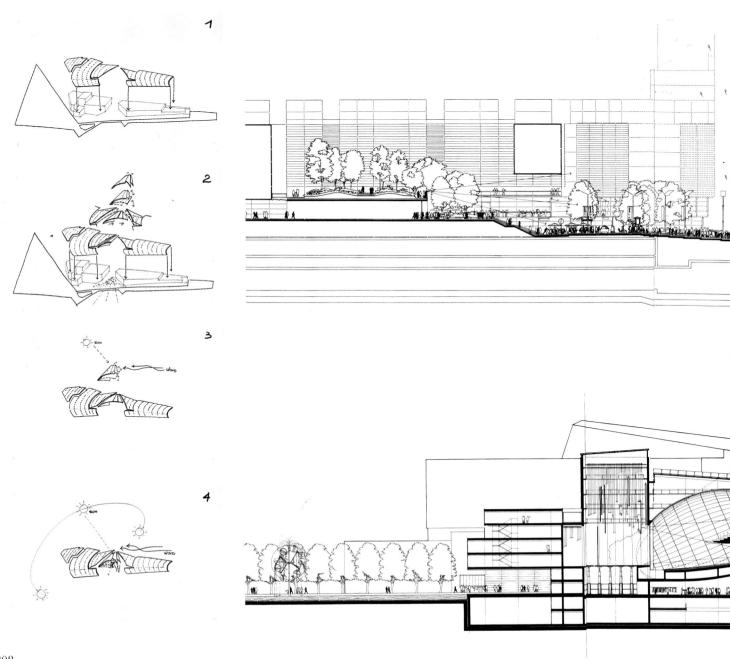

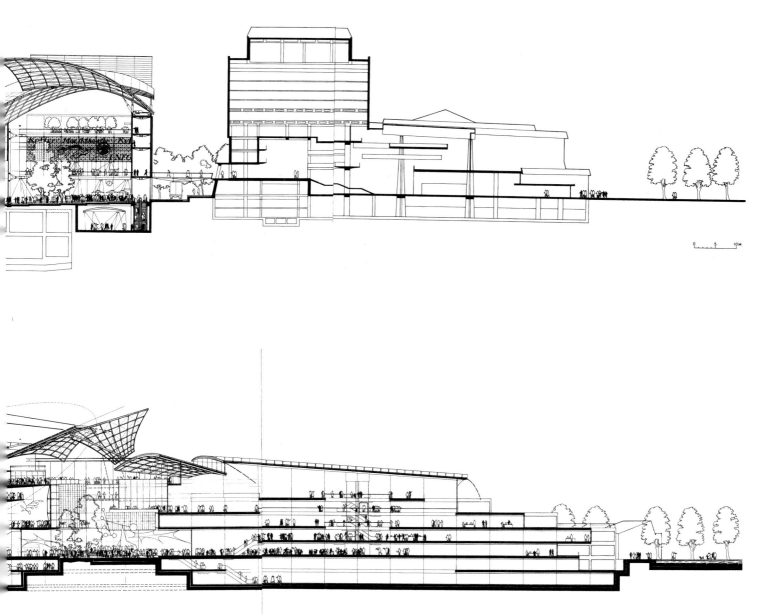

The Jean-Marie Tjibaou Kanak Cultural Centre, Nouméa, 1992

Design sketches.
Site plan.

In June 1988, as part of the agreements between the French government and New Caledonia for the forthcoming independence of the Pacific island, it was decided that a cultural centre dedicated to Melanesian Kanak traditions should be built and named after Jean-Marie Tjibaou.

Starting from a deep relationship with nature, typical of Melanesian culture, the design had two main guiding ideas: it aimed, on one hand, to evoke the Kanak skills in building with nature and in nature, and on the other, to use traditional local materials, such as wood and stone, together with modern materials, such as glass, aluminum and state of the art lightweight technologies. Thus, a very nature-conscious overall design ensued, blending history, architecture, archaeology and the social sciences. Situated on a tropical palm-covered promontory, the cultural centre is composed of a series of large shells: ogival pavilions from nine to twenty metres high arranged asymmetrically along a main axis. These pavilions contain the principal public areas: exhibition rooms, an auditorium and a restaurant. A circulation spine links up the various groups of pavilions and accommodates the heavier structures. Along a smaller perpendicular axis are the study services, such as the library and areas for researchers. The centre feels more like a promenade than a covered museum, since it is partly in the open air.

The shell structures are made by following a method that combines the memory of the Kanak culture and modern techniques. The curved walls are composed of three different diaphragms providing effective daylighting: a system of louvres, a laminated wood partition

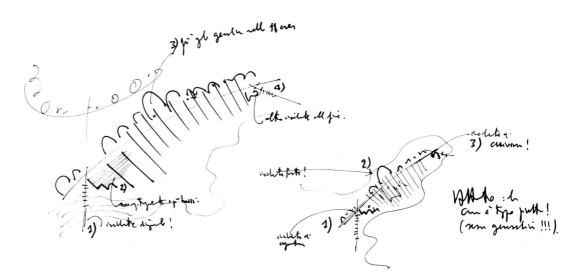

One of the wood and steel structures. Diagrams illustrating the natural ventilation system.

Longitudinal sections.

and a bamboo partition all contribute to filtering the light and sounds of the forest. The great shells "catch" the wind, providing natural ventilation by channelling fresh air through the lower part of the construction, while hot air is expelled through a convection system.

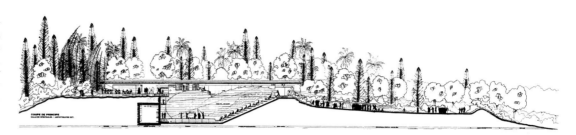

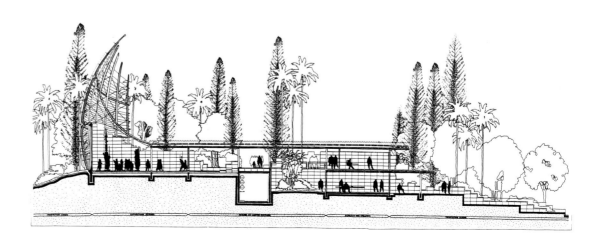

*Model of an ogival pavilion.
Design sketches.*

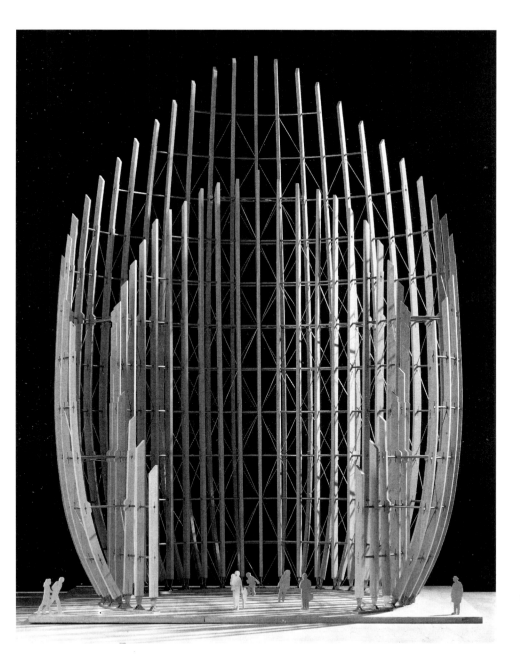
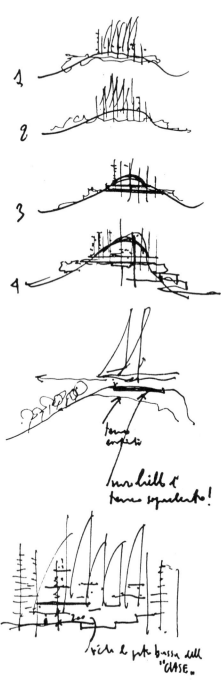

213

Elevation showing part of the cultural centre.
Design sketch.

Detail of a wood and steel structure.

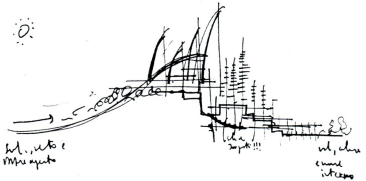

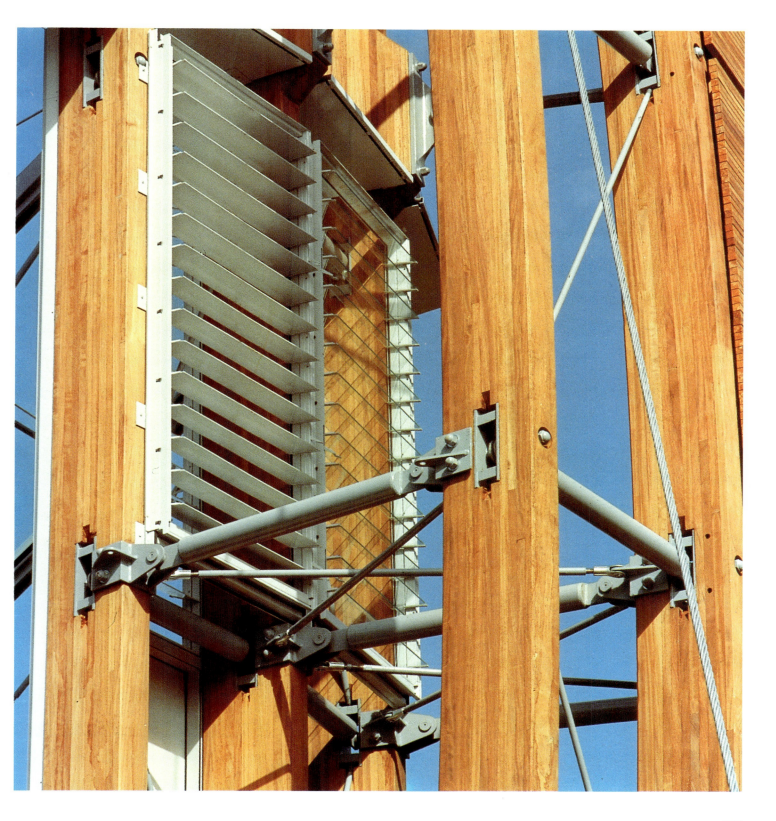

The Cy Twombly Pavilion, Houston 1992

Elevation showing the Cy Twombly Pavilion and the Menil Collection. Site plan.

The Renzo Piano Workshop's museum designing activities in Houston continue with this new building commissioned by the Menil Foundation. It is to house a collection of paintings and sculptures by the American artist Cy Twombly. Equally full of light as the Menil Collection, the new building has a completely different context with very distinctive features.

The roof is composed of several light-filtering layers – almost like the wings of a butterfly – that will allow outside climatic changes to be perceived inside. The top filtering layer is composed of a semi-opaque tent-like fabric, also used for the gallery ceiling. In contrast to the transparency of the roof, the outer walls are made of concrete blocks, thus marking the building off from the surrounding architecture.

Careful studies on light were conducted in collaboration with Ove Arup & Partners through a computer-controlled simulation using a mock-up of the building.

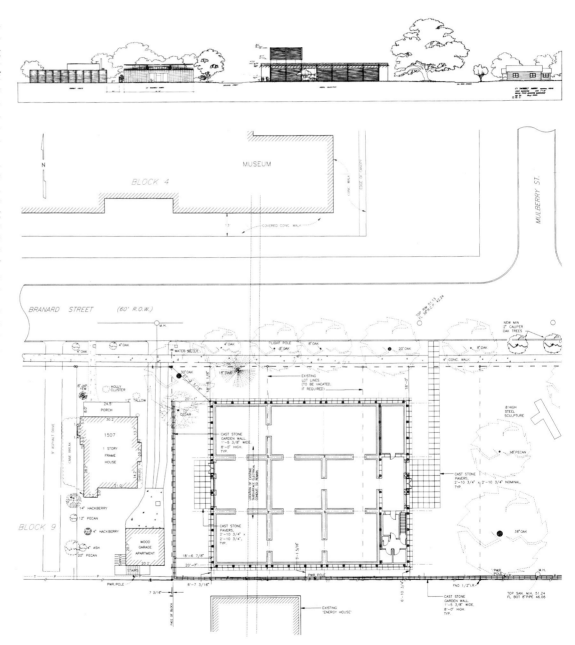

216

Exploded diagram and model views of the roof layers.

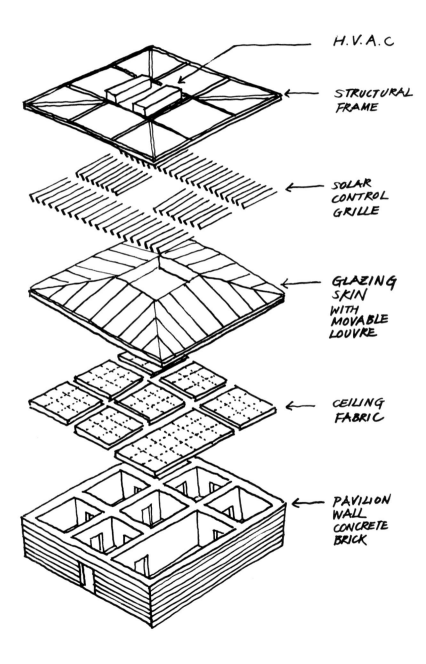

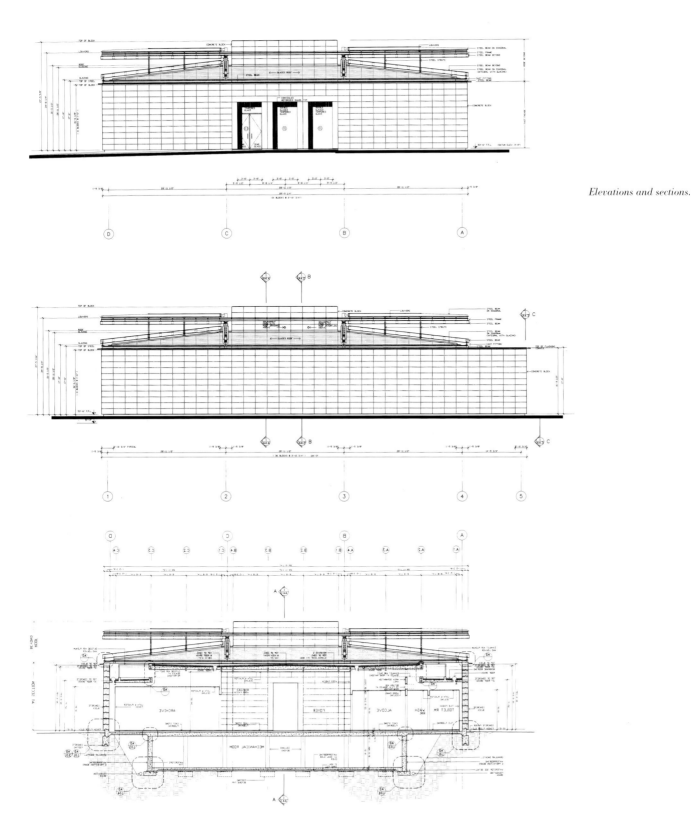

Elevations and sections.

View of the model.

Redevelopment of the Ile Séguin, Boulogne-Billancourt, Paris, 1993

Design sketches.
Aerial view of the project area.

The overall design form follows the shape of the island, once the site of a Renault factory, and expresses the relations established with the river through a series of varied elements. Along the north side the buildings are flush with the shore or project slightly forwards, whereas on the southern side, they are set back to create open spaces along the banks of the Seine. The long uniform frontages are interrupted and modified at places where river-related leisure facilities are situated. Walkways link a raised pedestrian area with the open square at the upstream point of the island. At the centre of the island is a slight depression. This is filled by a large park which runs the whole length of the depression and integrates with the buildings grouped at its two ends. In the overall form variations show only along the internal façades, where the buildings are differentiated by function and size. The open squares at the two points of the island are accessible to vehicular traffic and distribute the circulation to the various functional centres. The downstream tip of the island is connected to the Pont de Sèvres metro station and will become a reception centre with a library and conference rooms.

The upstream tip is to be equipped with shops, hotels, services and sports and leisure facilities. It could also be the site for a Renault social centre with a car museum in memory of the former factory on the island.

Along the eastern and western banks is housing flanked by buildings with activities linked to the reception centre.

Since the design clearly reveals the intention to preserve and highlight the original form of the island, the result appears to be a stratification of vegetation, street layouts and river courses which gave rise to the pre-existing texture underlying the local structure.

The abundant vegetation is the main feature of the island, which is covered in a thick wood interrupted by squares or open green patches. Trees and bushes have partly been planted to coincide with the original vegetation; elsewhere they are primarily a memory of the island's rural past. As the visitor penetrates towards the heart of the island the greenery gradually opens out into a botanical garden full of flowers and fruit trees.

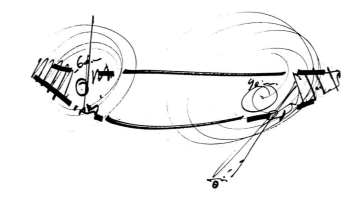

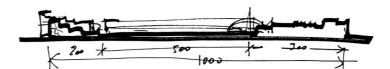

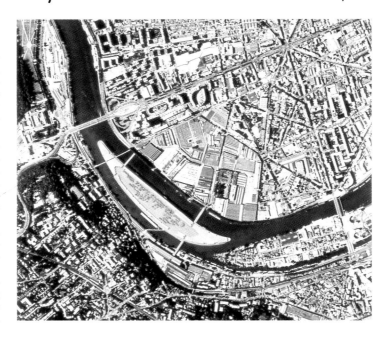

Site plans showing built area and greenery.

*Elevation and longitudinal section.
Views of the model.*

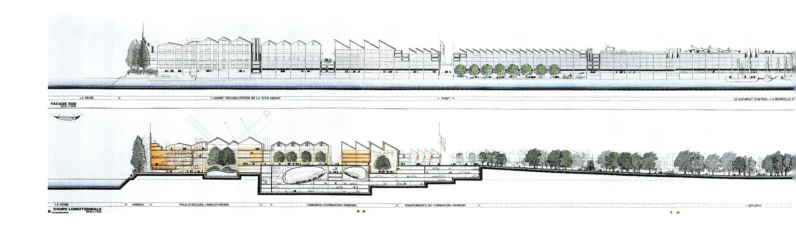

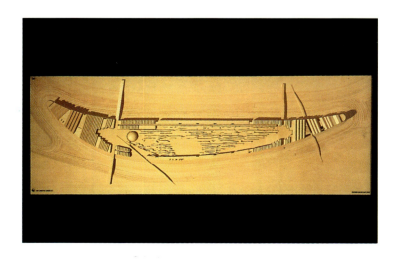

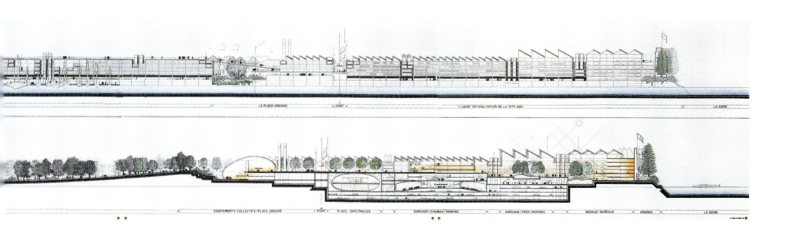

Pilot scheme for railway stations in Turin, Mestre, Venice and Bari, 1993

Sections showing the stations of Turin, Mestre, Venice and Bari.
Details of section of Mestre and Turin stations.

Turin
As part of the redevelopment project for a mixed-use centre and technological park in the former Fiat Lingotto works, the railway station of Turin Lingotto is relocated on the axis from Piazza Galimberti to the Fairs Centre in the redeveloped complex.
The new station is seen as a key element in revitalizing the whole area by linking up with domestic and international networks. The station will thus give a new centrality to an area at present considered marginal, and so contribute to ongoing urban renewal involving the removal of environmentally damaging activities away from the city centre. In planning terms, the scheme redesigns the confines between city and railway so that the areas contiguous to the new station will be rehabilitated in terms of urban quality, bringing much more life to the quarter.

Mestre
The town of Mestre (Venice) is separated from the neighbouring town of Marghera by an infrastructures channel (140 metres wide) containing the railway and a link road to the Mestre-Venice by-pass. With the aim of reorganizing the connecting area between Mestre and Marghera, the bridge-station typology is proposed. This structure becomes a new urban place straddling the railway and joining up the two towns. On the Mestre side, shifting the station would mean removing an important connection with the major thoroughfare of Via Piave. To overcome this problem, a satellite building has been designed to link up the street and the station entrance. The "satellite" accommodates complementary service functions to those inside the railway station.

Venice
The project is based on the premise that the road and rail terminal system in Venice should be redesigned to restore the historic centre to its island status. This is achieved by transferring both the Santa Lucia railway station and the Piazzale Roma road terminal.
The new station is situated on the dock along the Canale della Scomenzera, where there is easy access to the city across the bridge of Campo Sant'Andrea.
A new feature of the project is the departure from the usual typology of terminal stations: the new station has additional lines extending beyond the terminal for shunting and rerouting trains.
The concept of a bridge-station as a lively public place is played down in Venice. A marginal site has deliberately been chosen for the station, since it cannot possibly compete as a public gathering place with the far more dignified existing squares in the historic centre. The size of the station concourse is kept to the bare minimum for activities strictly connected with rail functions.

Bari
The area of the Bari Parco Sud railway station is located on a coastal stretch of the Bari-Lecce line. This part of the line is moved away from the coast bringing many advantages for the city of Bari: the elimination of a physical barrier separating the existing quarters from the coast, the possibility to extend the southern promenade of the city, which was interrupted in the 1930s; and the integration of the converted railway area with the new development in the Corso Perotti area.
The overall scheme includes a promenade along the coast, part of

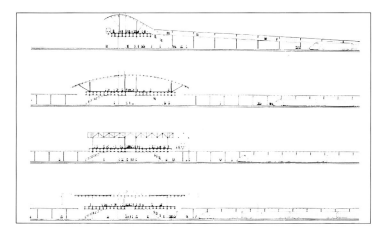

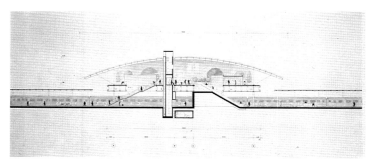

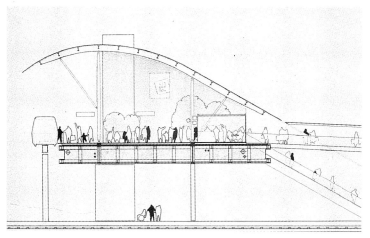

Model view of Mestre station.
Section of Mestre station.

which passes above a small sailing port, while the coast road is set back onto the axis of the current railway. At present the land in the area is not much more than a bare esplanade on which nothing can grow because of the prevailing sea winds. The landscape is thus redesigned in the manner of the Apulian countryside, by constructing a network of small walls at varying heights to create microclimates favouring the growth of vegetation.

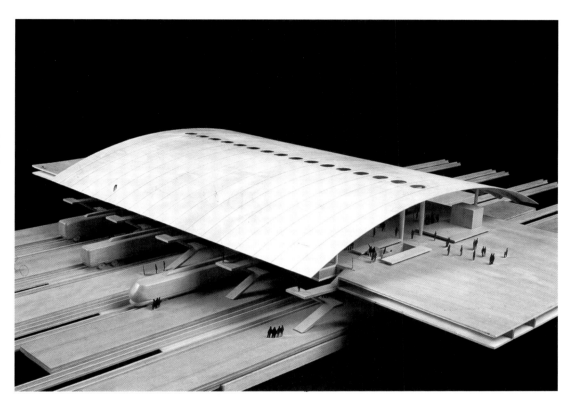

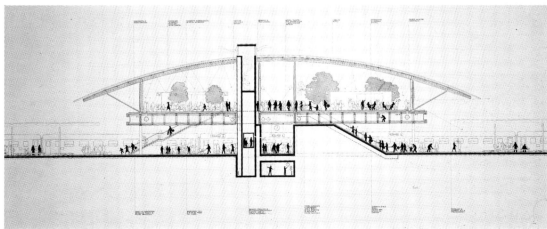

Perspective drawings of the stations of Turin, Mestre, Venice and Bari. Longitudinal section through Bari station.

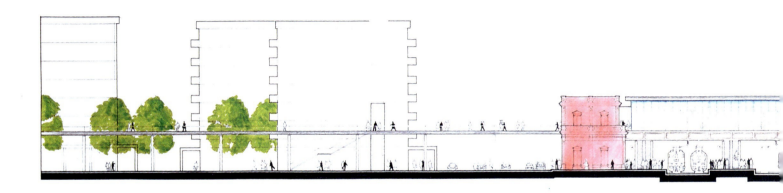

Redevelopment of the Teatro Margherita, Bari, 1993

The project area.
Elevation showing the main façade.
Site plan.

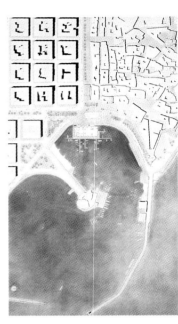

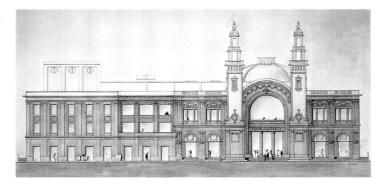

For the people of Bari the Teatro Margherita (a former theatre and cinema) is emblematic of popular culture in the 1930s, a time of great prosperity for the city.

The design aim is to reintegrate the building with the urban fabric of lively social, commercial and cultural activities in the city and join up the Murat quarter with the old town. These aims give rise to two requirements: the removal of barriers created by traffic and the creation of pedestrian passages and precincts. The area in front of the theatre and Piazza del Ferrarese, both free of traffic, are joined up by moving the fish market out of the ground floor of its present building and converting this structure into a covered public concourse.

In addition to small permanent shops, the concourse will host a part of the weekly market currently held in Piazza del Ferrarese: the theatre building is thus rejoined to the historic centre by a chain of pedestrian areas.

Redesigning the road layout contributes to solving the problem of the presently very congested area in front of the theatre. Two new underpasses linked to underground parking in Corso Vittorio Emanuele II and in Corso Cavour ensure that the area is totally traffic free.

The main elevation of the theatre stands like a stage set at the end of Corso Vittorio Emanuele II, while the virtual extension of the axis to the sea – highlighted by the great glazed arch – stretches out as far as the Barion and the lighthouse at the port entrance.

The theatre was originally built on a palafitte platform over the sea. But with time, the building has become increasingly firmly anchored to the land. Wharves serving a sailing club below road level have been

*Plans of various levels.
Longitudinal section.*

built round the original platform under the theatre, thus making it almost landlocked.

By reorganizing the layout of the surfaces and the wharves, the enchanting image of an object suspended over water is restored.

The large 1,200-seat theatre auditorium is suitable for films, congresses, conferences and recording television shows, but could also become a multimedia communications systems facility.

Further spaces in the theatre are to be used for production (recording studios, rehearsal rooms, television studios) and research (dubbing, copying and remixing of rare films or the preservation and updating of archives).

These functions will be complemented on the ground floor by activities related to images and sound: a music school, listening rooms, a radio-amateur centre, video-library and film club.

The centre also accommodates service activities related to communications systems, plus shops and galleries, a bar and a restaurant overlooking the sea, a newspaper kiosk, flower stand, automatic banking services, public telephones, etc.

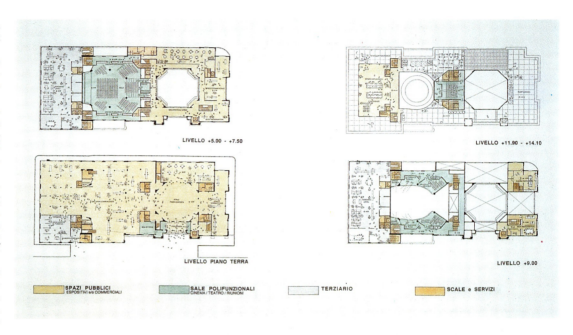

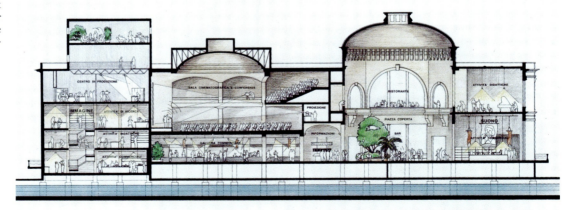

Brancusi Museum at the Georges Pompidou Centre, Paris, 1993–96

Site plan for the area round the Pompidou Centre.
Cross section of Pompidou Centre with surrounding area.

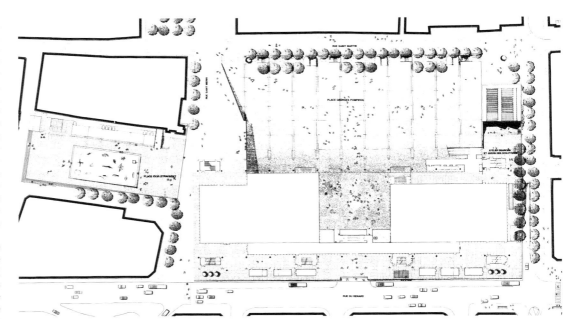

In his will the great Romanian artist Constantin Brancusi bequeathed his studio and all it contained to the French state. For their part, the French authorities promised to provide a new home for the artist's sculptures, sketches, work tables, equipment and furniture, possibly in the Musée National d'Art Moderne. The ambitious project aims at enabling the public to admire Brancusi's works in the most fitting environment – a reconstruction of the atelier in which they were created – but also takes into account all the usual museum requirements concerning the display, preservation and security of works of art.

The site for the atelier is a private sculpture garden in the Place Georges Pompidou, to be entered through the Centre. The project is part of the effort to reorganize the space around the Centre in the Beaubourg quarter. Externally, the new building closely reflects the architectural features of the Pompidou Centre, whereas inside the sequence of spaces is inspired by the volumes of the artist's atelier.

The museum will house the largest collection of works by Brancusi in the world: one hundred and forty-eight stone, marble, bronze or wooden sculptures; eighty-five carved plinths, mostly made of wood but also of plaster and marble; forty-one drawings and two paintings. The collection of original Brancusi photographs is also the largest of its kind in the world and includes four hundred and forty glass plates and over 1,100 original prints on paper. This museum is a unique contribution to the European artistic heritage, since apart from the early Romanian collections, all the other major Brancusi collections are in the United States.

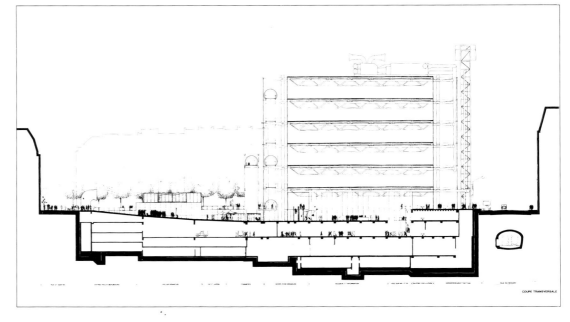

*Section through the Brancusi atelier.
Section through the underground car park.*

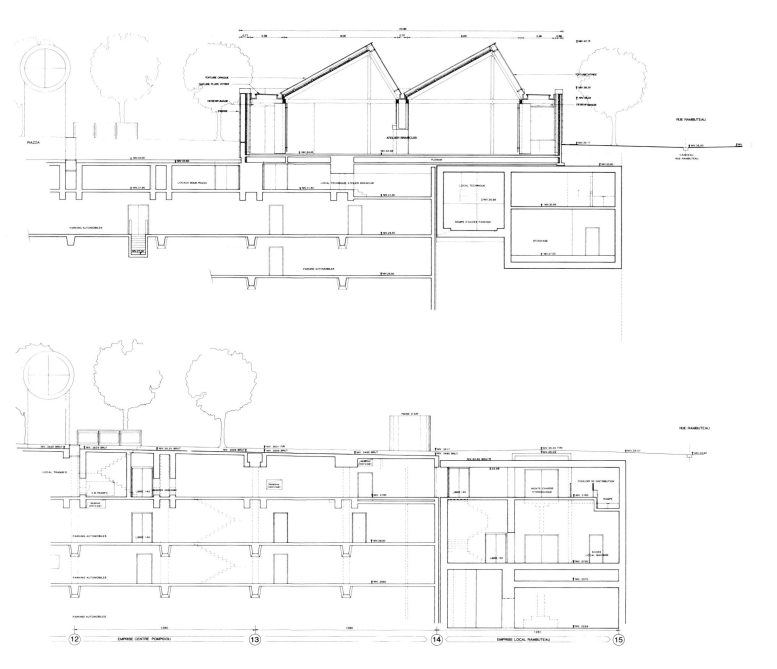

Section of the exhibition rooms.
Initial design plan.

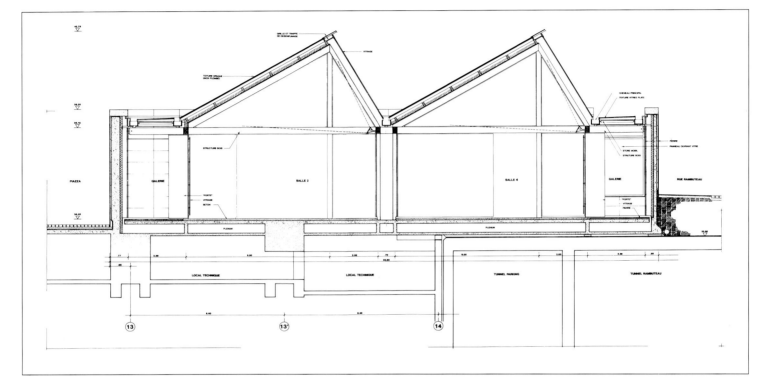
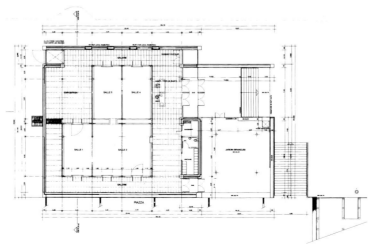

Ground-floor plan.

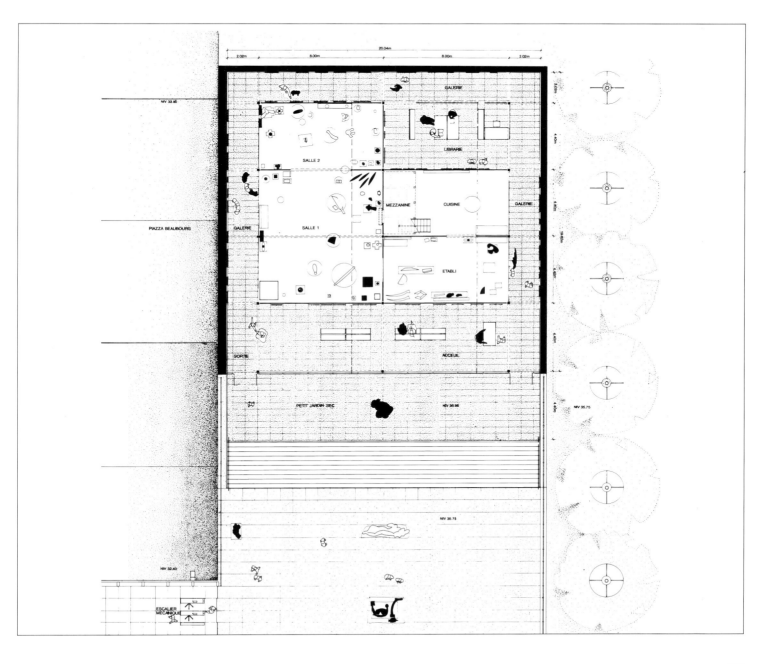

Exhibitions and Exhibition Designs

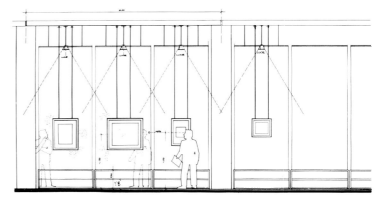

View of the Fiat Lingotto Centre. Section through the lighting system. Installation of the "Russian and Soviet Art 1870–1930" exhibition, Turin 1989.

The relation between the installation and the container is a major theme in Renzo Piano's approach to the world of exhibition design.

The "Russian and Soviet Art 1870–1930" exhibition in the Lingotto complex in summer 1988 was installed in the former Fiat works without any attempt to conceal the building's industrial past and technological structures. The only concession to decoration was the artificial lighting, which shaped the space through a system of light, emitted by shielded metal iodide lamps with pink filters and reflected on white panels.

In 1990 the "Automobile in Milan" exhibition was held in the former Ansaldo works. A mezzanine suspended by invisible cables at the back of a large industrial warehouse was used both as a video-library and a viewing point for the whole space containing the exhibited items illuminated by daylighting from the roof.

The "Jean Prouvé Constructeur" exhibition held at the Pompidou Centre in Paris realized one of the French architect's life-long dreams: a studio whose tables bring together teaching, action, thought, study, hand, head and heart. These tables gave order to the exhibition spaces and guided the visitor among documents, drawings and models.

In 1991 at the Palazzo della Ragione in Padua, Piano designed an exhibition on Galileo Galilei. Intended to be a model of Galileo's great workshop, the exhibition was a chronological reconstruction of the most important stages in the great scientist's explorations.

The design for "American Art 1930–1970" at the Lingotto centre in 1992 highlighted the rational aspects of the exhibition space by means of very simple white opaque walls and translucent partitions. On a large table at the centre of the exhibition hall were video installations and a well-stocked library, while all around the exhibited works were lit by direct illumination.

As part of the Christopher Columbus '92 Expo, Piano designed the set for "Ulysses and the White Whale", a play staged in the tent-like structure in Piazza delle Feste. The whole theatre consisted of a horizontally sliced-open whaling ship: the aft and starboard sides contained the audience, the deck was a long central stage and the prow and stern revealed structural ribs and beams.

In addition to the exhibition designs and thematic installations are a number of travelling displays illustrating the works of the Renzo Piano Building Workshop. These very distinctive exhibitions follow the development of projects explaining the various stages through sketches, original drawings, design sheets and models. They are basically didactic exhibitions conceived to illustrate both the design method and the planned works.

In the 1987 Chappelle de la Sorbonne exhibition all the featured projects were laid out on one long table, twenty metres by four, according to themes: the exhibition designs, the large-scale projects, technological works, environmental projects and work in historical contexts.

In 1989 the Royal Institute of British Architects set up a series of large tables around which to consult, read and discuss the drawings, models and design details by the Workshop; a similar exhibition travelled to the Urban Center, New York and to Madrid.

Cross section, plan and views of the "Automobile in Milan" exhibition, Ansaldo works, Milan 1990.

Views of the "Jean Prouvé Constructeur" exhibition, George Pompidou Centre, Paris 1990–91.

*"Padua and Galileo" designed for the
Palazzo della Ragione, Padua 1991.
Cross section.
Longitudinal section.
Design sketches.*

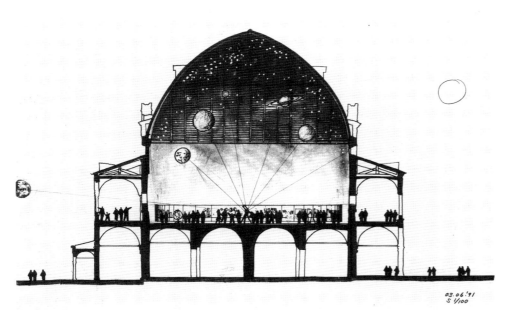
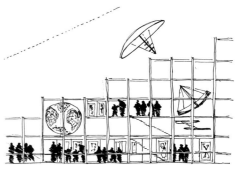
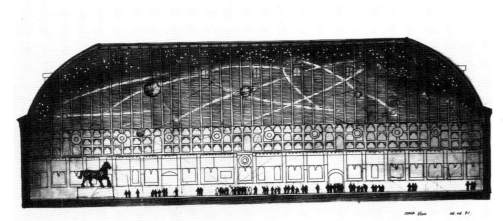
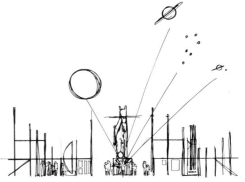

*View of the Fiat Lingotto façade during the "American Art 1930–1970" exhibition, Turin 1992.
Interiors and section of lighting system.*

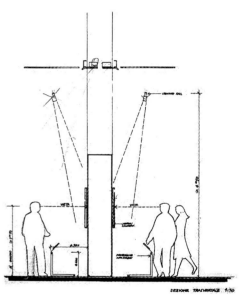

Preparatory work on "Ahab's ship" under the tensile structure in Piazza delle Feste at the Christopher Columbus '92 Expo, Genoa. Plan and sections of the ship-theatre.

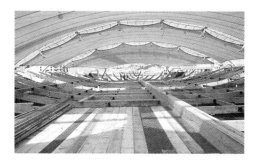
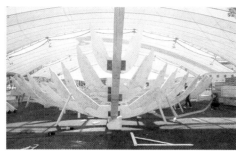

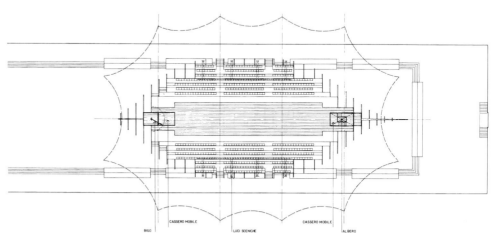
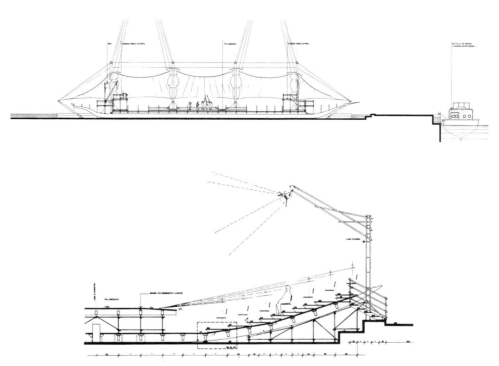

Cross section, plan and views of the exhibition "Works by Renzo Piano", Chapelle de la Sorbonne, Paris, 1987.

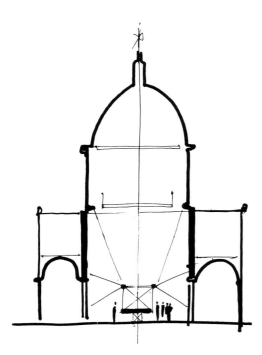

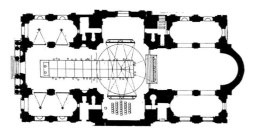

*Views and plan of the exhibition
"Renzo Piano Building Workshop –
25 Years of Projects", Royal Institute of
British Architects, London, 1989.*

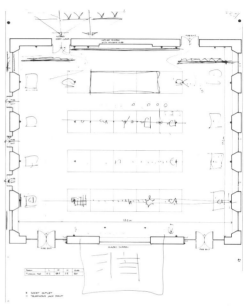

Views and design sketches of the exhibition "Renzo Piano Building Workshop: selected projects", Urban Center, New York, 1992–93.

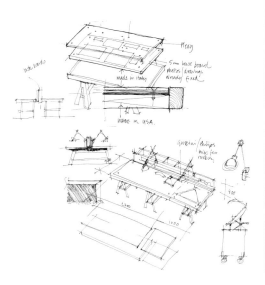
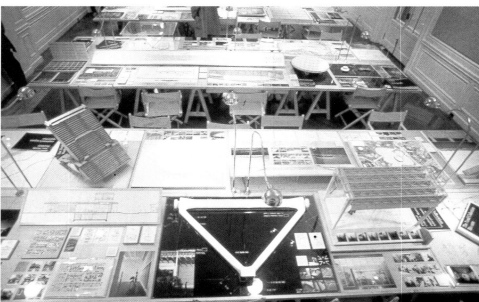

Views and plan of the exhibition "Renzo Piano Building Workshop" in the Ministerio de obras públicas, transportes y medio ambiente, Madrid, 1993.

Biography

Born in Genoa on 14 September 1937, Renzo Piano currently lives in Paris. He graduated from the Milan Polytechnic School of Architecture in 1964 and, subsequently gained practical building experience in his father's business in Genoa, where he had already begun designing under the guidance of Franco Albini. He then went on to work with Louis I. Kahn in Philadelphia and with Z.S. Makowsky in London. It was at this time he met Jean Prouvé whose friendship was to exert a decisive influence on his work.

Renzo Piano has collaborated with many architects and engineers: he began a long relationship with Richard Rogers in 1971 (Piano & Rogers), with Peter Rice (Atelier Piano & Rice) in 1977, and with Richard Fitzgerald in Houston in 1980; his chief collaborators in Genoa are Shunji Ishida, associate architect, Flavio Marano, associate engineer, and Alberto Giordano, general coordinator. In Paris he works with associate engineer Alain Vincent, and associate architects Noriaki Okabe and Bernard Plattner.

Renzo Piano has been a visiting professor to many European and American universities and has won recognition in numerous national and international competitions. He was awarded the 1978 International Union of Architects prize in Mexico City, and in 1981 the Compasso d'Oro (Italy) and an Honorary Fellowship of the AIA (American Institute of Architects).

In 1984 he was awarded the title of Commandeur des Arts et des Lettres and the Legion d'Honneur in Paris, while in London he was made an honorary fellow of the RIBA. In 1989 he was awarded the RIBA Royal Gold Medal for Architecture and was made a Cavaliere di Gran Croce by the Italian government. In 1990 he was awarded an honorary doctorate from the University of Stockholm and at Kyoto he received the Inamori Foundation Prize. In 1991 he won the Neutra Prize at Pomona, California and in 1992 he was given an honorary doctorate from the University of Delft.

Exhibitions of his work have been held in London, Paris, Milan, Rome, Venice, Genoa, Arezzo, Bologna, Bari, Naples, Helsinki, São Paulo, New York, Houston, Los Angeles, Philadelphia, Tokyo, Kyoto, Nice, Toronto, Boston, Sidney, Berlin, Vicenza, Marseille, Moscow, Osaka, Nagoya, Sapporo, Madrid and Pittsburgh.

Chronology

1964–65 Genoa
Reinforced polyester spatial frames
Design team: Studio Piano

1965 Genoa
Woodworking shop
Design team: Studio Piano, with the collaboration of R. Foni, M. Filocca, L. Tirelli
Contractors: E. Piano

1966 Pomezia (Rome)
Mobile structure for sulphur extraction
Design team: Studio Piano
Contractors: E. Piano

1966 Genoa
Space frame in small inflatable units
Design team: Studio Piano

1966 Genoa
Prestressed steel and reinforced polyester structure
Client: IPE, Genoa
Design team: Studio Piano with F. Marano
Contractors: E. Piano

1966 Milan
Shell structural systems: a pavilion for the XIVth Triennale
Client: Triennale of Milan
Design team: Studio Piano with F. Marano, O. Celadon, G. Fascioli

1967 Bologna
Reinforced concrete construction system
Client: Vibrocemento, Bologna
Design team: Studio Piano with F. Marano and G. Fascioli, assisted by R. Jascone

1968 Genoa
Industrialized construction system for a housing estate
Client: IPE, Genoa
Design team: Studio Piano with F. Marano, O. Celadon, G. Fascioli
Engineers: Sertec Engineering
Contractors: E. Piano

1968 Scarmagno (Ivrea)
Roofing for Olivetti works
Client: Olivetti Spa
Design team: Studio Piano
Roofing system: F. Marano, O. Celadon, G. Fascioli
Building design: Marco Zanuso, Edoardo Vittoria

1968–69 Genoa
Office workshop for the Renzo Piano Studio
Client: R. Piano
Design team: Studio Piano with F. Marano, G. Fascioli, T. Ferrari
Contractors: E. Piano

1968–70 Harrisburg, USA
Roofing components for the Olivetti Underwood works
Client: Olivetti Ltd, Harrisburg
Design team: Studio Piano
Roofing system: G. Fascioli
Building design: Louis I. Kahn
Engineers: Sertec Engineering

1968–71 Aybrook Street, London
Top-storey extension
Client: DRU (Design Research Unit)
Design team: DRU and Studio Piano & Rogers with M. Goldschmied, J. Young, P. Botschi, J. Kaplicky

1968–71 Cambridge
Fitzroy Street Shopping Centre
Client: Cambridge City Council
Design team: Studio Piano & Rogers with J. Young, M. Goldschmied, J. Morris

1969 Crema, Cremona
Roofing for Olivetti works
Client: Olivetti Spa
Design team: Studio Piano
Roofing system: F. Marano, G. Fascioli
Building design: Marco Zanuso, Edoardo Vittoria
Contractors: E. Piano

1969 Garonne, Alessandria
Open-plan house
Design team: Studio Piano with F. Marano, G. Fascioli, T. Ferrari
Contractors: E. Piano

1969–70 Osaka
Italian Industry Pavilion at the Osaka Expo
Design team: Studio Piano with F. Marano, G. Fascioli, G. Queirolo, T. Ferrari
Engineers: Sertec Engineering
Contractors: E. Piano

1970 Washington
Standardized hospital module
Client: ARAM (Associates for Rural Aids in Medicine), Washington
Design team: Studio Piano & Rogers with M. Goldschmied, J. Young, P. Flack

1970–71 Rome
Competition for a new system of prefabricated service stations
Client: Esso Standard Italiana, Rome
Design team: R. Piano, F. Marano, B. Bassetti

1971–73 Novedrate, Como
Office building for B & B Italia
Client: B & B Italia Spa, Como
Design team: Studio Piano & Rogers with C. Brüllmann, S. Cereda, G. Fascioli
Engineer: F. Marano

1971–77 Paris
The Georges Pompidou Cultural Centre
Client: Ministry of Cultural Affairs, Paris
Design team: Renzo Piano and Richard Rogers; G.F. Franchini (competition, programme for interiors), W. Zbinden with H. Bysaeth, J. Lohse, P. Merz, P. Dupont (infrastructures and services); L. Abbott with S. Ishida, H. Naruse, H. Takahashi (superstructures and mechanical services); E. Holt (façades and galleries); A. Stanton with M. Dowd, R. Verbizh (internal-external audiovisual systems); C. Brüllmann (environment and scenographic space); B. Plattner (coordination and site supervision); M. Davies with N. Okabe, K. Rupard, J. Sircus (IRCAM); J. Young with F. Barat, H. Diebold, J. Fendard, J. Huc, H. Schlegel (interiors); B. Merello, F. Marano (first design phase); F. Gouinguenet, C. Spielmann, C. Valensi (secretary)
Engineers: Ove Arup & Partners
Design team: P. Rice, L. Grut, R. Peirce (structure); T. Barker (technical installations); M. Espunosa (quantity surveying)
Contractors: GTM, Grands Travaux de Marseille, J. Thaury (director of works) with Krupp, Mont-a-Mousson, Pohlig (structures) CFEM (façades), Otis (lifts and escalators), Voyer (secondary structures), Industrielle de Chauffage, Saunier Duval (heating installations)

1972 Genoa
Ferro-cement pleasure craft
Client: ATIB Srl
Construction: Renzo Piano with R. Gaggero, F. Marano,

C. Brüllmann, G. Fascioli,
T. Ferrari

1972 Paris
Conversion of a river boat
Client: Piano & Rogers, Paris
Design team: Studio Piano &
Rogers
with C. Brüllmann, F. Marano

1972–74 Cusago, Milan
One-family housing
Client: Lucci, Giannotti, Simi, Pepe
Design team: Studio Piano &
Rogers with C. Brüllmann,
R. Luccardini, G. Fascioli, assisted
by R. Lucci, S. Lucci
Engineer: F. Marano

1973–74 Ashford
Chemical laboratory for perfume
production
Client: UOP Fragrances Ltd,
London
Design team: Studio Piano &
Rogers with M. Goldschmied,
J. Young, R. Bormioli, P. Flack,
N. Winder, P. Ullathorne
Engineering consultants: Anthony
Hunt Associates

1973–74 Paris
Atelier Paris
Client: Atelier Piano
Architects: Atelier Piano

1973–76 Ovada, Alessandria
Industrial Building
Client: ATIB Srl
Design team: Studio Piano &
Rogers with G. Fascioli
Engineer: F. Marano

1976 Cambridge
Electrical engineering workshop
Client: PAT Division, Cambridge
Design team: Studio Piano &
Rogers
with J. Young and
M. Goldschmied, M. Burckhardt,
D. Gray, D. Thom, P. Ullathorne
Engineering consultant: Felix
J. Samuely

1976
Telephone exchanges
Client: F.lli Dioguardi Spa
Design team: Piano & Rice &
Associates with S. Isbida and
N. Okabe

1977 Milan
Office system
Design team: Piano & Rice with
S. Ishida and N. Okabe

1977–80 Genoa
Studio workshop
Client: Studio Piano
Design team: Studio Piano

1977–80 Marne-la-Vallée, Paris
Housing and workshops
Client: Établissement Public de la
Ville Nouvelle de Marne-la-Vallée,
Paris
Design team: Piano & Rice &
Associates with B. Plattner
W. Zbinden, J. Lohse

1978 Selestat, Strasbourg
Kronenbourg factory building
Client: Kronenbourg
Design team: Piano & Rice &
Associates with M. Dowd,
B. Plattner
R. Verbizh, W. Zbinden, assisted
by N. Okabe, J. Lohse, C. Ostrej
Engineers: Gettec, Inex, Nnn

1978
Wall System
Client: F.lli Dioguardi Spa
Design team: Piano & Rice &
Associates with S. Ishida,
N. Okabe

1978 Cergy-Pontoise
Competition design for a
residential quarter
Design team: Piano & Rice &
Associates with M. Dowd,
B. Plattner, R. Verbizh,
W. Zbinden

1978 Dakar, Senegal
Mobile construction unit for
Senegal
Client: UNESCO; Dakar regional
office: M. Senghor; Breda of
Dakar
Design team: Studio Piano & Rice
& Associates with R. Verbizh,
O. Dellicour, S. Ishida

1978 Perugia
Industrialized system for
evolving-type homes
Client: Vibrocemento, Perugia
Coordinator: R. Jascone
Design team: Studio Piano & Rice
& Associates, S. Ishida, N. Okabe
with E. Donato, G. Picardi
Engineers: P. Rice, assisted by
F. Marano, H. Bardsley, with the
collaboration of Vibrocemento,
Perugia

1978–80 Turin
Fiat VSS experimental vehicle
Client: Fiat Auto Spa Turin;
IDEA Institute
Coordination: G. Trebbi; IDEA
Institute
Design team: Piano & Rice &
Associates with L. Abbott,
S. Ishida, N. Okabe, B. Plattner,
A. Stanton, R. Verbizh; IDEA
Institute with S. Boggio, F. Conti,
O. Di Blasi, W. De Silva,
M. Sibona F. Mantegazza
Engineers: Ove Arup & Partners
(under the supervision of
T. Barker)
Acoustics: S. Brown

1978–82 Corciano, Perugia
Quartiere Il Rigo
Client: Corciano Town Council
Design team: Studio Piano & Rice
& Associates with S. Ishida,
N. Okabe, L. Custer, chief
architects with E. Donato,
G. Picardi, O. Di Blasi
Engineers: P. Rice, assisted by
H. Bardsley, F. Marano with
Edilcooper, RPA Associates,
Vibrocemento
Site management: L. Custer with
F. Marano

**1978–82 San Luca di Molare,
Alessandria**
Holiday homes
Client: Immobiliare San Luca
Design team: Studio Piano with
S. Ishida, G. Picardi, E. Donato,
O. Di Blasi, F. Marano, G. Fascioli
Director of works: O. Di Blasi

1979
An experiment in educational
television: "Open Site"
Client: RAI, Rete 2
Programme by G. Macchi
Director: V. Lusvardi
Design team: Studio Piano & Rice
& Associates with S. Ishida,
N. Okabe, G. Picardi, S. Yamada,
M. Bonino, R. Biondo, G. Fascioli,
R. Gaggero
Screenplay by Magda Arduino

1979
Design for office-factory
Client: Studio Piano & Rice &
Associates
M. Dowd, chief architect

1979 Otranto, Lecce
Otranto neighbourhood
workshop:
an experiment in urban
reconstruction
Client: UNESCO (Division des
établissements humains et de
l'environnement socio-culturel)
S. Busuttil, W. Tochtermann
Design team: Studio Piano & Rice
& Associates, F.lli Dioguardi with

S. Ishida, N. Okabe, R. Verbizh,
E. Donato, G. Fascioli, R. Melai,
G. Picardi, R. Gaggero
Engineers: Ove Arup & Partners
(P. Beckmann) IDEA Institute,
Turin, assisted by G.P. Cuppini
G. Gasbarri, F. Marano,
F. Marconi, Editech, with the
collaboration of M. Fazio
(neighbourhood workshop) and
G. Macchi (RAI films) R. Biondo,
M. Bonino
Project coordination and
administration: G. Dioguardi
Programme by Magda Arduino

1979-81 Macolin, Switzerland
Prototype emergency home
Client: Département Affaires
Etrangères de la Confédération
Helvétique
Design team: Studio Piano & Rice
& Associates (competition)
B. Plattner, P. Rice (execution)

1980 Burano, Venice
Redevelopment plan for the
island of Burano
Client: Venice City Council
Design team: Studio Piano & Rice
& Associates, with the
collaboration of P.H. Chombard
De Lauwe, S. Ishida, Venice
University, with coordination by
the Fondazione Tre Oci, G.
Macchi, A. Macchi, assisted by
H. Bardsley, M. Calvi, L. Custer,
C. Teoldi
Programme by Magda Arduino

1980 Genoa
Multi-use food centre
Client: Genoa City Council
Design team: Studio
Piano/Building Workshop Srl
S. Ishida, F. Marano, E. Donato,
F. Doria, G. Fascioli with
F. Torrieri, Ansaldo Spa, Elsag
Spa, Molinari Appalti Srl,
Aerimpianti Spa,
Termomeccanica Spa

1980 Passaggio di Bettona, Perugia
Culture and exhibition centre
Client: Lispi
Design team: Studio Piano & Rice
& Associates/Building Workshop
Srl
S. Ishida, L. Custer, F. Marano,
with the collaboration of F. Icardi,
R. Ruocco

1980 Milan
Exhibition complex
Client: Nidosa – Gruppo Cabassi
Design team: Studio
Piano/Building Workshop Srl
S. Ishida, F. Doria, E. Frigerio,
A. Traldi, F. Marano, G. Trebbi
(coordinators), assisted by
M. Carroll, O. Di Blasi, R. Melai,
E. Miola, G. Fascioli, R. Gaggero
Film documentation: M. Arduino,
M. Bonino, S. Battini
Engineers: C. Giambelli,
D. Zucchi, Ove Arup & Partners
Consultants: Italian Promoservice
(exhibiting services); Richards
(transport) G. Lund (technical);
APT (fire prevention and security)

1980 Loano, Savona
Detailed plan for shore and park
Client: Loano City Council
Design team: Studio
Piano/Building Workshop Srl
S. Ishida, A. Traldi, F. Doria,
M. Carroll, G. Picardi
Engineer: Brizzolara

1980 Loano, Savona
Loano civic centre
Design team: Studio
Piano/Building Workshop Srl
S. Ishida, A. Traldi, F. Doria,
M. Carroll, G. Picardi

1980-81 Cremona
Arvedi tubular structural system
Client: Arvedi Spa
Design team: Studio Piano & Rice
& Associates/Building Workshop
Srl
S. Ishida, O. Di Blasi
Engineers: P. Rice, assisted by
H. Bardsley, with the collaboration
of the Arvedi technical
department, Gosi and Galli

1980-81 Milan
Load-bearing structure for the
Milanofiori Conference Centre
Client: WTC Milano
Design team: Studio
Piano/Building Workshop Srl
S. Ishida, F. Marano

1980-82 Bari
Neighbourhood workshop for
local maintenance work
Client: F.lli Dioguardi
Bari Design team: Studio
Piano/Building Workshop Srl and
F.lli Dioguardi with N. Costantino,
S. Pietrogrande, G. Ferracuti, S.
Ishida, F. Marano, E. Frigerio, E.
Donato, G. Fascioli C. Teoldi, SES
Engineering, L. Malgieri, assisted
by A. Aito, G. Amendola
Programme by Magda Arduino

1981 Berlin
IBA design for extension to the
Nationalgalerie and housing
Client: IBA, Berlin
Design team: Studio
Piano/Building Workshop Srl
S. Ishida, Ch. Süsstrunk (chief
architects) with F. Doria,
N. Okabe, A. Traldi

1981 Genoa
Redevelopment scheme for the
Molo quarter and services centre
Client: Genoa City Council
Design team: Studio
Piano/Building Workshop Srl
S. Ishida, A. Traldi with F.
Marano, A. Bianchi, E. Frigerio,
with the collaboration of
R. Ruocco, F. Icardi, R. Melai and
E. Miola
Planning aspects: V. Podestà,
G. Amadeo and Tekne Planning
with the legal consultancy of
F. Pagano
Programme by Magda Arduino

1981 Turin
Redevelopment of a city-centre
street block
Client: Turin City Council
Housing Department
Design team: Studio
Piano/Building Workshop Srl
S. Ishida, F. Marano, R. Ruocco,
F. Icardi and E. Frigerio
Programme by Magda Arduino

1981-83 Reggio Emilia
Building for the Banca Agricola
Commerciale, Automobile Club
Italiano and collective services
Client: Banca Agricola
Commerciale
Coordinator: S. Ferretti
Design team: Studio
Piano/Building Workshop Srl
S. Ishida, A. Traldi, F. Doria,
E. Donato, F. Marano,
C. Süsstrunk
Engineer: A. Rossi

1981-84 Montrouge, Paris
Redevelopment of the
Schlumberger industrial estate
Client: Compteurs Montrouge
(Groupe Schlumberger Ltd), Paris
Coordinators: Alain Vincent,
René Lafon, assisted by Gérard
Messand
Design team: Renzo Piano/Atelier
de Paris, Noriaki Okabe, Bernard
Plattner, assisted by T. Hartman,
J.F. Schmit, J. Lohse, P. Vincent,
G. Saint-Jean, J.B. Lacoudre,
S. Ishida, M. Alluyn, A. Gillet,

F. Laville, G. Petit, D. Rat,
C. Süsstrunk, M. Dowd
Consultants
Quantity surveyors: GEC, Paris,
R. Duperrier and F. Petit
Structural engineer: P. Rice,
London
Landscaping: A. Chemetoff, Paris,
assisted by M. Massot, C. Pierdet

1981–86 Houston
The Menil Collection Museum
Client: Menil Foundation
President: Dominique de Menil
Director: Walter Hopps
Vice-director: Paul Winkler
Design team: Piano & Fitzgerald
Architects, Shunji Ishida, Mark
Carroll, F. Doria, Mike Downs,
Chandra Patel, Bernard Plattner,
C. Süsstrunk
Consultants
Project management: P. Kelly,
assisted by L. Turner, E. Hickaby
Structural engineers: Ove Arup &
Partners (Peter Rice, Tom Barker,
Alistar Guthrie, Neil Nobel, John
Thornton)
Structures: Gentry Haynes &
Waley Assoc.
Service installations: Galewsky &
Johnston, Beaumont
Fire Prevention: R. Jensen,
Houston
Site supervisor: E.B. Brown, Fort
Worth
Contractors: E.G. Lowry, Houston

1982 Modena
Branch bank for the Banca
Agricola Commerciale
Client: Banca Agricola
Commerciale
Coordinator: S. Ferretti
Design team: Studio
Piano/Building Workshop Srl
S. Ishida, E. Frigerio
Engineers: Ceccoli, Jascone
Associates
Interiors: M. Dowd, J. Huc

Contractors: Contractant General,
GTM, Paris
Entreprises Generales: Albaric
Rontaix (Nord-France), Paris;
Bateg (Campenon-Bernard), Paris

1982
Competition for the OAPEC
headquarters in Kuwait
Client: Organization of Arab
Petroleum Exporting Countries
Design team: Studio
Piano/Building Workshop Srl
S. Ishida, A. Traldi, F. Doria,
B. Mehren, M. Carroll,
E. Frigerio, Tekne VRC with
C. Bottigelli, Parodi, Seratto

1982 Paris
Design for the 1989 Universal
Exposition
Client: French Ministry of Culture
Design team: Renzo Piano/Atelier
Piano, Noriaki Okabe, Bernard
Plattner, Jean François Schmit,
Bernard Vaudeville, G. Petit,
C. Clarisse
Engineering consultants: Ove
Arup & Partners (Peter Rice, John
Thornton with H. Bardsley)
Historical research: C. Hodeir

1982 Centocelle, Rome
Design for the new Torrespaccata
business centre
Client: Brioschi Finanziaria Spa,
Milan, Gruppo Cabassi
Design team: Renzo Piano
Building Workshop, Shunji
Ishida, Flavio Marano, Alessandro
Traldi, Renzo Venanzio Truffelli,
B. Mebren, M. Carroll, E.
Frigerio, A. Bianchi, F. Doria,
assisted by M. Mattei, F. Santolini
Structural engineers: Francesco
Clerici, Milan; Studio Alfa, Rome

1982 Turin
Alexander Calder retrospective at
the Palazzo a Vela

Client: Turin City Council, Toro
Assicurazioni
Exhibition curator: Giovanni
Carandente
Design team: Renzo Piano
Building Workshop, Shunji
Ishida, Ottavio Di Blasi, assisted
by Giorgio Fascioli, Flavio
Marano, Peter Terbuchte,
Alessandro Traldi, Enrico Frigerio
Engineering consultants: Ove
Arup & Partners
Tensile structure: Tensoteci, Milan
Lighting: Piero Castiglioni, Milan
Graphics: Pier Luigi Cerri, Milan

1982–84
IBM Travelling Exhibition
Client: IBM Europe
General coordinator:
G. L. Trischitta
Coordination of image:
R. Lanterio, F. Moisset
Design team: Renzo Piano
Building Workshop
Shunji Ishida, Alessandro Traldi,
assisted by Ottavio Di Blasi,
F. Marano, M. Carroll, R.
Gaggero, P. Nestler, A. Stanton,
François Doria, Giorgio Fascioli
Installation coordination: Atelier
Piano, Noriaki Okabe, assisted by
Jean Baptiste Lacoudre,
Paul Vincent
Engineering consultants: Ove
Arup & Partners London (Peter
Rice, Tom Barker)
Contractors: Calabrese
Engineering Spa, Bari

1983–94 Genoa
Metropolitan stations
Client: Genoa City Council
Concessionaire for the general
design and execution: Ansaldo
trasporti Spa, Genoa
Design team: Renzo Piano
Building Workshop
D.H. Hart, S. Ishida,
C. Manfreddo, F. Marano, Y. Tolu,

M. Varratta, M. Carroll, O. Di
Blasi, E. Frigerio, assisted by
A. Alborghetti, E. Baglietto,
K. Cussoneau, G. Fascioli,
N. Freedman, P. Maggiora,
M. Mallamaci, M. Mattei,
B. Merello, D. Peluffo
Model: D. Cavagna, E. Miola
Consultants:
Station structures: Mageco Srl
(L. Mascia, D. Mascia)
Line structures: Inco Spa, Genoa;
Reico Spa, Genoa
Service installations: Aerimpianti
Spa, Milan
Contractors: Imprese Riunite,
Genoa

1983 Omegna, Novara
Detailed plan of the Pietra area
Client: Omegna Town Council
Design team: Renzo Piano
Building Workshop
Shunji Ishida, Enrico Frigerio,
Donald L. Hart, Flavio Marano,
Alessandro Bianchi, assisted by
Maurizio Calosso, with the
collaboration of R. Ripamonti,
Francesca Santolini
Planning consultants: Studio
Ambiente Srl, Milan

1983 Paris
Renovation and extension of the
Centre Georges Pompidou
Client: Centre Georges Pompidou
Design team: Renzo Piano/Atelier
de Paris
Noriaki Okabe, Johanna Lohse,
Bernard Vaudeville, Paul Vincent
Engineering consultants: Albion,
Paris; Etienne Lenglume
Quantity surveying: GEC, Paris
(Robert Duperrier, Francis Petit)
Heating consultants: Inex, Paris
(Miroslav Jorgacevic, Charles
Henri Reiss)
Service installations: Cegef, Paris
(Eric Picard)
Lighting: Piero Castiglioni

1983 Genoa
Extension and urban integration of the Valpolcevera water purifier
Client: Genoa City Council
Design team: Renzo Piano Building Workshop
Shunji Ishida, Mark Carroll, Donald L. Hart, Flavio Marano, assisted by Paolo Beccio, Filippo Icardi, Lucio Ruocco, Italimpianti Spa

1983–84 Venice – Milan
Acoustic space for the opera *Il Prometeo* by L. Nono
Client: Teatro alla Scala, Milan
Design team: Renzo Piano Building Workshop
Shunji Ishida, Alessandro Traldi, Carmela Avagliano, Donald L. Hart, Marco Visconti
Consultants:
Structure and director of works: Maurizio Milan, Sandro Favero
Venice Contractors: F.lli Dioguardi Spa, Milan
Music: Luigi Nono
Texts edited by: Massimo Cacciari
Conductor: Claudio Abbado with Roberto Cecconi
Lights: Emilio Vedova
Live electronics: Experimental-Studio der Heinrich-Strobel-Stiftung des Südwestfunks e.V., Freiburg (Breisgau), L. Nono, H.P. Haller with R. Strauss and B. Noll
Computer technology: Biennale Computer-Music Workshop, Centro di Sonologia
Processing by: Padua University, L. Nono, A. Vidolin with S. Sapir and M. Graziani

1984 Sestriere, Turin
Holiday resort redevelopment scheme
Client: SAES Spa, Turin
Design team: Renzo Piano Building Workshop/Atelier de Paris Building Workshop
Shunji Ishida, Enrico Frigerio, Flavio Marano, assisted by Manuela Mattei, Renzo Venanzio Truffelli, Marco Visconti, Maurizio Varratta
Atelier de Paris: Alain Vincent, Noriaki Okabe, Thomas Hartman, assisted by J. Baptiste Lacoudre, Bernard Plattner, Nicolas Prouvé, Paul Vincent
Mapping and structural engineers: AI Engineering Srl, Turin
Planning consultants: AI Studio Srl, Turin

1984 Cremona
Design for a leisure centre
Client: Acciaieria Tubificio Arvedi
Design team: Renzo Piano Building Workshop
Shunji Ishida, Ottavio Di Blasi, assisted by Giorgio Fascioli Francesca Santolini
Documentary Consultants: Alan Stanton, London

1984 Genoa
Exhibition space
Client: Spazio espositivo Spa, Genoa
Design team: Renzo Piano Building Workshop
Shunji Ishida, Mark Carroll

1984 Houston
Menil collection: Orientation room, Cafeteria and Museum Shop
Client: Menil Foundation, Houston
Design team: Piano and Fitzgerald Architects
Shunji Ishida, Mark Carroll, Mike Downs, Thomas Hartman, assisted by Francesca Santolini
Engineering consultants: Ove Arup & Partners, London (Peter Rice, Tom Barker)

1984 Sestriere, Turin
Building for artificial snow machinery
Client: Sporting Club Sestriere Spa
Design team: Renzo Piano Building Workshop
Shunji Ishida, Enrico Frigerio, Flavio Marano, assisted by Giorgio Fascioli, Donald L. Hart, Manuela Mattei, Maurizio Varratta
Service installations: York Spa, France
Contractor: Cooperative of Cesena City Council workers and builders
Metal structures: F.lli Vaccarini, Alessandria

1984 Naples
Olivetti office building
Client: Coginvest Spa, Naples
General coordination: Gianni Di Meglio
Design team: Renzo Piano Building Workshop
Shunji Ishida, Mark Carroll, Flavio Marano, assisted by Giorgio Fascioli, Francesca Santolini, Maurizio Varratta
Consultants
Service installations: Santolo Cirillo, Naples
Director of works: Renzo Cecconi, Naples
Contractors: Cogeco Napoli Spa

1984 Lissone, Milan
The Gulf Center shopping and exhibition complex
Client: Ahmed Idris Nasreddin, Milan
Design team: Renzo Piano Building Workshop
Shunji Ishida, Flavio Marano, Francesca Santolini, Alessandro Traldi

1984 Nairobi, Kenya
Design for the Kenya Energy Laboratories
Client: Kenya Ministry of Energy
Design team: Renzo Piano Building Workshop in a joint venture with Cesen Building Workshop (Shunji Ishida, Mark Carroll), assisted by François Doria, Giorgio Fascioli, Francesca Santolini
Model: Edoardo Miola
Engineering consultants: Studio Phoebus, Catania

1984–85
Design of Indesit household appliances
Client: Indesit elettrodomestici Spa, Turin
Design team: Renzo Piano Building Workshop
Noriaki Okabe, Jean Baptiste Lacoudre, assisted by Nicolas Prouvé
Model: Denis Laville
Acoustic consultants: Peutz et Associés-Den Haag-Paris (H. Straatsma, Y. De Querel)
Industrialisation: S. Boggio, Turin

1984–85 Montecchio Maggiore, Vicenza
Offices
Client: Lowara, Montecchio Maggiore, Vicenza
Design team: Renzo Piano Building Workshop
Shunji Ishida, Ottavio Di Blasi, assisted by Giorgio Fascioli, Donald L. Hart, Manuela Mattei, Maurizio Varratta
Structures and director of works: Maurizio Milan, Sandro Favero, Venice
Service installations: Studio Sire, Venice
Contractors: Trevisan Tachera

1985 Le Bourget, Paris
Competition for the Le Bourget airport hangars renovation
Client: UTA Union Transport

Aériens, Paris
Design team: Renzo Piano/Atelier de Paris
Alain Vincent, Noriaki Okabe, Jean Baptiste Lacoudre, assisted by François Laville, Nicolas Prouvé
Consultants: GEC – Bureau d'études techniques, Paris
Quantity surveying: F. Petit

1985 Paris
250-unit housing complex
Client: Paris City Council
Design team: Renzo Piano/Atelier de Paris
Alain Vincent, Bernard Plattner, Jean François Schmit, assisted by Johanna Lohse
Consultants: GEC – Bureau d'études techniques, Paris
Quantity surveying: F. Petit

1985 Genoa
Tender for the construction of a fruit and vegetable market
Client: Genoa City Council
Design team: Renzo Piano Building Workshop
Holding company of contractors: Ansaldo Sistemi Industriali Spa, Genoa
Building Workshop: Shunji Ishida, Donald L. Hart, Flavio Marano, assisted by Giorgio G. Bianchi, Claudio Manfreddo

1985 Genoa
Regional conference centre
Client: Centro Congressi Spa, Genoa
Design team: Renzo Piano Building Workshop
Shunji Ishida, Donald L. Hart, Flavio Marano, Renzo Venanzio Truffelli
Structures and service installations: Ansaldo Sistemi Industriali Spa, Genoa; Italimpianti Spa, Genoa; Elsag

Spa, Genoa, assisted by Giorgio G. Bianchi

1985 Bari
Calabrese business centre
Client: Calabrese veicoli industriali Spa, Bari
Design team: Renzo Piano Building Workshop
Shunji Ishida, Enrico Frigerio, Flavio Marano, assisted by Manuela Mattei
Structures and service installations: Calabrese Engineering Spa, Bari

1985 Lecce
Branch of the Vallone bank
Client: Le Valli Immobiliare Srl, Lecce
Design team: Renzo Piano Building Workshop
Shunji Ishida, Enrico Frigerio, Manuela Mattei, assisted by Giorgio Fascioli, Flavio Marano, Marco Visconti
Structures, service installations and director of works: Calabrese Engineering Spa, Bari
Contractors: Brizio Montinari, Lecce

1985 Turin
Analysis of an exhibition space for prototype vehicles
Client: Centro Stile Fiat Spa, Turin
Design team: Renzo Piano/Atelier de Paris
Noriaki Okabe, Bernard Vaudeville
Consultants: Ove Arup & Partners, London (Peter Rice, Tom Barker)

1985 Marne-la-Vallée, Paris
Ministry of Finances College
Client: French Ministry of the Economy Finance
Design team: Renzo Piano/Atelier de Paris

Alain Vincent, Noriaki Okabe, Jean François Schmit, Jean Baptiste Lacoudre, assisted by Catherine Clarisse, Jean Luc Chassais, François Laville, Nicolas Prouvé
Cost control: Annie Benzeno; GEC, Paris
Documentation: Cecile Simon
Landscaping: Daniel Collin, Paris
Structures and service installations: Sodeteg, Paris

1985 Naples
Office tower block
Client: Coginvest Spa, Naples
General coordination: Gianni Di Meglio, Michele Mattei
Design team: Renzo Piano Building Workshop
Shunji Ishida, Mark Carroll, Donald L. Hart, Flavio Marano, assisted by Claudio Manfreddo, Francesca Santolini

1985–93 Cagliari
Bank and Offices
Client: Credito Industriale Sardo
Design team: Renzo Piano Building Workshop
E. Baglietto, R.V. Truffelli, G.G. Bianchi, M. Carroll, O. Di Blasi, D.L. Hart, S. Ishida, C. Manfreddo, F. Marano, F. Santolini, M. Varratta, assisted by M. Calosso, D. Campo, R. Costa, M. Cucinella
Model: S. Vignale, G. Sacchi, D. Cavagna
Installations: Mageco Srl Genoa (L. Mascia, D. Mascia), Manens Intertecnica Srl, Verona
Geological consultants: Pecorini, Cagliari; G. Gatti, Milan
Contractors: R. Tireddu, I.R.C. SO.G.DI.CO., Vibrocemento Sarda

1985 Cagliari
Area plan and extension of Council Chambers

Client: Cagliari City Council
Design team: Renzo Piano Building Workshop
Shunji Ishida, Mark Carroll, Ottavio Di Blasi, Flavio Marano, assisted by Francesca Santolini, Maurizio Varratta

1985 Genoa
Design of an emergency mobile unit (Magic box)
Client: Ansaldo Spa, Genoa
Design team: Renzo Piano Building Workshop
Shunji Ishida, Ottavio Di Blasi in a joint venture with Cesen
Engineering consultants: Calabrese Engineering Spa, Bari

1985 Savona
Redevelopment scheme for the Monticello area
Client: Savona City Council
Design team: Renzo Piano Building Workshop
Shunji Ishida, Donald L. Hart, Flavio Marano, assisted by Giorgio G. Bianchi
Planning consultants: Studio Ambiente Srl, Milan

1985 Genoa
Redevelopment scheme for industrial zone
Client: Azienda Municipalizzata Gas e Acqua
Design team: Renzo Piano Building Workshop
Shunji Ishida, Mark Carroll, Flavio Marano, assisted by Francesca Santolini, Maurizio Varratta

1985 Khania, Crete
Redevelopment of the historic Venetian shipyards
Client: UNESCO
Design team: Renzo Piano Atelier de Paris/Building Workshop
Atelier de Paris: Noriaki Okabe,

Thomas Hartman, Elena Karitaikis, Nicolas Prouvé
Building Workshop: Shunji Ishida, Giorgio G. Bianchi

1985 Murano, Venice
Design for the redevelopment of an industrial zone into a glass exhibition and educational centre
Clients: Società Veneziana Conterie Spa, Murano; Samim Spa, Rome Design team: Renzo Piano/Atelier de Paris
Alain Vincent, Bernard Plattner, assisted by Paul Vincent
Documentation: Cecile Simon

1985
Mobile office partition system
Client: Unifor, Milan
Design team: Renzo Piano/Atelier de Paris
Alain Vincent, Noriaki Okabe, Jean Baptiste Lacoudre, assisted by Nicolas Prouvé
Model: Jean Yves Richard
Acoustics consultants: Peutz et Associés, Paris
Engineering consultants: Albion, Paris (Etienne Lenglume)

1985 Genoa
Redevelopment of an industrial area into a business centre
Client: Ansaldo Spa, Genoa
Design team: Renzo Piano Building Workshop
Shunji Ishida, Mark Carroll, Renzo Truffelli, assisted by Maurizio Varratta, Francesca Santolini in a joint venture with Cesen

1985 Nancy
Competition for a scientific and technical documentation centre
Client: CNRS (Centre National de la Recherche Scientifique)
Design team: Renzo Piano/Atelier de Paris
Alain Vincent, Noriaki Okabe, Jean François Schmit, assisted by Isabelle Da Costa, Nicolas Prouvé
Engineering consultants: Sodeteg-Bureau d'études techniques, Paris

1985 Clermont-Ferrand
Auvergne Regional Headquarters
Client: Région d'Auvergne
Design team: Renzo Piano/Atelier de Paris
Alain Vincent, Noriaki Okabe, Paul Vincent, assisted by Thomas Hartman, Johanna Lohse, Catherine Clarisse, Nicolas Prouvé, Jean Lelay, Dominique Rat, Pierre Chatelain
Consultants:
Bureau d'etudes techniques: Seer, Clermont-Ferrand
Local architects: Douat, Forheaud, Harland – Clermont-Ferrand
Quantity surveyors: GEC, Paris
Landscape architects: Corajoud, Desvigne, Dalnoky, Paris
Acoustics: Gerard Noel, Clermont-Ferrand
Testing: Glitec Lyon
Contractors: Socae, Clermont-Ferrand
Model: Immo Maquette, Paris

1985
Research project for a continuous aluminum frame façade
Client: Aluminia Spa, Italia
Design team: Renzo Piano/Atelier de Paris
Alain Vincent, Bernard Plattner, assisted by Robert Van Santen, Bernard Vaudeville
Model: Denis Laville, Jean Yves Richard
Engineering consultants: Marc Mimram; Albion, Paris (Etienne Lenglume)
Acoustic Consultant: Peutz et Associés, Paris (Yves de Querel)
Thermal insulation consultant: Sodeteg, Paris (Dominique Rossignol)

1985 Rome
Television set for *Quark*, a programme by Piero Angela
Client: RAI, Rome
Design team: Renzo Piano Building Workshop
Shunji Ishida, Ottavio Di Blasi, assisted by Giorgio Fascioli

1985–94 Lyons
La Cité Internationale
Client: Spaicil-Cecil (conference centre); Ville de Lyon (museum); UGC (cinema)
Design team: Renzo Piano Building Workshop
P. Vincent, M. Cattaneo, A. Chaaya, A. El Jerari, G. Fourel, A. Gallissian, T. Hartman, M. Henry, M. Howard, C. Jackaman, J.B. Lacoudre, G. Modolo, J.B. Mothes, E. Novel, N. Okabe, M. Pimmel, D. Rat, M. Salerno, S. Scarabicchi, A.H. Téménidès, B. Tonfoni, C. Valentinuzzi, W. Vassal, B. Vaudeville, E. Verstrepen, M. Wollensak, assisted by C. Ardiley, A. Benzeno, M. Boudry, F. Canal, P. Charles, J.L. Chassais, H. Cocagne, G. Fourel, S. Eisenberg, B. Kurtz, J. Lelay, K. McLone, J. Moolhijzen, G. Mormina, D. Nock, A. O'Carroll, S. Planchez, T. Rolland, M. Schessler, Y. Surti, E. Tisseur
Model: J.P. Allain, P. Darmer, O. Dorzy, C. d'Ovidio, M. Fau, M. Goudin, G. d'Ovidio, A. Schultz
Landscaping: M. Corajoud; Vegetude
Back-up studio: Curtelin-Richard-Bergeret; A. Catani (cinema)
Partner: R. Plottier (first phase)
Administration: Syllabus (Alain Vincent)
Engineer: Syllabus (Sophie Gunera)
Quantity surveyors: GEC Ingénierie
Acoustics: Peutz
Lighting: Joel, Piero Castiglioni (first phase)
Façades: CSTB
Signs: Pierre Bernard
Conference centre installations: Barbanel
Conference centre structures: ESB
Conference centre scenography: Labeyrie
Equipment: Merlin
Museum: Agibat (structures), Courtois (ventilation), HGM (technical installations)
Cinema: B.E. Belzunce (structures), Inex (ventilation), Claude Fusée (technical installations)
Fountain: Jetdil
Synthesis: Sari Ingénierie (first phase)
Concept: Ove Arup & Partners (first phase)

1985 Milan
Competition for the redevelopment of the Pirelli Bicocca area
Client: Industrie Pirelli Spa, Milan
Design team: Renzo Piano Building Workshop
Shunji Ishira, Ottavio Di Blasi, Enrico Frigerio, Donald L. Hart, assisted by Giorgio G. Bianchi, Klaus Dreissigacker, Manuela Mattei, Marco Visconti
Planning consultants: Alberto Secchi, Milan
Quantity surveyor: Alain Vincent
Structural engineers: Ove Arup & Partners, London
Model: Edoardo Miola, Genoa

1985–87 Novara
Research Institute for Light Metals

Client: Aluminia Spa, Italia
Design team: Renzo Piano/Atelier de Paris
Alain Vincent, L. Pennisson, Bernard Plattner, Bernard Vaudeville, assisted by Jean Lelay, Ronnie Self, Robert Van Santen
Model: Jean Yves Richard
Quantity surveyor: Annie Benzeno
Structural engineers: M. Mimram, Paris; Sodeteg, Paris
Façades: Italstudio
Back-up studio: Omega, Turin
Landscaping: M. Desvigne; Immo Maquette

1985–86 Fegino, Genoa
Renovation of office building
Client: Ansaldo Spa, Genoa
Design team: Renzo Piano Building Workshop
Shunji Ishida, Renzo Venanzio Truffelli, Giorgio Grandi, assisted by Giorgio Fascioli, Claudio Manfreddo, Marco Visconti in a joint venture with Cesen
Structural engineers and director of works: Ansaldo Divisione Impianti Spa, Genoa
Service installations: Aerimpianti Spa, Milan
Contractors: Coopsette Scrl, Reggio Emilia

1985–87 Paris
Municipal workshops
Client: Paris City Council
Design team: Renzo Piano/Atelier de Paris
Alain Vincent, Bernard Plattner, Jean François Schmit, assisted by Jean Luc Chassais, Catherine Clarisse, Jean Baptiste Lacoudre
Quantity surveyor: Annie Benzeno
Consultants: GEC – Bureau d'etudes tecniques (F. Petit), Paris
Contractors: Dumez, Paris

1985–96 Turin
Redevelopment of the Fiat Lingotto Works
Client: Lingotto Srl
Design team: Renzo Piano Building Workshop
S. Ishida, P. Ackermann, E. Baglietto, A. Calafati, M. Carroll, M. Cattaneo, A. Carisetto, G. Cohen, F. Colle, I. Corte (CAD), P. Costa, M. Cucinella, S. De Leo, A. De Luca, S. Durr, K. Fraser, A. Giovannoni, D. Guerrisi (CAD), C. Hays, G. Hernandez, C. Herrin, W. Kestel, G. Langasco (CAD), P. Maggiora, D. Magnano, M. Mariani, K.A. Naderi, T. O'Sullivan, A. Piancastelli, D. Piano, G. Robotti (CAD), E. Rossato, A. Sacchi, S. Scarabicchi, P. Sanso, L. Siracusa (CAD), A. Stadlmayer, R.Y. Truffelli, M. Varratta, N. Van Oosten, H. Yamaguchi, assisted by S. Arecco, F. Bartolomeo, N. Camerada, M. Carletti, R. Croce Bermondi, I. Cuppone, A. Giovannoni, M. Nouvion, P. Pedrini, M. Piano
Model: D. Cavagna, E. Miola, P. Varratta
Consultants
Structural engineers: Ove Arup & Partners; AI Engineering; Fiat Engineering
Acoustics: Arup Acoustics, Müller Bbm
Quantity surveying: Davis Langdon, Everest
Theatre: Techplan
Exhibition space administration: ECL
Road system: CSST
Lighting: P. Castiglioni
Graphics: P.L. Cerri, Eco Spa
Fittings: F. Santolini
Back-up studio: Studio Vitone and Associates, F. Levi, G. Mottino
Director of works: Studio Program, (I. Castore), R. Montauti, B. Roventini, G. Vespignani, S. Rum, E. Bindi
Contractors: Fiat Engineering, Turin
Temporary associations of firms: Recchi, Pizzarotti, Guerrini, Rosso, Borini and Prono; Del Favero, Maltauro and Aster

1986 Amiens
Competition for the Jules Verne Theme Park
Client: City of Amiens
Design team: Renzo Piano/Atelier de Paris
Landscaping: Michel Corajoud, Cristine Dalnoky, Michel Desvigne Structural engineer: Marc Mimram
Atelier de Paris: Alain Vincent, Noriaki Okabe, Bernard Vaudeville, assisted by Bruno Hubert, Robert Van Santen, Martin Veith
Model: Denise Laville

1986
Design for the Lady Bird Pavilion in the IBM Travelling Exhibition
Client: IBM Europe
Design team: Renzo Piano Building Workshop
Shunji Ishida, Klaus Dreissigacker, Marco Visconti
Consultants:
Structural engineers: Ove Arup & Partners (Peter Rice, Tom Barker)

1986 Milan
Crystal table system
Client: Fontana Arte, Milan
Design team: Renzo Piano Building Workshop
Shunji Ishida, Ottavio Di Blasi

1986 Ravenna
Sports centre
Client: Ravenna City Council
Design team: Renzo Piano Building Workshop
S. Ishida, F. Marano, M. Cucinella, O. Di Blasi, E. Fitzgerald, D. Magnano, C. Manfreddo, S. Montaldo, F. Moussavi, F. Pierandrei, S. Smith, M. Visconti, Y. Yamaguchi, assisted by E. Baglietto, G. Fascioli, N. Freedman, M. Mallamaci, M. Mattei, B. Merello, D. Peluffo
Model: M. Bassignani, D. Cavagna
Consultants
Structural engineers: Ove Arup & Partners (P. Rice, R. Hough); M. Milan, S. Favero, Venice
Contractors: Di Penta, Rome

1986 Rhodes, Greece
Redevelopment of the fortifications and the historic centre
Client: UNESCO
Design team: Renzo Piano Building Workshop
Shunji Ishida, Giorgio G. Bianchi
Consultants:
Local coordination: Rhodes City Council, Stamatis Sotirakis
Historic research: Danila De Lucia
Photographic documentation: E. Sailler

1986 La Valletta, Malta
Redevelopment of the Bastions and City Gate
Client: The Maltese Government
Design team: Renzo Piano Building Workshop
B. Plattner, A. Chaaya, with the collaboration of P. Callegia, D. Felice, K. Zammit Endrich
Consultants: M. Mimram

1986 Rome
Design for a head office
Client: Italscai Spa, Rome
Design team: Renzo Piano Building Workshop
Shunji Ishida, Renzo Venanzio Truffelli, assisted by Giorgio G. Bianchi, Giorgio Grandi

1986 Vicenza
Rehabilitation of the Palladian Basilica and City Hall
Client: Vicenza City Council
Design team: Renzo Piano Building Workshop
G. Grandi, G. Bianchi, P. Bodega S. Ishida, M. Michelotti
Model: G. Sacchi
Consultants
Structural engineers: Ove Arup & Partners; M. Milan, S. Favero
Lighting: Sivi
Quantity surveyors: S. Baldelli, A. Grasso

1987 Sistiana, Trieste
Design for the Bay of Sistiana Redevelopment Scheme
Client: Finsepol Spa, Trieste
Design team: Renzo Piano Building Workshop
B. Plattner, L. Couton, A. Chaaya, P. Copat, R. Self, M. Salerno, with the collaboration of E. Agazzi, F. Joubert, R. Keiser, B. Leboudec, O. Lidon, J. Lohse, R.J. Van Santen, G. Torre, O. Touraine
Model: O. Doizy, A. Schultz
Consultants
Structural engineers: Ove Arup & Partners, (P. Rice, A. Day), M. Milan Studio Boghetto; Manens Intertecnica
Environmental studies: CMS
Back-up studio: Studio Architetti Associati, Venice (G. Pauletto, G. Furlan, G. Galli)
Landscaping: M. Desvigne, C. Dalnoky
Planning consultants: Studio Ambiente Milan; Sodeteg, Paris

1987 Grenoble
European Synchrotron Radiation Facility
Client: ESRF
Design team: Renzo Piano Building Workshop
N. Okabe, J.L. Chassais, C. Clarisse, J.B. Lacoudre, J. Lelay, P. Merz, C. Morandi, A. O'Carroll, S. Planchez, R.J. Van Santen, P. Vincent
Consultants
Structural engineers: Ove Arup & Partners (P. Rice)
Environmental control: Ove Arup & Partners (T. Barker)
Lighting: Ansaldo
Fire prevention: Initec
Landscaping: M. Corajoud
Planning: Seri Renault Novatome; Interatome Germany; USSI

1987 Urbino
Petriccio multi-use complex
Client: Costruzioni Edili Bertozzini Spa
Design team: Renzo Piano Building Workshop
S. Ishida, F. Marano, G.G. Bianchi

1987 Trani
Sports centre
Client: Trani Town Council
Design team: Renzo Piano Building Workshop
S. Ishida, F. Marano, R.V. Truffelli, D. Campo, R. Costa, E. Frigerio, C. Manfreddo
Consultants
Quantity surveyors: S. Baldelli A. Grasso, M. Montanari
Model: S. Vignale

1987 Sestriere, Turin
Kandahar Center
Client: Kandahar Center
Design team: Renzo Piano Building Workshop
S. Ishida, F. Marano, E. Frigerio, P. Maggiora
Consultants
Structural engineer: Raineri
Contractors: Macciotta

1987 Genoa
Design for the AMIU business centre
Client: AMIU, Genoa
Design team: Renzo Piano Building Workshop
S. Ishida, F. Marano, G. Grandi E. Baglietto
Consultants
Service installations: Tradeco Srl, Milan (G. Chiesa)
Quantity surveyor: S. Baldelli
Structural engineers: Mageco Srl, Genoa (L. Mascia, D. Mascia)

1987 Urbino
Study for an infrastructure network
Client: Urbino City Council
Design team: Renzo Piano Building Workshop
S. Ishida, F. Marano, G.G. Bianchi, assisted by S. Smith

1987 Newport Beach
Design for an American Contemporary Art Museum
Client: Newport Harbor Art Museum
Design team: Renzo Piano Building Workshop
S. Ishida, M. Carroll, A. Arancio, N. Freedman, F. Pierandrei, M. Desvigne, Blurock partnership
Consultants
Structural engineers: Ove Arup & Partners, London/Los Angeles (P. Rice, T. Barker)

1987-88 Pompeii
Development of the archaeological city of Pompeii
Client: IBM
Design team: Renzo Piano Building Workshop
S. Ishida, G.G. Bianchi, N. Freedman, G. Grandii, E. Piazza, A. Pierandrei, S. Smith

1987-90 Paris
IRCAM: Institute for Research and Coordination of Acoustics and Music
Client: Ministry of Culture, CNAC Georges Pompidou, IRCAM
Design team: Renzo Piano Building Workshop
P. Vincent, N. Okabe, J. Lelay, M. Davies, K. Rupard, J. Sircus, W. Zbinden, assisted by F. Canal, J.L. Chassais, A. O'Carroll, N. Prouvé
Model: O. Doizy, J.Y. Richard
Consultants
Structural engineers: Ove Arup & Partners
Acoustic consultant: V. Peutz
Scenographic consultant: G.C. François
Structures and service installations: AXE IB
Quantity surveyors: GEC Ingéniérie
Director of works: Gemo
Foundations and steel structure: Sicmeg
Façades: Durand
Lifts: CG2A

1987-90 Charenton le Pont, Paris
Bercy II Shopping Centre
Client: GRC
Design team: Renzo Piano Building Workshop
N. Okabe, J.F. Blassel, S. Dunne, M. Henry, K. McBryde, A. O'Carrol, B. Plattner, R. Rolland, M. Salerno, N. Westphal, assisted by M. Bojovic, D. odel: Y. Chapelain, O. Doizy, J.Y. Richard
Consultants
Structural engineers: Ove Arup & Partners (P. Rice, A. Lenczner); Otra (J.P. Rigail) J.L. Sarf; OTH SI (J. Herman)
Site supervisor: Veritas
Testing: Copibat
Landscaping: M. Desvigne,

C. Dalnoky
Interiors: Crighton Design Management
Contractors: Tondela NF, Cosylva EI, SPPR

1987–90 Monfalcone
Crown Princess
Client: P&O, Fincantieri
Design team: Renzo Piano Building Workshop
S. Ishida, N. Okabe, K. McBryde, M. Carroll, R. Costa, M. Cucinella, R.J. Van Santen, F. Santolini, R. Self, S. Smith, O. Touraine, with the collaboration of G.G. Bianchi, G. Grandi, N. Freedman, D.L. Hart, P. Maggiora, C. Manfreddo, F.R. Ludewig
Model: D. Cavagna
Consultants: Studio Architetti Associati, Venice
Air-resistance testing: Danish Maritime Institute, Lyngby
Shipbuilders: Fincantieri Monfalcone, Trieste

1987–90 Bari
San Nicola Stadium
Client: Bari City Council
Design team: Renzo Piano Building Workshop
S. Ishida, F. Marano, O. Di Blasi, L. Pellini
Model: D. Cavagna, G. Sacchi
Consultants
Landscaping: M. Desvigne
Structural engineers: Ove Arup & Partners (P. Rice, T. Carfrae, A. Lenczer); M. Milan, Venice
Reinforced concrete: Studio Vitone, Bari
Test on precast elements: N. Andidero
Director of works: J. Zucker, M. Belviso
Contractors: Bari 90 Srl

1988 Venice
Design for Venice Expo 2000

Client: Venice Expo 2000
Design team: Renzo Piano Building Workshop
Shunji Ishida, Giorgio Bianchi, Renzo V. Truffelli, assisted by Alessandro Pierandrei, Fabrizio Pierandrei

1988–91 Paris
Rue de Meaux Housing
Client: RIVP, le Mutuelles du Mans
Design team: Renzo Piano Building Workshop
B. Plattner, F. Canal, C. Clarisse, T. Hartman, U. Hautch, J. Lohse, R.J. Van Santen, J.F. Schmit
Structural engineers: Gec Ingéniérie
Landscaping: M. Desvigne, C. Dalnoky, P. Conversey
Contractors: Dumez

1988 Lecco, Como
Meridiana Shopping and Office centre
Client: Colombo Costruzioni Spa
Design team: Renzo Piano Building Workshop
S. Ishida, F. Marano, G. Grandi, P. Bodega, V. Di Turi, C. Manfreddo, F. Santolini, S. Schafer, I. Corte (CAD), S. D'Atri (CAD), assisted by A. Bordoni

1988–90 Matera
Design for the Redevelopment of the Sassi quarter
Client: Camera di Commercio, Matera
Design team: Renzo Piano Building Workshop
S. Ishida, F. Marano, G.G. Bianchi, D. Campo, M. Cattaneo
Structural engineers: Ove Arup & Partners (P. Rice, T. Barker)

1988–90 Saint Quentin-en-Yvelines,
Guyancourt Thomson Works
Client: Thomson CSF
Design team: Renzo Piano Building Workshop
P. Vincent, A. Vincent, A. Gallissian (Thomson 1), M. Henry (tower), A. El Jerari, L. Le Voyer, A. O'Carrol, D. Rat (Thomson 2), A.H. Téménidès, assisted by C. Ardilley, C. Bartz, M. Bojovic, F. Canal, G. Fourel, A. Guez, B. Kurtz
Model: O. Doizy, C. d'Ovidio
Consultants
Ventilation installations and quantity surveying: GEC Ingéniérie (F. Petit, F. Thouvenin, C. Baché)
Structural Engineers: Ove Arup & Partners (P. Rice, R. Hough)
Administration: Ouvrage Snc
Landscaping: M. Desvigne, C. Dalnoky, assisted by P. Convercey
Testing: Copitec (C. Knezovic), Planitec (M. Lopez)
Acoustics: Peutz
Contractors: Durand, Danto Rogeat Savoie, Villequin

1988–92 Genoa
Christopher Columbus International Exposition '92
Client: Genoa City Council – Ente Colombo '92
Contractor and project management: Italimpianti, Genoa
Design team: Renzo Piano Building Workshop
S. Ishida, E. Baglietto (Italian Pavilion), G.G. Bianchi (cotton warehouses, scenography Moby Dick, Italian Pavilion), P. Bodega, M. Carroll (aquarium, Italian Pavilion), O. De Nooyer (Il Bigo) G. Grandi (customs warehouses, services), D. L. Hart (conference centre), C. Manfreddo (services, Mandraccio, press office, Molo Vecchio), V. Tolu, R.V. Truffelli (customs warehouses), assisted by A. Arancio, M. Calosso, E. Carreri, M. Cucinella, S. D'Atri (CAD), S. De Leo (CAD), G. Fascioli, E.L. Hegerl, G. Langasco (CAD), M. Mallamaci, G. McMahon, M. Michelotti, P. Persia (CAD), A. Pierandrei, F. Pierandrei, S. Smith, R. Venelli, L. Vercelli, S. Shingu (sculptor)
Consultants
Structural engineers: Ove Arup & Partners (P. Rice); L. Mascia, D. Mascia, P. Costa, L. Lembo, V. Nascinbene, B. Ballerini, G. Malcangi, Sidercard, M. Testone, G.F. Visconti
Service installations: Manes Intertecnica, Verona
Historic buildings supervisor: M. Semino
Aquarium: Cambridge Seven Ass. Boston, USA (P. Chermayeff)
Technical supervisors: F. Doria, M. Giacomelli, S. Lanzon, B. Merello, M. Nouvion, G. Robotti, A. Savioli
Quantity surveyors: Sted, Genoa (S. Baldelli, A. Grasso)
Acoustics: D. Commings, Paris
Lighting: P. Castiglioni
Aquarium director of works: E. Piras, Genoa
Local supervisor: L. Moni
Scenography: Scene, Paris
Naval engineers: Cetena
Italian Pavilion exhibition curator: G. Macchi
Graphics: Origoni/Steiner
Contractors: Italimpianti

1988–94 Osaka
Kansai International Airport Main Passenger Terminal Building
Client: Kansai International Airport Co. Ltd
Competition design: Renzo Piano

Building Workshop Paris
Partners: R. Piano, N. Okabe, Ove Arup & Partners International Ltd (P. Rice, T. Barker)
Architects and engineers: Renzo Piano Building Workshop Japan Renzo Piano, Noriaki Okabe, Nikken Sekkei Ltd (Kimiaki Minai); Ove Arup & Partners International Ltd (Peter Rice)
Analysis of airport functions: Paul Andreu, Paris Airport
Analysis of runway: Misao Matsumoto, Japanese airport consultant
Competition team: Renzo Piano Building Workshop, Paris
Partners: R. Piano, N. Okabe
Design Team: J.F. Blassel, R. Brennan, A. Chaaya, L. Couton, R. Keiser, L. Koenig, K. McBryde, S. Planchez, R. Rolland, G. Torre, O. Touraine, assisted by G. le Breton, M. Henry, J. Lelay, A. O'Carrol, M. Salerno, A.H. Téménidès, N. Westphal
Consultants
Structural engineers: Ove Arup & Partners International Ltd
Landscaping: M. Devigne
Master plan: Renzo Piano Building Workshop, Japan
Partners: R. Piano, N. Okabe
Design Team: J.F. Blassel, A. Chavela, I. Corte, K. Fraser, R.S. Garlipp, M. Goerd, G. Hall, K. Hirano, A. Ikegami, S. Ishida, A. Johnson, C. Kelly, T. Kimura, S. Larsen, J. Lelay, K. McBryde, T. Miyazaki, S. Nakaya, N. Takata, T. Tomuro, O. Touraine, M. Turpin, M. Yamada, H. Yamaguchi, T. Yamaguchi, assisted by A. Autin, G. Cohen, A. Golzari, B. Gunning, G. Hastrich, M. Horie, I. Kubo, S. Medio, K. Miyake, S. Montaldo, S. Mukai, K.A. Naderi, S. Oehler, T. O'Sullivan, P. Persia,
F. Pierandrei, M. Rossato, R. Shields, T. Takagawa, T. Ueno, K Uezono, J.M. Weill, T. Yamakoshi
Structural engineers: Ove Arup & Partners International Ltd
Acoutics: Peutz et Associés (Y. Dekeyrel)
Glazed surfaces: R. Van Santen
Quantity surveyors: David Langdon & Everest; Futaba Quantity Surveying Co., Ltd
Landscaping: Koung Nyunt, Toshi Keikan
Working project: Renzo Piano Building Workshop Japan
Partners: R. Piano, N. Okabe
Design Team: A. Ikegami, T. Kimura, T. Tomuro, Y. Ueno, assisted by S. Kano, A. Shimizu
Endwall Glazing Development: RFR (J.F. Blassel); Sekkei Inc. (S. Okumura)

1989 Turin
Russian and Soviet Art 1870–1930 exhibition at the Lingotto Centre
Client: Fiat Lingotto
Design team: Renzo Piano Building Workshop
M. Varratta, S. Ishida, M. Cattaneo, M. Rossato, with the collaboration of G. Carandente
Lighting: P. Castiglioni
Graphics: P. Cerri
Installations: Bodino

1989 Amsterdam
Science and Technology Museum
Client: NINT
Design team: Renzo Piano Building Workshop
S. Ishida, O. De Nooyer, H. Yamaguchi, J. Fujita, with the collaboration of I. Corte, D. Guerrisi, E. Piazze, A. Recagno, K. Shannon, F. Wenz, Y. Yamaoka
Model: M. Bassignani, D. Cavagna
Coordination: A. Giordano
Consultants
Structural engineers: Ove Arup & Partners (P. Rice, T. Barker, J. Wernick)
Director of works: Brink Groep
Back-up studio: Bureau Bouwkunde (D. Hoogstad)
Structural Engineers: D3BN (J. Kraus)
Service installations: Huisman en Van Muijen BV (R. Borrett)
Acoustics: Peutz & Associés BV

1989 Turin
Towards the New Lingotto exhibition
Client: Fiat
Design team: Renzo Piano Building Workshop
P. Bodega, M. Cucinella, J. Desscombe, S. Durr, E. Frigerio, S. Ishida, P. Maggiora, F. Marano, A. Piancastelli, M. Rossato, M. Varratta, S. Vignale, with the collaboration of I. Corte (CAD)
Landscaping: M. Desvigne, C. Dalnoky
Model: E. Miola
Video: Cinema Srl (M. Arduino)
Consultants
Graphics: Grosz
Installations: Bodino

1989–91 Vesima, Genoa
UNESCO Workshop Research Laboratory
Client: UNESCO
Design team: Renzo Piano Building Workshop
M. Cattaneo, F. Marano, S. Ishida, M. Lusetti, M. Nouvion, with the collaboration of M. Calosso, M. Carroll, M. Desvigne, O. Di Blasi, D. Piano, R.V. Truffelli, M. Varratta, M.C. Verdona
Model: D. Cavagna
Consultants
Geological studies: A. Bellini, L. Gattoronchieri
Structural engineer: P. Costa
Bionic research: C. Di Bartolo (CRSN)
Contractors: Edilindustria Spa Andidero
Landscaping: Nuovo Verde, Ratti
Greenhouse, roofs and glazing: Focchi, Siv, Pati, Montefluos
Interiors: Gruppo Bodino
Wooden structures: Habitat legno
Cable-car: Maspero elevatori
Louvres: Model System Italia

1989–95 Kumamoto
Bridge in the Ushibuka Archipelago
Client: Kumamoto Prefecture Department for the Environment and Fisheries
Design team: Renzo Piano Building Workshop
N. Okabe, S. Ishida, M. Yamada, with the collaboration of J. Lelay, T. Ueno
Model: D. Cavagna
Consultants
Structural engineers: Ove Arup & Partner (P. Rice, J. Nissen, P. Brooke, J. Batchelor), Mayeda Enginnering Co. (T. Matsumoto, S. Tsuchiya, S. Kawasaki)

1990 Milan
The Automobile, Production and Design 1879–1949 exhibition
Clients: Milan City Council, Alfa Romeo
Design team: Renzo Piano Building Workshop
S. Ishida, F. Marano, M. Carroll. O. Di Blasi, M. Varratta, with the collaboration of M. Nouvion, R. Trapani
Consultants
Structural engineer: L. Mascia
Lighting: P. Castiglioni
Graphics: F. Origoni & A. Steiner
Installations: Bodino

1990 Turin
American Art 1930–1970 exhibition
Client: Lingotto Srl
Design team: Renzo Piano Building Workshop
M. Cattaneo, S. Ishida, M. Varratta
Curators: A. Codignato, N. Bevilacqua
Consultants
Lighting: P. Castiglioni
Graphics: P. Cerri
Installations: Bodino

1990 Turin
Andy Warhol: Early New York Years Exhibition
Client: Lingotto Srl
Design team: Renzo Piano Building Workshop
M. Varratta, S. Ishida
Curators: A. Codignato, D. Desalvo
Consultants
Lighting: P. Castiglioni
Graphics: Grosz, ECO
Installations: Bodino

1990 Turin
The Car Culture exhibition
Client: Lingotto Srl
Design team: Renzo Piano Building Workshop
M. Varratta, S. Ishida, M. Cucmella, P. Maggiora, A. Piancastelli, M. Rossato, S. Vignale
Curators: A. Bassignana, A. Marchis, A. Signetto
Consultants
Graphics: Grosz
Model: E. Miola
Installations: Bodino

1991 San Giovanni Rotondo, Foggia
Design for the Church of Padre Pio
Client: Frati Minori Cappuccini
Design team: Renzo Piano Building Workshop
K. Fraser, G. Grandi, P. Bodega, I. Corte (CAD), S. D'Atri (CAD), B. Ditchburn, V. Di Turi, E. Fitzgerald, S. Ishida, L. Lin, F. Marano, M. Palmore, P. Persia (CAD), with the collaboration of H. Hirsch
Model: M. Bassignani, D. Cavagna
Coordination: Alberto Giordano
Consultants
Structural engineers: Ove Arup & Partners (P. Rice, T. Barker, J. Wernick), R. Calzona
Acoustics: Müller-Bbm
Back-up studio: G. Muciaccia, Foggia
Liturgical consultant: G. Grasso, Genoa
Quantity surveyors: Sted (A. Grasso, S. Baldelli)
Planning: G. Amadeo

1991 Padua
Padua and Galileo exhibition
Client: Padova City Council
Design team: Renzo Piano Building Workshop
S. Ishida, N. Okabe, P. Ackerman, M. Cattaneo, with the collaboration of C. Garbato
Model: D. Cavagna
Consultants
Coordination: G. Macchi
Lighting: P. Castiglioni
Consultant scientific committee from Padua University:
E. Bellone, M. Bonsembiante, R. Hipschman

1992 Berlin
Design for Potsdamer Platz
Client: Daimler Benz AG: dlM debis Immobilienmanagement GmbH; Project manager: Drees & Sommer, Stuttgart
Design team: Renzo Piano Building Workshop
Christoph Kohlbecker,
B. Plattner, S. Baggs, E. Baglietto,
R. Baumgarten, G. Bianchi, P. Charles, C. Hight, S. Ishida, M. Kramer, N. Mecattaf, J. Moolhuijzen, F. Pagliani, L.I. Penisson, D. Putz, M. Rossato Piano, J. Ruoff, C. Sapper, S. Schafer, R.V. Truffelli, L. Viti, with the collaboration of E. Belik, G. Carreira, A. Chaaya, I. Corte (CAD), O. De Nooyer, J. Fujita, W. Grasmug, D. Guerrisi (CAD), G. Langasco (CAD), N. Miegeville, E. Del Moral, H. Nagel, G. Ong, Ph. Regnier (CAD), B. Tonfoni, R. Sala, K. Shannon, F. Wenz, H. Yamaguchi
Model: J.P. Allain, D. Cavagna, P. Darmer, M. Goudin
Coordination: A. Giordano
Consultants
Structural engineers: Ove Arup & Partners, Gh/Arup, Boll/Arup, IBB, Burrer, Falkner Weiske & Partners, Hunt & Partner, R. Preston + Klimasystem (RP + K)
Acoustics: Müller Bbm
Planning and organization: Quickborner team
Fire prevention: Debis Risk Consult
Road network: Studiengesellschaft Verkehr mbH
Housing administration: Blumenauer Immobilien
Sales administration: Warburg & Schluter, Ece

1992 Nouméa
The Jean-Marie Tjibaou Kanak Cultural Centre
Design team: Renzo Piano Building Workshop
P. Vincent, A. Chaaya, A. El Jerari, A. Gallissian, M. Henry, D. Mirallie, G. Modolo, J.B. Mothes, F. Pagliani, D. Rat, A.H. Téménidès, W. Vassal, with the collaboration of R. Baumgarten, C. Catino, J. Moolhuijzen, R. Phelan
Model: D. Cavagna, O. Doizy, P. Darmer, A. Schultz
Consultants
Structural engineering and ventilation: Ove Arup & Partners (P. Rice, T. Barker, J. Wernick); CSTB (J. Gandemer): Agibat (D. Quost, J. Gandemer)
Ethnologist: A. Bensa
Landscaping: M. Desvigne, C. Dalnoky; Vegetude (C. Guinaudeau)
Quantity surveyors: GEC Ingénierie (F. Petit, C. Baché, T. Plantagenest)
Acoustics: Peutz & Associés (Y. Dekeyrel, J.M. Marion)
Scenography: Scène (J.H. Manoury)
Planning: Gemo
Supervisors: Qualiconsult (J.L. Rolland)

1993 Bari
Redevelopment of the Teatro Margherita
Client: Fratelli Dioguardi Spa
Design team: Renzo Piano Building Workshop
S. Ishida, F. Marano, E. Baglietto, M. Cattaneo, R. Fernandez Prado, F. Pierandrei, S. Nobis
Consultants: G. Amendola; Beacon
Project management: Studio Gorjux Architetti Associati; Studio Tecnico Lab, Sovrintendenza beni AA.AA.AA.SS.: Studio Vitone & Associati

1993 Boulogne-Billancourt, Paris
Design for the ile Séguin
Client: Mission Billancourt
Design team: Renzo Piano Building Workshop
P. Vincent, A. Chaaya, E. Novel, T. Roland, M. Salerno, with the collaboration of S. Barone,

C. Catino, P. Charles,
H. Chattenay, A. El Jerari,
M. Henry, J. Moolhuijzen,
B. Tonfoni, W. Vassal
Model: P. Darmer, O. Doizy
Consultants
Landscaping: M. Desvigne,
C. Dalnoky

1993 Genoa
Design for the Molo quarter
Design team: Renzo Piano
Building Workshop
S. Ishida, D.L. Hart, with the
collaboration of M. Menzio,
C. Leoncini

1993
Pilot scheme for railway stations
in Turin, Mestre, Venice and Bari
Client: Italfer Sis TAV (FS-Italian
State Railways)
Steering committee: Susanna
Agnelli, Giuseppe De Rita, Carlo
Maria Guerci, Renzo Piano
Design team: Renzo Piano
Building Workshop
S. Ishida, R.V. Truffelli,
E. Baglietto, M. Cattaneo,
J. Cohen, K. Fraser, D. Hart,
C. Marfreddo, O. De Nooyer,
D. Piano, F. Pierandrei,
S. Scarabicchi, with the
collaboration of N. Baldassiri,
M. Belviso (CAD), I. Corte (CAD),
A. Ewing, M. Fawcett, J. Fujita,
D. Guerrisi (CAD), A. Hopkins,
N. Malby, G. Pauletto (CAD),
M. Penna, T. Reynolds, G.
Robotti, K. Shannon, F. Wenz,
H. Yamaguchi
Model: M. Bassignani,
D. Cavagna, P. Varratta
Structural engineer: P. Costa
Supervisor: Sted
Compatibility with railway
structures: G. Scorza

1993–96 Paris
Plan for the reorganization of the
Georges Pompidou Centre area
and Brancusi Museum
Client: CNAC Georges Pompidou
Design team: Renzo Piano
Building Workshop
B. Plattner, R. Self, J.L.
Dupanloup, A. Galissian,
R. Phelan, assisted by
C. Aasgaard, Z. Berrio, C. Catino,
P. Chappell, J. Darling, P. Satchell
Structural engineering and
quantity surveying: GEC
Ingéniérie Mechanical services:
Inex
Car parks: Isis

Renzo Piano Building Workshop, Genoa, Paris, Osaka

Partners:
Mark G. Carroll
Shunji Ishida
Flavio Marano
Noriaki Okabe
Bernard Plattner
Renzo Venanzio Truffelli
Paul Vincent

Design team:
Camilla Aasgaard
Jean Philippe Allain
Alessandra Alborghetti
Michele Allevi
Stefano Arecco
Susan Baggs
Emanuala Baglietto
Roger Baumgarten
Giorgio G. Bianchi
Marjolijne Boudry
Danila Campo
Maria Cattaneo
Antoine Chaaya
Patrick Charles
Geoffrey Cohen
Shelly Comer
Ivan Corte
Loïc Couton
Stefano D'Atri
Alessandro De Luca
Vittorio Di Turi
Jean Luc Dupanloup
Stacy Eisenberg
Ahmed El Jerari
Lukas Epprecht
Kenneth Fraser
Junya Fujita
Alain Gallissian
Maurizio Garrasi
Alessandro Gortan
Giorgio Grandi
Domenico Guerrisi
Donald L. Hart
Pascal Hendier
Maìre Henry
Christopher Hight
Michelle Howard
Charles Hussey
Akira Ikegami
Charlotte Jackman

Shin Kanoo
Tetsuya Kimura
Misha Kramer
Giovanna Langasco
Claudia Leoncini
Richard Librizzi
Lorraine Lin
Paola Maggiora
Domenico Magnano
Claudio Manfreddo
Katheryne McLone
William Mathews
Nayla Mecattaf
Catheryne McLone
Gianni Modolo
Joost Moolhuijzen
Jean-Bernard Mothes
Olaf de Nooyer
Eric Novel
Grace Ong
Michael Palmore
Filippo Pagliani
Lionel Penisson
Ronan Phelan
Marie Pimmel
Daniele Piano
Matteo Piano
Fabrizio Pierandrei
Dominizue Putz
Dominique Rat
Milly Rossato
Joachim Ruoff
Maria Salerno
Carola Sapper
Susanna Scarabicchi
Stefan Schäfer
Ronnie Self
Aki Shimizu
Yasmin Surti
Anne-Hélène Temenides
Vittorio Tolu
Taichi Tomuro
Bruno Tonfoni
Yoshiko Ueno
Maurizio Varratta
William Vassal
Eric Verstrepen
Lorenzo Viti
Hiroshi Yamaguchi

Models:
Jean-Philippe Allain
Dante Cavagna

Coordination:
Alberto Giordano

Research and publications:
François Bertolero
Daniela Capuzzo
Isabella Carpiceci
Carla Garbato
Elisabeth Nodinot
Noriko Takiguchi

Administration:
Kathy Bassière
Gianfranco Biggi
Philippe Goubet
Sonia Oldani
Michele Ras
Angela Sacco
Hélène Teboul
Alain Vincent

Secretaries:
Rosella Biondo
Stefania Canta
Eva Kruse
Sylvie Milanesi
Hiroko Nishikawa

Collaborators

Camilla Aasgaard
Laurie Abbot
Maria Accardi
Peter Ackermann
Kamran Afshar Naderi
Emilia Agazzi
Alessandra Alborghetti
Jean Philippe Allain
Michele Allevi
Michel Alluyn
Arianna Andidero
Sally Appleby
Andrea Arancio
Catherine Ardilley
Magda Arduino
Stefano Arecco
P. Audran
Veronique Auger
Frank August
Alexandre Autin
Carmela Avagliano
Patrizio Avellino
Rita Avvenente
Carlo Bachschmidt
Alessandro Badi
Susan Baggs
Emanuela Baglietto
Antonella Balassone
Nicolò Baldassini
François Barat
Henry Bardsley
Giulia Barone
Sonia Barone
Fabrizio Bartolomeo
Cristopher Bartz
Bruno Bassetti
Kathy Bassière
Sandro Battini
Roger Baumgarten
Paolo Beccio
Annie Benzeno
Jan Berger
Eva Belik
François Bertolero
Alessandro Bianchi
G. Giorgio Bianchi
Gianfranco Biggi
Gregoire Bignier
Germana Binelli
Judy Bing

Rosella Biondo
Jean François Blassel
A. Blassone
William Blurock
Paolo Bodega
Marko Bojovic
Sara Bonati
Manuela Bonino
Gilles Bontemps
Andrea Bosch
Pierre Botschi
Marjolijne Boudry
Sandrine Boulay
Ross Brennan
Gaelle Breton
Maria Cristina Brizzolara
Cuno Brullmann
Michael Burckhardt
Christiane Bürklein
Hans-Peter Bysaeth
Alessandro Calafati
Patrick Callegia
Maurizio Calosso
Michele Calvi
Nunzio Camerada
Danila Campo
Florence Canal
Andrea Canepa
Stefania Canta
Daniela Capuzzo
Alessandro Carisetto
Monica Carletti
Elena Carmignani
Isabella Carpiceci
Emanuele Carreri
Mark Carroll
Elena Casali
Marta Castagna
Cristiana Catino
Maria Cattaneo
Enrica Causa
Dante Cavagna
Simone Cecchi
Giorgio Celadon
Ottaviano Celadon
Alessandro Cereda
Antoine Chaaya
Patricia Chappell
Patrick Charles
Jean Luc Chassais

Hubert Chatenay
Pierre Chatelain
Ariel Chavela
Laura Cherchi
Raimondo Chessa
Cristopher Chevalier
Catherine Clarisse
Geoffrey Cohen
Franc Collect
Daniel Collin
Shelly Comer
Giulio Contardo
Philippe Convercey
Pier Luigi Copat
Colman Corish
Monica Corsilia
Ivan Corte
Giacomo Costa
Raffaele Costa
Loic Couton
Paolo Crema
Raffaella Croce Belmondi
A. Croxato
Mario Cucinella
Irene Cuppone
Catherine Cussoneau
Lorenzo Custer
Stefano D'Atri
Catherine D'Ovidio
Isabelle Da Costa
Paul Darmer
Lorenzo Dasso
Mike Davies
Silvia De Leo
Alessandro De Luca
Simona De Mattei
Olaf De Nooyer
Daniela Defilla
S. Degli Innocenti
Alessio Demontis
Julien Descombes
Michel Desvigne
Carmelo Di Bartolo
Ottavio Di Blasi
Brian Ditchburn
Maddalena Di Sopra
Vittorio Di Turi
Helene Diebold
John Doggart
Olivier Doizy

Eugenio Donato
François Doria
Michael Dowd
Mike Downs
Klaus Dreissigacker
Delphine Drouin
Frank Dubbers
Susan Dunne
Jean Luc Dupanloup
Philippe Dupont
Susanne Durr
John Dutton
Mick Eekhout
Stacy Eisenberg
Ahmed El Jerari
Kenneth Zammit Endrich
Lukas Epprecht
Alison Ewing
Roberta Fambri
Roberto Faravelli
Giorgio Fascioli
Maxwell Fawcett
David Felice
Alfonso Femia
Jacques Fendard
Agostino Ferrari
Maurizio Filocca
Laurent Marc Fischer
Richard Fitgerald
Eileen Fitzgerald
Peter Flack
Renato Foni
M. Fordam
Gilles Fourel
Gianfranco Franchini
Kenneth Fraser
Nina Freedman
Marian Frezza
Enrico Frigerio
Junya Fujita
Rinaldo Gaggero
Alain Gallissian
Andrea Gallo
Maurizio Garrasi
Carla Garbato
Robert Garlipp
G. Gasbarri
Angelo Ghiotto
M. Giacomelli
Davide Gibelli

260

Alain Gillette
Sonia Giordani
Alberto Giordano
Antonella Giovannoni
Marion Goerdt
Marco Goldschmied
Enrico Gollo
Anahita Golzari
Alessandro Gortan
Philippe Goubet
Françoise Gouinguenet
Robert Grace
Giorgio Grandi
Cecil Granger
Don Gray
Nigel Greenhill
Magali Grenier
Paolo Guerrini
Domenico Guerrisi
Alain Gueze
Barnaby Gunning
Greg Hall
Donald Hart
Thomas Hartman
Gunther Hastrich
Ulrike Hautsch
Christopher Hays
Eva Hegerl
Pascal Hendier
Pierre Henneguier
Maìre Henry
Gabriel Hernandez
Caroline Herrin
Christopher Hight
Kohji Hirano
Harry Hirsch
Andrew Holmes
Eric Holt
Abigal Hopkins
Masahiro Horie
Helene Houizot
Michelle Howard
Jean Huc
Ed Huckabi
Frank Hughes
Charles Hussey
Filippo Icardi
Frediano Iezzi
Akira Ikegami
Djenina Illoul

Paolo Insogna
Shunji Ishida
Charlotte Jackman
Angela Jackson
Tobias Jaklin
Amanda Johnson
Frederic Joubert
Shin Kanoo
Jan Kaplicky
Elena Karitakis
Robert Keiser
Christopher Kelly
Paul Kelly
Werner Kestel
Irini Kilaiditi
Tetsuya Kimura
Laurent Koenig
Tomoko Komatsubara
Akira Komiyama
Misha Kramer
Eva Kruse
Betina Kurtz
Frank La Riviere
Jean Baptiste Lacoudre
Antonio Lagorio
Giovanna Langasco
Antonio Langorio
Stig Larsen
Denis Laville
François Laville
Jean Lelay
Renata Lello
Claudia Leoncini
Laurent Le Voyer
Olivier Lidon
Lorraine Lin
Bill Logan
Johanna Lohse
Federica Lombardo
François Lombardo
Steve Lopez
Riccardo Luccardini
Simonetta Lucci
Rolf-Robert Ludewig
Claudine Luneberg
Massimiliano Lusetti
Paola Maggiora
Domenico Magnano
Nicholas Malby
Milena Mallamaci

Natalie Mallat
Claudio Manfreddo
Flavio Marano
Andrea Marasso
Francesco Marconi
Massimo Mariani
Alberto Marré Brunenghi
Cristina Martinelli
Daniele Mastragostino
Manuela Mattei
William Mathews
Marie Helene Maurette
Ken Mc Bryde
Katheryne McLone
Grainne Mc Mahon
Nayla Mecattaf
Simone Medio
Barbara Mehrrn
Roberto Melai
Mario Menzio
Eveline Mercier
Benny Merello
Peter Metz
Marcella Michelotti
Paolo Migone
Sylvie Milanesi
Emanuela Minetti
Edoardo Miola
Takeshi Miyazaki
Gianni Modolo
Sandro Montaldo
Elisa Monti
Joost Moolhuijzen
Denise Morado Nascimento
Gerard Mormina
Ingrid Morris
Jean Bernard Mothes
Farshid Moussavi
Mariette Muller
Philip Murphy
Andrea Musso
Hanne Nagel
Shinichi Nakaya
Hiroshi Naruse
Roberto Navarra
Pascale Negre
Andrew Nichols
Hiroko Nishikawa
Susanne Nobis
David Nock

Elisabeth Nodinot
Marco Nouvion
Eric Novel
Anna O'Carrol
Tim O'Sullivan
Alphons Oberhoffer
Stefan Oehler
Noriaki Okabe
Antonella Oldani
Sonia Oldani
Grace Ong
Patrizia Orcamo
Stefania Orcamo
Roy Orengo
Carlos Osrej
Piero Ottaggio
Nedo Ottonello
Antonella Paci
Filippo Pagliani
Michael Palmore
Giorgia Paraluppi
Chandra Patel
Pietro Pedrini
Luigi Pellini
Danilo Peluffo
Gianluca Peluffo
Lionel Penisson
Mauro Penna
Patrizia Persia
Gil Petit
Ronan Phelan
Paul Phillips
Alberto Piancastelli
Carlo Piano
Daniele Piano
Lia Piano
Matteo Piano
Enrico Piazze
Marie Pimmel
Gennaro Picardi
Alessandro Pierandrei
Fabrizio Pierandrei
M. Pietrasanta
Sandra Planchez
Bernard Plattner
Monica Poggi
Andrea Polleri
Roberta Possanzini
Fabio Postani
Nicolas Prouvé

Costanza Puglisi
Dominique Putz
Gianfranco Queirolo
Michele Ras
Maria Cristina Rasero
Dominique Rat
Neil Rawson
Judith Raymond
Antonella Recagno
Luis Renau
Tom Reynolds
Elena Ricciardi
Kieran Rice
Nemone Rice
Peter Rice
Jean Yves Richard
Gianni Robotti
Giuseppe Rocco
Richard Rogers
Renaud Rolland
Emilia Rossato
Bernard Rouyer
Lucio Ruocco
Joachim Ruoff
Ken Rupard
Antonella Sacchi
Angela Sacco
Jean Gerard Saint
Riccardo Sala
Maria Salerno
Maurizio Santini
Francesca Santolini
Paulo Sanza
Carola Sapper
Paul Satchell
Alessandro Savioli
Susanna Scarabicchi
Maria Grazia Scavo
Stefan Schäfer
Helga Schlegel
Giuseppina Schmid
Jean François Schmit
Maren Schuessler
Andrea Schultz
Ronnie Self
Barbara-Petra Sellwig
Mario Semino
Patrik Senne
Anna Serra
Kelly Shannon
Randy Shields
Aki Shimizu
Madoka Shimizu
Cecile Simon
Thibaud Simonin
Alessandro Sinagra
Luca Siracusa
Jan Sircus
Alan Smith
Stephanie Smith
Richard Soundy
Claudette Spielmann
Adrian Stadlmayer
Alan Stanton
David Summerfield
Yasmin Surti
Christian Süsstrunk
Jose Lu Taborda Barrientos
Hiroyuki Takahashi
Norio Takata
Noriko Takiguchi
Hélène Teboul
Anne Hélène Téménidès
Carlo Teoldi
Peter Terbuchte
G.L. Terragna
David Thom
John Thornhill
Cinzia Tiberti
Luigi Tirelli
Elisabeth Tisseur
Vittorio Tolu
Taichi Tomuro
Bruno Tonfoni
Graciella Torre
Laura Torre
Olivier Touraine
Alessandro Traldi
Renata Trapani
Renzo Venanzio Truffelli
Leland Turner
Mark Turpin
Yoshiko Ueno
Kiyomi Uezono
Peter Ullathorne
Colette Valensi
Maurizio Vallino
Antonia Van Oosten
Robert Jan Van Santen
Michael Vaniscott
Maurizio Varratta
Paolo Varratta
Claudio Vaselli
William Vassal
Francesca Vattuone
Bernard Vaudeville
Martin Veith
Reiner Verbizh
Maria Carla Verdona
Eric Verstrepen
Silvia Vignale
Antonella Vignoli
Mark Viktov
Alain Vincent
Paul Vincent
Patrick Virly
Marco Visconti
Lorenzo Viti
Louis Waddell
Jean Marc Weill
Florian Wenz
Nicolas Westphal
Chris Wilkinson
Niel Winder
Martin Wollensak
George Xydis
Masami Yamada
Sugako Yamada
Hiroshi Yamaguchi
Tatsuya Yamaguchi
Emi Yoshimura
John Young
Gianpaolo Zaccaria
Lorenzo Zamperetti
Antonio Zanuso
Martina Zappettini
Walter Zbinden
Maurizio Zepponi
Massimo Zero

Bibliography

Articles

R. Piano, R. Foni, G. Garbuglia, L. Tirelli, M. Filocco, *Una struttura ad elementi standard, per la copertura di medie e grandi luci*, in "La Prefabbricazione", January 1966.

Z.S. Makowski, *Structural plastics in Europe*, in "Arts & Architecture", August 1966, pp. 20–30.

M. Scheichenbauer, *Progettare con le materie plastiche*, in "Casabella", 316, 1967.

Ricerca sulle strutture in lamiera e in poliestere rinforzato, in "Domus", 448, March 1967, pp. 8–22.

Il grande numero, in "Domus", 466, September 1968.

Nuove tecniche e nuove strutture per l'edilizia, in "Domus", 468, November 1968, p. 6.

Uno studio-laboratorio, in "Domus", 479, October 1969, pp. 10–14.

R. Piano, *Progettazione sperimentale per strutture a guscio*, in "Casabella", 335, 1969.

R. Piano, *Experiments and projects with industrialised structures in plastic material*, in "PDOB", 16–17, October 1969.

Z.S. Makowski, *Plastic structures of R. Piano*, in "Systems, Building and Design", February 1969, pp. 37–54.

R. Piano, *Nasce con le materie plastiche un nuovo modo di progettare architettura*, in "Materie plastiche e elastometri", 1, 1969.

Z.S. Makowski, *Les structures et plastiques de R. Piano*, in "Plastique Batiment", 126, February 1969, pp. 10–17.

R. Piano, *Italie recherche de structures*, in "Techniques & Architecture", XXX, 5, 1969, pp. 96–100.

Z.S. Makowski, *Strukturen aus Kunststoff von Renzo Piano*, in "Bauen + Wohnen", 4, April 1970, pp. 112–121.

Un cantiere sperimentale, in "Casabella", 349, 1970.

R. Piano, *Il padiglione dell'Industria italiana all'Expo 70 di Osaka*, in "Acciaio", 11, November 1970.

A. Cereda, *Alcune recenti esperienze nel campo della industrializzazione edilizia. Tre architetture di Renzo Piano*, in "Lipe", 3, March 1970, pp. 1–12.

R. Piano, *Architecture and Technology*, in "AA Quarterly", 3, vol. 2, July 1970, pp. 32–43.

Renzo Piano, in "Architectural Design", 3, March 1970, pp. 140–145.

Italian industry Pavillon, Expo 70, Osaka, in "Architectural Design", 8, August 1970, p. 416.

Il poliestere rinforzato protagonista del padiglione dell'industria italiana, in "Materie plastiche e elastometri", 5, May 1970, pp. 470–477.

Rigging a roof, in "The Architectural Forum", 2, vol. 132, March 1970.

Renzo Piano verso una pertinenza tecnologica dei componenti, in "Casabella", 352, 1970, p. 37.

L'Italia a Osaka, in "Domus", 484, March 1970.

Industrialisierung, in "Deutsche Bauzeitung", 4, April 1971, pp. 405–407.

Industrial building, in "The Architectural Forum", April 1971.

Piano & Rogers: Beaubourg, in "Domus", 503, October 1971, pp. 1–7.

R. Piano, *Per un'edilizia industrializzata*, in "Domus", 495, February 1971, pp. 12–15.

R. Piano, *L'acciaio nell'edilizia industrializzata*, in "Acciaio", 11, November 1971, pp. 1–4.

Le materie plastiche nella produzione edilizia per componenti, in "Materie plastiche e elastometri", 5, May 1971.

Grand Piano, in "Industrial Design", 68, vol. 18, October 1971, pp. 40–45.

M. Cornu, *Concours Beaubourg "est-ce un signe de notre temps?"*, in "Architecture Mouvement Continuité", 23, November 1971, pp. 8–9.

Projet des Lauréats, in "Techniques & Architecture", 3 speciale, 34, February 1972, pp. 48–55.

Les projet Laureat, in "Paris project", 7, pp. 48–57.

Paris: Centre Beaubourg, in "Deutsche Bauzeitung", 9, September 1972, pp. 974–976.

A Parigi, per i Parigini l'evoluzione del progetto Piano + Rogers per il Centre Beaubourg, in "Domus", 511, June 1972, pp. 9–12.

Aktualität: Esso Tankestellen Wettbewerb in Italien, in "Bauen + Wohnen", 6, 1972, p. 280.

Padiglione dell'industria italiana all'Expo 70 di Osaka, in "Casabella", suppl. 363, March 1972.

Centre Culturel du Plateau Beaubourg, in "L'Architecture d'Aujourd'hui", 168, July/August 1973, pp. 34–43.

Piano + Rogers, in "L'Architecture d'Aujourd'hui", 170, November/December 1973, pp. 46–58.

Centre Plateau Beaubourg, in "Domus", 525, August 1973.

Edificio per gli uffici B&B a Novedrate, in "Domus", 530, January 1974, pp. 31–36.

Beaubourg en trasparence, in "Architecture Interieure", 141, June/July 1974, pp. 72–77.

Piano, in "Zodiac", 22, pp. 126–147.

Centre Beaubourg à Paris, in "Techniques & Architecture", 300, September/October 1974, p. 58.

Factory, Tadworth, Surrey, in "The Architectural Review", 934, December 1974, pp. 338–345.

Piano & Rogers, *B&B Italia Factory*, in "Architectural Design", 4, 1974, pp. 245–246.

Le Centre Beaubourg, in "Chantiers de France", 68, 1974, pp. 1–6.

Expressive Einheit von Tragkonstruktion und Installationsanlagen, in "Bauen + Wohnen", 2, February 1974, pp. 71–74.

A Parigi musica underground, in "Domus", 545, April 1975, pp. 9–12.

R. Bordaz, *Le Centre Georges Pompidou*, in "Construction", 9, September 1975, pp. 5–30.

Etablissement public du Centre Beaubourg, Paris, in "Werk oeuvre", 2, February 1975, pp. 140–148.

P. Rice, *Main Structural Framework of the Beaubourg Centre, Paris*, in "Acier. Stahl. Steel", XL, 9, September 1975, pp. 297–309.

Piano & Rogers, *Piano + Rogers*, in "Architectural Design", 45, May 1975, pp. 75–311.

F. Marano, *Una struttura tubolare per un nuovo edificio per uffici a Novedrate*, in "Acciaio", 2, February 1975, pp. 1–7.

P. Rice, L. Grut, *Renzo Piano. La struttura del C. Beaubourg a Parigi*, in "Acciaio", 9, September 1975, pp. 3–15.

K. Menomi, *Nel prato una struttura policroma. Edificio per uffici B&B*, in "Ufficio stile", LX, 6, 1976, pp. 76–79.

Piano + Rogers: Architectural method, in "A + U", 66, 1976, pp. 63–122.

L'Ircam institut de recherche et coordination acoustique-musique, in "Chanteurs de France", 93, September 1976, pp. 2–13.

Ircam design process, in "Riba Journal", 2, 1976, pp. 61–69.

Strukturen und Hüllen, in "Werk oeuvre", 11, 1976, pp. 742–748.

Piano & Rogers, *Beaubourg furniture internal system catalogue*, in "Architectural Design", 46, July 1976, pp. 442–443.

Novedrate Italia Edificio per uffici.

in "AC", XXII, 82, April 1976, pp. 35-37.
P. Restany, C. Casati, *Parigi: l'oggetto funziona!*, in "Domus", 575, October 1977, pp. 1-11.
Le défi de Beaubourg, in "AA", 189, February 1977, pp. 40-81.
Frankreichs Centre National d'Art et de Culture G. Pompidou in Paris, in "Bauwelt", 11, March 1977, pp. 316-334.
Piano & Rogers, in "Riba Journal", 1, January 1977, pp. 11-16.
Centre National d'Art et Culture Georges Pompidou, in "Domus", 566, January 1977, pp. 3-37.
Centre Georges Pompidou, in "AD Profiles", 2, 1977.
Piano & Rogers 4 progetti, in "Domus", 570, May 1977, pp. 17-24.
The Pompidolium, in "The Architectural Review", CLXI, 963, May 1977, pp. 270-294.
M. Fadda, *Dal Beaubourg al progetto collettivo*, in "Laboratorio", 1, April/June 1977, pp. 69-73.
G. Neret, *Le Centre Pompidou*, in "Connaissance des Arts", 1977, pp. 3-15.
Y. Futagawa, *Centre Beaubourg: Piano + Rogers*, in "CA Globe Architecture", 44, 1977, pp. 1-40.
Le Centre Beaubourg, in "Ministère des Affaires Culturelles Ministére de L'Education National", 1977.
Staatliches Kunst- und Kulturzentrum Georges Pompidou, Paris, in "DLW - Nachrichten", 61, 1977, pp. 34-39.
Intorno al Beaubourg, in "Abitare", 158, October 1977, pp. 69-75.
R. Piano, *Mobilités de hypothèses alternatives de production*, in "Werk-Archithese", 11-12, November/December 1977, p. 32.
C. Mitsia, M. Zakazian, C. Jacopin, *Eiffel vs Beaubourg*, in "Werk-Archithese", 9, 1977, pp. 22-29.
J. Bub,W. Messing, *Centre National d'Art et Culture de G. Pompidou ein Arbeitsbericht von zwei Architekturstudenten*, in "Bauen + Wohnen", 4, April 1977, pp. 132-139.
R. Piano, *Per un'edilizia evolutiva*, in "Laboratorio", 2, September/November 1977, pp. 7-10.
Piano & Rogers, in "Architectural Design", 7-8, vol. 47, 1977, pp. 530.
G. Lentati, *Centro Beaubourg, un'architettura utensile*, in "Ufficio stile", X, 5, 1977, pp. 74-87.
P. Chemetov, *L'opera Pompidou*, in "Techniques & Architecture", 317, December 1977, pp. 62-63.
M. Cornu, *Ce diable de Beaubourg*, in "Techniques & Architecture", 317, December 1977, pp. 64-66.
A. Darlot, *Le Centre National d'Art et de Culture G. Pompidou*, in "Revue Française de l'electricité", L, 259, December 1977, pp. 48-55.
R. Continenza, *Il Centro nazionale d'arte e cultura G. Pompidou a Parigi*, in "L'ingegnere", LIII, 6, June 1978, pp. 187-198.
A. Paste, *Il Centro d'arte e di cultura G. Pompidou*, in "L'Industria delle Costruzioni", 76, February 1978, pp. 3-30.
Centro Beaubourg Paris, in "Informes de la Construciòn", XXX, 299, April 1978, pp. 13-23.
G. Biondo, E. Rognoni, *Materie plastiche e edilizia industrializzata*, in "Domus", 585, August 1978, pp. 25-28.
Tipologie evolutive, in "Domus", 583, June 1978, pp. 12-13.
Esperienze di cantiere. Tre domande a R. Piano, in "Casabella", 439, September 1978, pp. 42-51.
Tipologie evolutive, lo spazio costruito deve adattarsi all'uomo, in "Domus, sup. 587, October 1978, pp. 30-31.
Ircam, in "AA", 199, October 1978, pp. 52-63.
Da uno spazio uguale due case diversissime, in "Abitare", 171, January/February 1979, pp. 2-21.
Wohnboxen in Mailand, in "MD", 6, June 1979.
L. Wright, *Heimatlandschaft*, in "The Architectural Review", 990, 166, August 1979, pp. 120-123.
R. Continenza, *L'opera di Piano & Rogers*, in "L'ingegnere", LIV, 10, October 1979, pp. 469-485.
Mobiles-Quartiers Laboratorium, in "Bauen + Wohnen", 9, September 1979, pp. 330-332.
Per il recupero dei Centri storici. Una proposta: Il Laboratorio di quartiere, in "Abitare", 178, October 1979, pp. 86-93.
Una recentissima proposta di Renzo Piano: Laboratorio mobile per lavori di recupero edilizio, in "Modulo", 7-8, 1979, p. 855.
Il Laboratorio di quartiere a Otranto, in "Domus", 599, October 1979, p. 2.
L. Rossi, *Piano + Rice + Ass. Il Laboratorio di quartiere*, in "Spazio & Società", 8, December 1979, pp. 27-42.
Renzo Piano. The Mobile Workshop in Otranto, in "ILA & UD Annual Report Urbino" 1979, pp. 60-63.
Operazione di recupero, in "Casabella", 453, December 1979, p. 7.
R. Continenza, *Architettura e tecnologia aspetti dell'opera di R. Piano e R. Rogers*, in "Costruttori Abruzzesi", II, 1979, pp. 15-18.
Free-Plan Four House Group, in "Toshi Jutaku", February 1980, pp. 14-23.
Enveloppes identiques-diversité interne Milano-Cusago I, in "AC 97", 25, 97, January 1980, pp. 6-11.
Fiat's magi carpet ride, in "Design", 379, July 1980, p. 58.
Centre Georges Pompidou, in "Nikkei Architecture", 8, August 1980, p. 83-85.
Contemporary design in two cities, in "Building & Remodelling Guide", July 1980, pp. 108-113.
La technologie n'est pas toujours industrielle, in "AA", 212, December 1980, pp. 51-54.
Art news, in "The Geiutsu Sheischo", September 1980.
C.G. Pompidou, in "AA", 213, February 1981, pp. 92-95.
M.T. Mirabile, *Centro Musicale a Parigi*, in "L'Industria delle Costruzioni", 114, April 1981, pp. 68-69.
Sul mestiere dell'Architetto, in "Domus", 617, May 1981, pp. 27-29.
Wohnhausgruppe bei Mailand, in "Die Kunst", 6, June 1981.
P. Santini, *Colloquio con R. Piano*, in "Ottagono", XVI, 61, June 1981, pp. 20-27.
Pianoforte, in "Building Design", 556, July 1981, pp. 11-14.
R. Pedio, *Renzo Piano Itinerario e un primo bilancio*, in "L'Architettura", 11, November 1981, pp. 614-662.
G. Lentati, *Quale Ufficio?*, in "Ufficio stile", 6, 1981, pp. 60-69.
R. Piano, *Renzo Piano, Genova*, in "Casabella", 474-475, November/December 1981, pp. 95-96.
Rainieri, Valli, *Progetto e partecipazione*, in "Edilizia Popolare", 163, November/December 1981, pp. 66-68.
Piano in Houston, in "Skyline", January 1982, p. 4.
Renzo Piano monografia, in "AA", 219, February 1982.
Fiat vettura sperimentale e sottosistemi, in "Abitare", 202, March 1982, pp. 8-9.
Italia, in "Nikkei Architecture", 2, February 1982, pp. 52-56.
M. Dini, *La città storica*, in "Area", 5, June/July 1982, p. 47.
S. Fox, *A Clapboard Treasure House*, in "Cite", August 1982, pp. 5-7.
Renzo Piano still in tune, in "Build-

ing Design", 606, August 1982, pp. 10–11.

Piano demonstration in Texas, in "Progressive Architecture", 9, 1982.

M.T. Carbone, *Sei progetti e un fuoco di paglia*, in "Costruire per Abitare", 5, December/January 1982-83, pp. 76–78.

Tecnoarchitettura vettura sperimentale e sottosistemi, in "Ottagono", March 1982.

People's office e ufficio fabbrica, in "Ufficio stile", 4, April 1982, pp. 49–52.

Abitacolo e abitazione, in "Casabella", 484, October 1982, pp. 14f.

Renzo Piano, in "The Architectural Review", 1028, October 1982, pp. 57–61.

L. Scacchetti, *Si chiude la scena, comincia il congresso*, in "Costruire per Abitare", 3, October 1982, pp. 117–120.

Il Centro Congressi del World Trade Center Italiano, in "Ufficio stile", XV, 67, 1982, pp. 24–30.

La macchina espositiva, in "Abitare", 212, March 1983, pp. 90–91.

A.L. Rossi, *La Macchina climatizzata*, in "Domus", 638, April 1983, pp. 10–15.

P.A. Croset, *Parigi 1989*, in "Casabella", XLVII, 490, April 1983, pp. 18–19.

M.T. Carbone, *Renzo Piano: il Molo, gli specchi, il cantiere di quartiere*, in "Costruire", 5, December/January 1982-83, pp. 76–78.

G. Ferracuti, *Il Laboratorio di Quartiere*, in "Recuperare", 4, March/April 1983, pp. 120–123.

Tra il dire e il fare, in "Costruire", 9, May 1983, p. 71.

C. Béret, *L'espace-flexible*, in "Art Press", 2, June/August 1983, pp. 22–23.

Designs on the future, in "Wave", April 1983, pp. 51–54.

B. Costantino, *Taller de Barrio: coloquio con Renzo Piano y Gianfranco Dioguardi*, in "Modulo", 11, June 1983, pp. 20–33.

Des Technologies nouvelles pour l'habitat ancien, in "Techniques & Architecture", 348, June/July 1983, pp. 51–61.

O. Pivetta, *Postindustriale sarà lei*, in "Costruire", 12, September 1983, pp. 100–105.

Piano Machine, in "The Architectural Review", CLXIX, 1038, August 1983, pp. 26–31.

M. Pawley, *Piano's progress*, in "Building Design", 23, September 1983, pp. 32–34.

M. Brändli, *L'allestimento di Renzo Piano per la mostra di Calder*, in "Casabella", XLVII, 494, September 1983, pp. 34–36.

J.P. Robert, *Un chantier experimental a Montrouge*, in "Le Moniteur", 40, September 1983, pp. 60–67.

O. Fillion, *Schlumberger à Montrouge*, in "Architecture Interieure", 196, September 1983, pp. 118–123.

Un boulevard flottant, in "Urbanisme", 197, September 1983, pp. 44–45.

S. Boidi, *Io, il mestiere, i miei sentimenti*, in "Costruire", 14, November 1983, pp. 82, 83, 112.

Calder a Torino, in "Domus", 644, November 1983, pp. 56–59.

Renzo Piano, artisan du futur, in "Technique & Architecture", 350, 1983, pp. 121–138.

L. Rossi, *La cultura del fare*, in "Spazio & Società", VI, 23, September 1983, pp. 50–62.

Piano Rehab, in "The Architectural Review", CLXXIV, 1041, November 1983, pp. 68–73.

M. Margantini, *Instabil Sandy Calder*, in "Modo", 64, November 1983.

R. Pedio, *Retrospettiva di Calder a Torino*, in "L'Architettura", XXIX, 12, December 1983, pp. 888–894.

R. Rovers, *Recent werk van Renzo Piano*, in "Bouw", 25, December 1983, pp. 9–12.

G. Plaffy, *R. Piano: Sub-systems automobile*, in "Omni", 1, January 1984, pp. 112–115.

O. Boisière, *Paris × Paris*, in "Domus", 646, January 1984, pp. 22–27.

Una tensostruttura per l'insegna della mostra di Calder a Torino, in "Acciaio", XXV, 2, February 1984, pp. 53–57.

M. Fazio, *A Torino Calder*, in "Spazio & Società", 25, March 1984, pp. 66–69.

Lingotto: Piano/Schein, in "Building Design", May 1984, pp. 26–28.

M. Zardini, *Venti idee per il Lingotto*, in "Casabella", 502, May 1984, pp. 30, 31.

UUL, Unità Urbanistiche Locali, in "Costruire", 20, June 1984, pp. 36.38.

A. Pélisser, *Renzo Piano: participer inventer de nouvelles méthodes de travail et de nouvelles maisons*, in "Histoires de Participer", 93, February 1984, pp. 64–69.

P. Rumpf, *Fiat-Lingotto: Chance oder Danaergeschenk für Turin?*, in "Bauwelt", 17, May 1984, pp. 733.

Y. Pontoizeau, *Renovation du site industriel Schlumberger, Montrouge*, in "L'Architecture d'Aujourd'hui", 233, June 1984, pp. 14–23.

Exposition itinerante de technologie informatique, in "Techniques & Architecture", 354, June/July 1984, pp. 144, 145.

R. Marchelli, *Un involucro di policarbonato per una mostra itinerante*, in "Materie plastiche e elastometri", 7-8, July/August 1984, pp. 424–427.

Ibm Exhibit Pavilion, Paris Exposition, in "A+U", 168, September 1984, pp. 67–72.

A. Castellano, *Venti Progetti per il futuro del Lingotto*, in "La mia casa", 170, September 1984, pp. 48–51.

Una mostra itinerante per far conoscere il computer, in "Abitare", 227, September 1984, pp. 4–6.

The Menil Collection, in "Arts & Architecture", 1, 1984, pp. 32–35.

C. Di Bartolo, *Creatività e progetto*, in "Modo", 8, 73, October 1984, pp. 36–40.

Y. Pontoizeau, *Projects & Realisations*, in "L'Architecture d'Aujourd'hui", 235, October 1984, pp. 59–65.

Tecnologia: tecnologie leggere, in "Modulo", 10, October 1984, pp. 1003–1009.

L'Expo-Ibm, in "GA Document", 11, November 1984.

Beaubourg analogo, in "Rassegna", VI, 19, September 1984, pp. 94–97.

Un'arca veneziana per i suoni di "Prometeo", in "AD Mondadori", IV, 42, November 1984, pp. 48–50.

Arcadian Machine, in "The Architectural Review", CLXXVI, 1053, November 1984, pp. 70–75.

A. Mladenovic, *Renzo Piano*, in "Nas Dom", XVIII, 9, September 1984, pp.26–29.

S. Boeri, P.A. Croser, *Dinosaur with a brain*, in "Blueprint", 12/95, November 1984, pp. 12, 13.

Riflessioni sul "Prometeo", in "Casabella", XLVIII, 507, November 1984, pp. 38, 39.

R. Pedio, *Exhibit Ibm, padiglione itinerante di tecnologia informatica*, in "L'Architettura", XXX, 11, November 1984, pp. 818–824.

A. Castellano, *Renzo Piano e l'Arca del Prometeo*, in "La mia casa", 173, December 1984, pp. 48–53.

Piano + Nono, in "The Architectural Review", CLXXVI, 1054, December 1984, pp. 53–57.

Renzo Piano and his Methods, in "SD 85-01 High-Tech", 244, January 1985, pp. 47–67.

G. Simonelli, *La grande nave lignea*, in "Modulo", 3, March 1985, pp. 164–170.
Prometeo, in "Interni", 348, March 1985, p. 73.
A. Burigana, *Renzo Piano*, in "Architectural Digest", V, 47, April 1985, pp. 32–38.
A. Castellano, *L'architettura sperimentale di Renzo Piano*, in "La mia casa", 176, April 1985, pp. 32–53.
G. Sansalone, *Questo gruppo spara su tutto*, in "Costruire", 27, March 1985, p. 49.
E. Caminati, *L'arte di costruire*, in "Costruire", 29, May 1985, pp. 162–168.
J. Glancey, *Piano Pieces*, in "The Architectural Review", 1059, May 1985, pp. 58–63.
R. Piano, *Music space for the Opera "Prometeo" by L. Nono*, in "A + U", 177, June 1985, pp. 67–74.
J.M.H., *Restructuration d'un site industriel a Montrouge*, in "Techniques & Architecture", 359, April/May 1985, pp. 42–53.
France: le printemps des musées, in "Le Moniteur", May 1985.
M. Milan, *Il Prometeo*, in "Acciaio", XXVI, 4, April 1985, pp. 166–170.
Ibm, in "Architects Magazine", 11, 1985, pp. 249–250.
Il Prometeo, in "Daidalos", 17, September 1985, pp. 84–87.
P. Buchanan, *The traps of technology*, in "Forum", 29, 1985, pp. 138–144.
O. Fillion, *Nature, la revanche*, in "Archi-Crée", 207, August/September 1985, pp. 64–69.
E. Hubeli, *Künstliches und Natürliches*, in "Werk, Bauen + Wohnen", 11, November 1985, pp. 23–28.
J.P. Robert, *La Schlumberger a Montrouge di Renzo Piano*, in "Casabella", XLIX, 517, October 1985, pp. 26–29.
Italia 1984, in "L'industria delle Costruzioni", XIX, 168, October 1985, pp. 64–73.
Cité Descartes, in "Techniques & Architecture", 362, October 1985, pp. 135–137.
A. Pélisier, *Entretien avec Renzo Piano*, in "Techniques & Architecture", 362, October 1985, pp. 101–111.
Des chantiers permanents, in "L'Architecture d'Aujourd'hui", 242, December 1985, pp. 12–15.
Urban conversion of the Schlumberger Factories, in "Global Architecture", 14, December 1985.
C. Negro, *Un architetto per Lione*, in "Costruire", 37, February 1986, pp. 86–89.
Eine mobile Oper und ein "Quartierlabor", in "Werk, Bauen + Wohnen", 4, April 1986, pp. 4–9.
Reazione spaziale di Renzo Piano negli uffici Lowara a Vicenza, in "Architettura", April 1986, pp. 246–253.
Un open space trasparente, in "Habitat-Ufficio", June/July 1986, pp. 48–55.
Houston, Texas, De Menil Museum, in "Abitare", 247, September 1986, pp. 382–384.
M. Prusicki, *Renzo Piano, Progetto Lingotto a Torino*, in "Domus", 675, September 1986, pp. 29–37.
D. Mangin, *Piano de A à W*, in "L'Architecture d'Aujourd'hui", 246, September 1986, pp. 1–37.
F. Zagari, *Progetto Bambù*, in "Abitare", 248, October 1986, pp. 28–31.
Aspettando Colombo, in "Costruire", 44, October 1986, pp. 42–49.
A. Robecchi, *La religiosa attesa dell'atto*, in "Costruire", 45, November 1986, pp. 126–130.
Vicenza, Una mostra di Renzo Piano, in "Abitare", 249, November 1986, pp. 111.
O. Boissière, *Il Museo de Menil a Houston*, in "L'Arca", 2, December 1986, pp. 28–35.
D. Smetana, *Piano and Palladio, virtuoso duet*, in "Progressive Architecture", December 1986, p. 25, 33.
M. Vogliazzo, *Conversando con Renzo Piano*, in "Grand Bazaar", December 1986, pp. 22–25.
Immeuble de bureaux, in "Architecture Contemporaine", 1986, pp. 182–185.
Le Synchrotron de Grenoble, in "Le Moniteur", January 1987, pp. 58f.
A. Castellano, *Il Forum industriale*, in "L'Arca", 3, January/February 1987, pp. 29–37.
Piano lessons, in "AJ", 21, January 1987, pp. 20–21.
Piano solo, in "Building Design", 23, January 1987, pp. 14–15.
B. Galletta, *Concorso per la sede del Credito industriale sardo, a Cagliari*, in "L'Industria delle Costruzioni", 183, January 1987, pp. 27–33.
Piano's sketches for the final composition, in "Design week", 23, January 1987.
E.M. Farrelly, *Piano Practice*, in "The Architectural Review", 1081, March 1987, pp. 32–59.
Facciata continua strutturale, in "Domus", 681, March 1987.
R. Piano, *La modernità secondo Piano*, in "L'Arca", 5, April 1987, pp. 59–65.
B. Nerozzi, *L'Architettura ritrovata*, in "Gran Bazaar", 55, April/May 1987, pp. 47–54.
P. Papandemetriou, *The responsive box*, in "Progressive Architecture", May 1987, pp. 87–97.
Trennwand System aus glasfaserverstärktem Beton, in "Detail", 27, May 1987, pp. 1–4.
Simplicity of form, ingenuity in the use of daylight, in "Architecture", May 1987, pp. 84–91.
H.F. Debailleux, *Piano à Houston*, in "Beaux-Arts Magazine", 47, June 1987, pp. 68–73.
R. Ingersoll, *Pianissimo, the very quiet Menil Collection*, in "Texas Architecture", 3, May/June 1987, pp. 40–47.
R. Banham, *In the neighborhood of art*, in "Art in America", June 1987, pp. 124–129.
M. Filler, *A quiet place for Art*, in "House & Gardener", 7, June 1987.
A. Benedetti, *Ristrutturazione e riuso di un'area industriale a Montrouge, Parigi*, in "L'Industria delle Costruzioni", 188, June 1987, pp. 6–23.
R. Piano, *Uno stadio per Bari*, in "Domus", 684, June 1987, p. 7.
Renzo Piano, lo Stadio di Bari e il sincrotone di Grenoble, in "Casabella", 536, June 1987, pp. 54–63.
M. Keniger, *The Art of Assembly*, in "Australia Architecture", 5, June 1987, pp. 63–67.
E. Ranzani, E. Gazzoni, *Renzo Piano, Museo Menil, Houston*, in "Domus", 685, July/August 1987, pp. 32–43.
Renzo Piano: Menil Collection a Houston, in "Ilaud", 1986–87, pp. 76–77.
E.M. Farrelly, *The quiet game*, in "The Architectural Review", 1087, September 1987, pp. 70–80.
L. CApril, *Il Museo con la cassaforte sul tetto una nuova contestazione di Renzo Piano*, in "Arte", 177, September 1987, p. 25.
G.K. Koenig, *Piano: la Basilica palladiana non si tocca*, in "Ottagono", 86, September 1987, pp. 48–53.
A homely gallery, in "The Architect", September 1987, pp. 38–41.
Piano, retour près de Beaubourg, in "L'Architecture d'Aujourd'hui", 253, October 1987, pp. 48–50.
The de Menil Collection, in "Transaction", October 1987, pp. 44–51.
S. Ishida, *The Menil Art Museum*, in "SD", November 1987, pp. 48–50.

R. Banham, S. Ishida, *Renzo Piano*, in "A+U", 206, November 1987, pp. 39-122.

J.F. Pousse, *Renzo Piano: la métamorphose de la technologie* (Menil, Schlumberger, Lingotto Lovara), in "Techniques & Architecture", 374, October/November 1987, pp. 146-165.

S. Heck, *Piano's entente cordiale*, in "Riba Journal", November 1987, pp. 28-35.

A. Castellano, *Poesia e geometria per Bari*, in "L'Arca", November 1987, pp. 80-85.

V. Magnago Lampugnani, E. Ranzani, *Renzo Piano: sovversione, silenzio e normalità*, in "Domus", 688, November 1987, pp. 17-24.

Konstruktionen für das Licht, in "Werk, Bauen + Wohnen", December 1987, pp. 30-39.

Sammlung Menil in Houston, in "Baumeister", December 1987, pp. 36-41.

C. Ellis, *Umbau eines Industriekomplex und Landschaftsgestaltung in Montrouge, Paris*, in "Bauwelt", January 1988, pp. 29-31.

R. de la Nouve, I. Cazes, *Donjon Final. La tour de l'Ircam sera le campanile du beau Bourg*, in "Sept à Paris", 6, January 1988, pp. 34-35.

V. Borel, E. Daydé, *L'Ircam au Faite*, in "Sept à Paris", 6, January 1988, p. 35.

F. Irace, *Destinazione museo*, in "Abitare", 261, January 1988, pp. 192-197.

Wood framing (Ibm), in "Progressive Architecture", February 1988, p. 92.

M. Giordano, *La catarsi genovese del '92*, in "L'Arca", 14, March 1988.

D. Marabelli, *Leggera e integrata*, in "Modulo", 140, April 1988, pp. 478-483.

L'invention constructive, les avancées technologiques, in "Architecture et Informatique", 27, May/June 1988, pp. 20-23.

Menil – Sammlung in Houston, in "DBZ", June 1988, pp. 795-798.

Menil Collection Museum in Houston, Texas, in "Detail", 3, May/June 1988, pp. 285-290.

Atélier Municipaux, Paris 19ème, in "Usine", 1988, pp. 82-85.

G. de Bure, *Renzo Piano: l'homme aux semelles de vent*, in "Decoration International", 102, February 1988, pp. 110-113.

Genua, in "Werk, Bauen + Wohnen", 9, September 1988, pp. 48-55.

Il lingotto, in "Rassegna", X, 35, September 1988, 110-113.

Osaka, in "Building Design", 918, January 1989, p. 1.

G. Picardi, *Flying High*, in "Building Design", 920, January 1989, pp. 26-28.

R. Ingersoll, *Pianissimo – La discreta collecion Menil*, in "Arquitectura Viva", 4, January 1989, pp. 15-19.

R. Radicioni, *Quale Piano e per chi?*, in "Spazio & Società", XII, 45 January, 1989, pp. 104-106.

Museo a Houston (Texas), in "Abacus", V, 17, January/February/March 1989, pp. 28-39.

A. Pelissier, *Kansai: la course contre le temps*, in "Techniques & Architecture", 382, February 1989, pp. 65-68.

Football Stadium, in "GA Document", 23, February/March 1989, pp. 44-46."

F. Mellano, *Vuoti a rendere*, in "Modulo", 149, March 1989, pp. 272-281.

P. Davey, *Piano's Lingotto*, in "The Architectural Review", 1105, March 1989, pp. 4-9.

Il concorso per il nuovo aeroporto di Osaka, in "Casabella", LIII, 555, March 1989, pp. 22-23.

Kansai International Airport, in "Architectural Design", 3-4, March/April 1989, pp. 52-60.

Arvedi space, in "Acciaio", XXX, 4, April 1989, pp. 168-173.

D. Ghiarardo, *Piano Quays – aeroporto di Osaka*, in "The Architectural Review", CLXXXV, 1106, April 1989, pp. 84-88.

S. Redecke, *La cultura del fare*, in "Bauwelt", 3, April 1989, pp. 614-617.

Italy's Brunel, in "Blueprint", 56, April 1989, pp. 52-54.

M. Desvigne, *Musée d'art moderne à Newport*, in "L'Architecture d'Aujourd'hui", 262, April 1989, pp. 50-51.

Il Building Workshop di Renzo Piano compie 25 anni, in "L'Arca", 26, April 1989, p. 118.

M. Desvigne, *Ensemble touristique dans la baie de Sistiana*, in "L'Architecture d'Aujourd'hui", 262, April 1989, pp. 52-54.

Concorso Kansai International Airport, in "The Japan Architect", 2, 1989, pp. 191-197.

L'artificio assoluto, in "Gran Bazaar", 67, April/May 1989, pp. 29-34.

V. Magnago Lampugnani, *Il concorso per l'aeroporto internazionale di Kansai*, in "Domus", 705, May 1989, pp. 34-39.

Renzo Piano: una mostra e la presentazione del progetto Lingotto, in "Abitare", 274, May 1989, p. 149.

F. Montobbio, *Prospettive ed evoluzione verso un nuovo disegno della città*, in "Urbanistica", 95, June 1989, pp. 110-113.

E. Marcheso Moreno, *What makes a Museum Environment Successful* in "Architecture", June 1989.

Turin-Gênes, in "CREE", June/July 1989.

Bari bowl, in "Construction Today", July 1989, p. 26.

Salir a la luz ampliacion de Ircam, in "A & V", 17, 1989, pp. 75-77.

A gate for Malta, in "Building Design", 22, September 1989, pp. 20-21.

Home for a Hero, in "Building Design", 22, September 1989, pp. 22-25.

M. Dini, *Oltre lo styling*, in "Architetti Liguria", IX, 7, September/October 1989, p. 30.

C. Davies, *Piano quarter*, in "The Architectural Review", CLXXXVI, 112, October 1989, pp. 60-75.

C. Mulard, *Le musée d'art de Newport Harbor, par Renzo Piano*, in "CREE", 232, October/November 1989, p. 27.

Raison de forme: Centre Commercial de Bercy, in "Techniques & Architecture", 386, October/November 1989, pp. 114-123.

Extension de l'Ircam, Paris, in "Techniques & Architecture", 386, October/November 1989, pp. 114-123.

E. Ranzani, *Renzo Piano: Allestimento al Lingotto*, in "Domus", 711, December 1989, pp. 14-16.

Una mostra al Lingotto, in "Rassegna", XI, 40/4, December 1989, pp. 90-93.

Piano plays nature's theme, in "World Architecture", 2, 1989, pp. 72-77.

Fusion Horizontale, in "Techniques & Architecture", 387, December/January 1989-90, pp. 144-145.

O. Di Blasi, *Renzo Piano: Libreria, Te- so, Fontana Arte*, in "Domus", 712, January 1990, pp. 76-79.

F. Lenne, *Une usine modulaire en foret*, in "Le Moniteur", 4499, February 1990, pp. 64-67.

Stade de Bari, Italie, in "L'Architecture d'Aujourd'hui", 267, February 1990, pp. 120-121.

F. Bertamini, *Il regalo di Colombo*,

in "Costruire", 81, February 1990, pp. 27–30.
E. Ranzani, *Ampliamento dell'Ircam a Parigi*, in "Domus", 713, February 1990, pp. 38–47.
C. Mattongo, *I sassi di Renzo*, in "Costruire", 83, April 1990, pp. 68–70.
J. Melvin, *Special Report: Shopping Centres*, in "Building Design", April 1990, pp. 11–19.
G. Lorenzelli, *All'ultimo stadio*, in "Costruire", 84 May 1990, p. 46.
E. Ranzani, *Renzo Piano, stadio di calcio e atletica leggera, Bari*, in "Domus", 716, May 1990, pp. 33–39.
Bari, in "Stadt Bauwelt", 24, May 1990, pp. 1220–1221.
Schmuckstücke und Skandale, in "Deutsche Bauzeitung", 5, May 1990, pp. 163–164.
V. Magnago Lampuagnani, *La terminal de la isla*, in "Arquitectura Viva", 12, May/June 1990, p. 14.
R. Laera, C. Riccardi, *Bari: Il nuovo stadio, un fiore nel deserto*, in "Il Nuovo Cantiere", estratto, June 1990, pp. 10–11.
A. Demerle, *Le stade de Bari*, in "Le Moniteur Architecture", 12 June 1990, pp. 32–39.
Grand Stand, in "New Civil Engineering", 7, June 1990, pp. 10–11.
M. Barda, *Bari: estadio San Nicola*, in "Architectura Urbanismo", VI, 30, June 1990, pp. 34–35.
J.M. Montaner, *Innovacion en la arquitectura de museos*, in "Architectural Digest", 31, June 1990, pp. 118–122.
Libreria Teso, in "Techniques & Architecture", 390 June/July 1990, p. 162.
Monographic issue on Cruise Princess, in "GB Progetti", 1990.
M. Beretta, *203.000 kilometri di coda*, in "Oice", 4–5, July/October 1990, pp. 71–72.
R. Ingersoll, *La trastienda del Mundial*, in "Arquitectura Viva", 13, July–August 1990, pp. 52–53.
Parigi: Un dirigibile in legno e acciaio, in "Il Nuovo Cantiere", XXIV, 7–8, July/August 1990, pp. 14–16.
Extension of the Ircam Studios in Paris, in "Detail", 4, August/September 1990, pp. 395–398.
A. Castellano, *La nave delfino*, in "L'Arca", 41, September 1990, pp. 72–81.
F. Irace, *Tempo di Musei*, 288, September 1990, pp. 280–287.
Soft Shore, in "The Architectural Review", 1123, September 1990, pp. 71–73.
Ort und Stadium, in "Werk, Bauen + Wohnen", 9, September 1990, pp. 22–29.
L.P. Puglisi, *I sassi di Matera: recupero di palazzo Venusio e del suo intorno*, in "L'Industria delle Costruzioni", XXIV, 227, September 1990, pp. 48–52.
G.F. Brambilla, *Renzo Piano: ampliamento dell'Ircam*, in "Costruire in laterizio", III, 17, September/October 1990, pp. 358–361.
Raumschiff mit Zentraler Bühne: Fußballstadion in Bari, in "Architektur Aktuell", 139, October 1990, pp. 82–85.
Industrial Revolution, in "Building Design", 19, October 1990, p. 30.
R. Piano, *Abitazioni a tipologia evolutiva a Corciano*, in "Edizioni Over", 1990, pp. 21–22.
Centre Georges Pompidou, in "Connaissance des Arts", 1990, pp. 1–76.
V. Magnago Lampugnani, *Renzo Piano Building Workshop*, in "A & V", 23, 1990, pp. 1–88.
The San Nicola Stadium, in "The Arup Journal", XXV, 3, 1990, pp. 3–8.
B. Marzullo, *Centri Storici: a Genova per noi*, in "Il Nuovo Cantiere", XXIV, 11, November 1990, pp. 38–40.
Monographic issue, in "A & V", Edizioni Avisa, 23, Madrid 1990.
Parte il Metrogenova, in "Vetro Spazio", 19, December 1990, pp. 10–16.
L'automobile, produzione e design a Milano 1879–1949, in "Rassegna", XII, 44, December 1990, pp. 98–101.
Transatlantici, in "Rassegna", XII, 44, December 1990.
Le Grand Souffle: Stade de Carbonara, Bari, Italie, in "Techniques & Architecture", 393, December/January 1990–91, pp. 44–49.
J. Ferrier, *Usine optronique Thomson-Guyancourt 1990*, in "Usines", vol. 2, Editions de Moniteur, 1991, pp. 64–73.
Ponti per il Porto di Ushibuka, in "Space Design", 1, 1991, pp. 88–91.
Fontana Arte: Teso, in "Abitare", 292, January 1991, p. 145.
Antologia 3, in "Casabella", LV, 575–576, January/February 1991, p. 89.
Verselbständigter Turm, in "Baumeister", 3, March 1991, pp. 20–21.
V. Travi, *Trieste: la baia delle meraviglie*, in "Il Nuovo Cantiere", 3, March 1991, pp. 55/56.
S. Ishida, N. Okabe, *Renzo Piano Building Workshop*, in "GA Document", 28, March 1991, pp. 60–95.
The Menil Collection Museum, in "Space Design", 3, 1991, pp. 74–76.
Un nuovo porto antico per Genova, in "Presenza Tecnica", IX, 2, March/April 1991, pp. 10–23.
Kansai International Airport, in "GA Document", 29, April 1991, p. 70.
Fja, *Eastern Promise*, in "The Architectural Review", 1131, May 1991, pp. 83–90.
Raumschiff, in "DB", 5, May 1991, pp. 64–67.
E. Ranzani, *La trasformazione della città: Genova*, in "Domus", 727, May 1991, pp. 44–71.
B. Marzullo, *Aree dismesse: due progetti importanti. L'area Caleotto*, in "Cantiere", XXV, 5, May 1991, pp. 48–49.
J.P. Menard, *Détail: Renzo Piano Façades en briques et composite*, in "Le Moniteur Architecture", 21, May 1991, pp. 51–61.
Monographic issue on Columbus exhibition, in "GB Progetti", 7, May/June 1991.
Piano a Bercy, in "L'Architecture d'Aujourd'hui", 269, June 1991, pp. 162–166.
Kansai International Airport Passenger Terminal Building Design Development Process, in "Space Design", 1991, pp. 6–9.
Expo 92: un grande progetto di recupero, in "Allestire", VIII, 73, June/July 1991, pp. 50–54.
Piano à Bercy, in "L'Architecture d'Aujourd'hui", 269, June 1991, pp. 162–166.
R. Morganti, *Centro commerciale a Bercy II, Parigi*, in "L'Industria delle Costruzioni", XXV, 236, June 1991, pp. 22–30.
Lyon, Cité International de la Tête d'Or, in "Techniques & Architecture", 395, April/May 1991, pp. 52–57.
Complesso residenziale a Parigi, in "Domus", 729, July/August 1991, pp. 27–39.
French Connection, in "The Architectural Review", CLXXXIX, 1133, July 1991, pp. 59–63.
Côté Jardin, in "Techniques & Architecture", CLXXXIX, 1133, July 1991, pp. 38–47.
La facciata strutturale in alluminio, in "Ufficio stile", XXIV, September 1991, pp. 138–149.
Il ruolo dell'acciaio inox nel metrò di Genova, in "Inossidabile", 105, September 1991, p. 8.
C. Mattogno, *Piano torna al*

Beaubourg, in "Costruire", 101, October 1991, pp. 107.

M.J. Dumont, *Renzo Piano, l'aéroport du Kansai à Osaka*, in "L'Architecture d'Aujourd'hui", 276, September 1991, pp. 45-50.

J. Cervera, *A flor de piel*, in "Arquitectura Viva", 20, September/October 1991, pp. 42-47.

Centre Cultural Kanak à Nouméa, in "L'Architecture d'Aujourd'hui", 277, October 1991, pp. 9-13.

La sede dell'Isml sperimenta una facciata continua di nuova concezione, in "AxA", I, 2, September 1991, pp. 50-57.

F. Peyouzere, *Le Centre National d'Art et de Culture Georges Pompidou*, in "Architecture Intérieure", 246, December/January 1991-92, pp. 87.

Leucos, *Il vetro in architettura*, in "Abitare", 303, January 1992, pp. 42-43.

Piano, in "Le Moniteur", 27, January 1992, pp. 18.

Logements Rue de Meaux, Paris XIXe, in "Le Moniteur", 27, January 1992, pp. 84-85.

Piano's magic carpet, in "The Architectural Review", 1139, January 1992.

Fiat factory gets Renzo Piano retread, in "Architectural Record", 1, January 1992, pp. 18.

Progetto per l'esposizione internazionale Genova 1992, in "Phalaris", 18, January/February 1992, pp. 44-47.

Renzo Piano, attraverso Parigi, in "Arredo Urbano", 47-48, January/April 1992, pp. 116-121.

A. Castellano, *Renzo Piano, Aeroporto Kansai*, in "Abitare", 305, March 1992, pp. 229-234.

P. Buchanan, *Pacific Piano*, in "The Architectural Review", 1141, March 1992, pp. 61-63.

T. Fisher, *Flights of Fantasy*, in "Progressive Architecture", March 1992.

P. Righetti, *La nuova sede del Credito industriale sardo*, in "Modulo", 179, March 1992, pp. 170-180.

Kansai International Airport, in "The Architect", 46, March 1992, pp. 60-65.

L. Gelhaus, *Il Grande Bigo*, in "Rassegna", 41/1, March 1992, pp. 114-117.

Una città e il mare, in "L'Arca", 59, April 1992, pp. 6-15.

T. Fisher, *The Place of Sports*, in "Progressive Architecture", 4, April 1992, pp. 94-95.

M. Barda, *Um Aeroporto sobre o mar*, in "A+U", 41, April/May 1992, pp. 54-63.

F. Bertamini, G. Salsalone, *La scoperta di Genova*, in "Costruire", 108, May 1992, pp. 26-38.

M. Toffolon, *Sotto le ali di una tenda*, in "Modulo", 181, May 1992, pp. 488-491.

F. Irace, *Piano per Genova-La città sul mare*, in "Abitare", 308, June 1992, pp. 133-136.

M. Champenois, *Piano, rénovation du port de Gênes*, in "L'Architecture d'Aujourd'hui", 281, June 1992, pp. 78-85.

Genèse d'un Paysage, in "Teräsrakenne", 402, June/July 1992, pp. 88-93.

Gênes d'un Paysage, in "Techniques & Architecture", 402, June/July 1992, pp. 88-93.

R. Ingersol, S. Ishida, *Renzo Piano Building Workshop: Shopping Center Bercy; Bari Soccer Stadium; Subway Station, Genoa*, in "A+U", 262, July 1992, pp. 70-114.

C.F. Kusch, *Internationale Columbus Austellung, Genoa*, in "DBZ", 7, July 1992, pp. 1033-1035.

C. Minoletti, *Genova Domani*, in "Quaderni", 12, July 1992, pp. 19-24.

Una corte per Abitare, in "Abitare", 308, July/August 1992, p. 192.

Z. Freiman, *Perspectives Genoa's historic port reclaim*, in "Progressive Architecture", 8, August 1992, pp. 78-85.

R. Maillinger, *Colombo '92 in Genua*, in "Baumeister", 8, August 1992, pp. 40-45.

La città e il mare – L'area del porto vecchio, 311, October 1992, pp. 60-65.

C. Garbato, *Il porto Vecchio*, in "Sport & Città", 3, September 1992, pp. 10-16.

N. Baldassini, *Genova. Le celebrazioni Colombiane*, in "Flare", 7, October 1992, pp. 4-13.

P. Righetti, *Gli ex Magazzini del Cotone*, in "Modulo", 185, October 1992, pp. 1024-1033.

J.C. Garcias, *Deux Etoiles Italiennes*, in "L'Architecture d'Aujurd'hui", 283, October 1992, pp. 92-97.

G. Paci, *Il delfino Bianco*, in "Casa Vogue", 245, October 1992, pp. 58-61.

F. De Pasquali, *Per la Caterìstica e l'acciaio, uno sviluppo che viaggia in parallelo*, in "Acciaio", 4, October 1992, pp. 23-27.

Colombo '92 – Esposizione di Genova, Sala Congressi-Auditorium Aquarium, in "Habitat-Ufficio", 58, October/November 1992, pp. 62-63.

S. Ishida, *Unesco Workshop, Columbus International Exposition, Thomson CSF Factory*, in "GA Document", 35, November 92.

P. Rumpf, *Progetti per l'area di Potsdamer Platz, Berlino*, in "Domus", 744, December 1992, pp. 44-55.

Esposizione Internazionale 1992 nel porto antico, in "L'Architettura", 446, December 1992, pp. 862-863.

Dal bullone al territorio, in "L'Architettura", 446, December 1992, pp. 884-886.

Colombo '92 Esposizione di Genova, in "Habitat-Ufficio", 58, October/November 1992, pp. 62-63.

Futagawa, *Renzo Piano, Unesco Laboratory Columbus International Expo '92, Thomson CSF Factory*, in "GA Document", 35, November 1992, pp. 40-59.

Un sistema, illuminotecnico funzionale, in "Rassegna", 52/4, December 1992, pp. 94-97.

Trompe l'oeil, in "Werk, Bauen + Wohnen", 5, May 92, pp. 54-57.

Un sistema, illuminotecnico funzionale, in "Rassegna", 52/4, December 92.

A. Valenti, *Berlino. Renzo Piano a Potsdamer Platz: L'Eclettico e il disciplinato dell'Architettura*, in "Arredo Urbano", 50-51, September 1992, pp. 30-33.

D. Cruickshank, *Cross Roads Berlin*, in "The Architectural Review", 1151, January 1993, pp. 20-28.

D. Cruickshank, *Genoa Drama*, in "The Architectural Review", 1151, January 1993, pp. 36-41.

G. Ullmann, *Zwischen Seelandschaft und Piazza*, in "Werk, Bauen + Wohnen", 1-2, January/February 1993, pp. 41-48.

L. Pogliani, *Piano per tre*, in "Costruire", 117, January 1993, pp. 48.

E. Morteo, *Renzo Piano*, in "Domus", 748, April 1993, pp. 87-89.

E. Regazzoni, *Unesco & Workshop*, in "Abitare", 317, April 1993, pp. 156-169.

Un Modello su cui muoverci, in "L'Arca", 68, February 1993, p. 98.

Er(b)folge am Potsdamer Platz, in "Baumeister", 2, February 1993.

Elektronikfabrik in Guyancourt, in "Detail", 6, February 1993, pp. 593-597.

Das Experiment im Werk, Renzo Piano, in "Detail", 6.

Mecanico e Organico, in "Arquitectura Viva", 29, March/April 1993, pp. 52-59.

Renzo Piano Spazio Scenico per Moby Dick "Ulisse e la Balena Bianca", in "Domus", 29, March/April 1993.

D. Albrecht, *Renzo Piano Exhibit in NY*, in "Architecture", 2, February 1993, pp. 22-23.

P. Arcidi, *Renzo Piano Exhibit opens in NY*, in "Progressive Architecture", 2, February 1993, pp. 19.

Renzo Piano Aeroporto di Kansai, Osaka, in "Domus", 1, January 1993, pp. 52-59.

C. Sattler, *Potsdamer Platz – Leipziger Platz, Berlin 1991*, in "AD Profiles", 1, January/February 1993, pp. 18-23.

R. Piano, *Un nuevo rodaje para el Lingotto*, in "Diseno Interir", 24, April 1993, pp. 26-27.

D.O. Mandrelli, *Lungo il fiume, tra gli alberi*, in "L'Arca", 71, May 1993, pp. 4-11.

R. Stefanato, *Trasporto Ferroviario, speranze tra i binari*, in "Olce temi", 1, January 1993, pp. 33-37.

Crown Princess, in "Interni", 427, January/February 1993, pp. 120-121.

Sistemazione degli spazi esterni dell'industria Thomson a Guyancourt, in "Casabella", 597/8, January/February 1993, pp. 110-111.

A.L. Nobre, *Renzo Piano, presença na America*, in "Architectura Urbanismo", 47, May 1993, p. 28.

S. Brandolini, *Il terminal passeggeri del Kansai International Airport nella baia di Osaka*, in "Casabella", 601, May 1993.

Genova Acquario Oceanico. Protezione delle superfici esterne in cemento, in "Arkos", 20, May 1993, p. 30.

Lingotto: una completa gamma illuminotecnica ad alto contenuto tecnologico, in "Rassegna", 53, March 1993, pp. 90-93.

Lingotto Fiere: montanti eccezionali per diaframmi luminosi, in "Proporzione", 1, June 1993, pp. 32-40.

N. Baldassini, *La luce nell'architettura High-Tech*, in "Flare", 8, May 1993, pp. 26-28.

Le Centre Culturel Jean-Marie Tjibaou, in "MWA VEE", 1, May 1993, pp. 48-53.

J. Sainz, *Hipergeometriàs, el ordenador en el studio de Renzo Piano*, in "Arquitectura Viva", 30, May/June 1993, pp. 96-97.

Haltestelle Brin in Genua, in "Detail", 4, August/September 1993, pp. 414-417.

M. Tardis, *La grande Vague*, in "Techniques & Architecture", 408, June/July 1993, pp. 114-121.

R.P. Red, *Solitäre in der periurbanen Wüste*, in "Werk, Bauen + Wohnen", July/August 1993, pp. 20-25.

Ushibuka Fishing Port Connecting Bridge, in "JA", 10, 1993, pp. 212-217.

Kansai International Airport, Passenger Terminal Building, in "JA", 11, 1993.

Osaka: "Aeroporto", in "GB Progetti", 19, September 1993, p. 4.

F. Premoli, *Amsterdam: "Musei"*, in "GB Progetti", 19, September 1993, p. 16.

Ushibuka – Giappone: Ponti, in "GB Progetti", 21, November 1993, p. 10.

Kansai International Airport P.T.B., in "JA", 3/11, 1993, pp. 54-69.

G. Messina, *Progetti di Renzo Piano in mostra itinerante*, in "L'Industria delle Costruzioni", 266, December 1993, pp. 64-65.

Nuovo Teatro Margherita, in "Casabella", 607, December 1993, pp. 38.

R. Dorigati, *Un parco culturale per la città il Lingotto*, in "L'Arca", 78, January 1993, pp. 48-53.

JM A. Enjuto, *Arquitectura en la confluencia de los limites*, in "Lapiz", 98, December 1993, pp. 45-49.

M. Rognoni, *Un Edificio Residenziale a Parigi: Rue de Meux*, in "Maiora", 18, December 1993, pp. 4-11.

Presentato a Bari, il progetto per l'ex teatro Margherita, in "L'Industria delle Costruzioni", 267, January 1994, p. 74.

Remo Dorigati, *Un Parco Culturale per la Città, il Lingotto*, in "L'Arca", 78, January 1994, pp. 48-53

Robert Keiser, *Flugzeugträger*, in "Werk, Bauen + Wohnen", No. 4, April 1994, pp. 49-53.

Angelo Bugatti, *Un lingotto di tecnologia*, in "Costruire", No. 132, May 1994, pp. 125-128.

Berlino – Riqualificazinoe area della Potsdamer Platz, in "GB Progetti", No. 23, March 1994, p. 11.

Special Feature: Kansai Airport, GA Japan, No. 9, July/August 1994, pp. 24-80.

Museo Beyeler a Riehen, Basilea, in "Domus", No. 2, 1994, pp. 30-33.

Dietmar Danner, *Woge – Der Kansai-Airport in der Bucht von Osaka*, in "AIT", July/August 1994, pp. 26-35.

Peter Buchanan, *Padre Pio Pilgrimage Church: Italy*, in "Scroope", No. 6, 1994/95, pp. 28-29.

L'Auditorium al Lingotto di Torino, in "Casabella", No. 614, July/August 1994, pp. 52-59.

Dan Cruikshank, *Piano Forte*, in "Perspectives", No. 5, September 1994, pp. 34-37.

The Hills are Alive, in "Building Design", September 1994, pp. 16-19.

Luca Gazzaniga, *Renzo Piano Building Workshop, Aereoporto Internazionale di Kansai, Osaka, Giappone*, in "Domus", No. 764, October 1994, pp. 60-61.

Marten Kloos, *Het juiste gebaar*, in "Archis", No. 6, June 1994, pp. 5-7.

Riichi Miyake, *Special report Renzo Piano Building Workshop. Creating Harmony from Technology and Nature*, in "Approach", No. 3, Autumn 1994, pp. 1-23.

Aldo Castellano, *Kansai International Airport*, in "L'Arca", No. 86, October 1994, pp. 2-27.

Laura Verdi, *Un nuovo Lingotto per Torino*, in "Modulo", No. 204, September 1994, pp. 284-291.

Maria Claudia Clemente, *Leggero come l'aria*, in "Costruire", No. 137, October 1994, pp. 46-49.

Kansai International Airport Passenger Terminal Building, in "JA", No. 15, Autumn 1994.

Valerio Cappelli, *Il nuovo Auditorium di Roma, una sfida Urbanistica*, in "Amadeus", No.11(60), November 1994, pp. 43-45.

Clemens F. Kusch, *Hafenanlage von Genua*, in "Deutsche Bauzeitung", November 1994, pp. 67-70.

Nick Baker, *Tears in the reunited city*, in "Building Design", November 1994, p. 22.

Peter Buchanan, *Kansai*, in "Architectural Review", No. 1173, November 1994, pp. 30-81.

Robert Keiser, *Vorwärtsstrategien*, in "Werk, Bauen + Wohnen", No. 11, pp. 6-17.

Books

International Conference on Space Structures, exhibition catalogue, London 1966.

E. Poleggi, G. Timossi, *Porto di Genova. Storia e attualità*, Genoa 1977.

Ircam, Paris 1977.

G. Marinelli, *Il centro Beaubourg a Parigi: Macchina e segno architettonico*, Bari 1978.

Costruire e Ricostruire, Udine 1978.

R. Piano, M. Arduino, M. Fazio, *Antico è bello*, Roma-Bari 1980.
A. Fils, *Das Centre Pompidou in Paris*, Munich 1980.
G. Donin (ed.), *Renzo Piano: Pezzo per Pezzo*, exhibition catalogue, Rome 1982.
La Modernité, un projet inachevé, exhibition catalogue, Paris 1982.
M. Dini, *Renzo Piano: progetti e architetture 1964–1983*, Milan 1983 (French edition: Paris 1983; English edition: *Renzo Piano: Projects and buildings 1964–1983*, New York 1984).
Storia di una Mostra Torino 1983, Milan 1983.
L. Nono, *Verso Prometeo*, Venice 1984.
R. Piano, *Chantier ouvert au public*, Paris 1985.
L. Milella, *Nuovo è bello*, Roma-Bari 1985.
Associazione Industriali provincia di Genova, *Genova ieri, oggi, domani*, Genoa 1985.
1992 Genova Città di Colombo: Immagini e progetti, Genoa 1986.
R. Piano, *Dialoghi di cantiere*, Bari 1986.
Renzo Piano: progetti e architetture 1984–1986, Milan 1986.
L. Miotto, *Renzo Piano*, exhibition catalogue, Paris 1987.
R. Piano, R. Rogers, *Du Plateau Beaubourg au Centre Georges Pompidou*, Paris 1987.
A+U, *Renzo Piano Building Workshop, 1964–1988*, Tokyo 1989.
Renzo Piano, exhibition catalogue, Tokyo 1989.
Eco, Zeri, Piano, Graziani, *Le Isole del tesoro*, Milan 1989.
P. Goldberger (ed.), *Renzo Piano, Buildings and Projects 1971–1989*, New York 1989.
S. San Pietro (ed.), R. Piano, *Il Nuovo Stadio di Bari*, Milan 1990.
M. Mastropiero (ed.), "*Colombo '92: la città, il porto, l'esposizione*", Quaderni di Mostrare, Milan 1992.
C. Garbato, M. Mastropiero (eds.), *Renzo Piano Building Workshop Exhibit/Design*, Milan 1992.
Peter Buchanan, *Renzo Piano Building Workshop Complete Works*, London, 1994–95. (German edition: *Renzo Piano. Architekt*, Stuttgart 1994–95.)

Photographic Credits

Gianni Berengo Gardin. 37, 41, 42 above, 43, 47, 50, 51, 56, 57, 80, 83, 94, 97, 98, 100, 101, 103, 110–114, 117, 124 below, 127, 146, 147, 155, 162 below, 163, 164 right, 165, 166
Sergio Cigliuti 53
Michel Denancé 31, 34, 40, 99, 105, 109, 123, 124 above, 125, 132–135, 138–141, 153
Fregoso-Basalto 177 above, 179, 180 right, 181–183
Stefano Goldberg 178 right
Roland Halbe 58, 61
Paul Hester 20, 24, 25, 27, 28 below
Kanji Hiwatashi 162 above
Alistair Hunter 19, 23 above, 28 above on right
Shunji Ishida 23 below, 36, 145, 151, 152, 177 below, 178 left, 180 left
Kawatetsu 167
Minetti 30
Renzo Piano 21
Publifoto 142, 174
Hickey Robertson 28 above on left, 29
Salviati 66
Skyfront 154 below
Ben Smuse 17
Mauro Vallinotto 42

Cover photograph:
Gianni Berengo Gardin

For all other illustrative material we thank Renzo Piano Building Workshop.